Bridge to an Unseen Shore

The publisher and the University of California Press Foundation gratefully acknowledge the generous support of the Richard and Harriett Gold Endowment Fund in Arts and Humanities.

Bridge to an Unseen Shore

NEW AGE MUSIC AS VISIONARY ART

Jacob Smith

UNIVERSITY OF CALIFORNIA PRESS

University of California Press
Oakland, California

Library of Congress Cataloging-in-Publication Data

Names: Smith, Jacob, author
Title: Bridge to an unseen shore : new age music as visionary art / Jacob Smith.
Description: Oakland, California : University of California Press, [2026] | Includes bibliographical references and index.
Identifiers: LCCN 2026019430 (print) | LCCN 2026019431 (ebook) | ISBN 9780520426238 cloth | ISBN 9780520426252 paperback | ISBN 9780520426269 ebook
Subjects: LCSH: New Age music—History and criticism | Visions in art—History—20th century | New Age movement—History
Classification: LCC ML3529 .S65 2026 (print) | LCC ML3529 (ebook) | DDC 782.42164—dc23/eng/20260501
LC record available at https://lccn.loc.gov/2026019430
LC ebook record available at https://lccn.loc.gov/2026019431

GPSR Authorized Representative: Easy Access System Europe, Mustamäe tee 50, 10621 Tallinn, Estonia, gpsr.requests@easproject.com

35 34 33 32 31 30 29 28 27 26
10 9 8 7 6 5 4 3 2 1

CONTENTS

Introduction

IN MARCH 1973, an astronomer named Luboš Kohoutek discovered a previously unknown comet hurtling through space between Jupiter and Mars. By November, the comet would be visible in the early morning sky, and by some estimations, it would glow as brightly as a full moon. The immanent arrival of Comet Kohoutek sparked extensive discussion and became the subject of planetarium lectures, newspaper editorials, late-night television conversations, novelty songs, and *Peanuts* cartoons. The public's interest was not purely scientific, and there were many speculations about the comet's cosmic significance. The fact that it would appear around Christmas amplified its spiritual overtones. Was this a new Star of Bethlehem signaling the return of the Messiah? Did it presage the cataclysmic end of the world or the inauguration of a new era of peace and enlightenment? The psychologist-turned-LSD-advocate Timothy Leary published a pamphlet in which he called the comet a "starseed" and claimed that it was part of an interstellar communication network that was bringing new life to humanity as a "bright reminder of our extraterrestrial origin and future."[1]

The idea that the comet would usher in a new phase in human consciousness inspired an event in January 1974 called the Kohoutek Celebration of Consciousness. This two-day celebration in the San Francisco Civic Auditorium featured talks, musical performances, and workshops in what the organizers called an "alchemical mix" of approaches to the "new art/science of consciousness." Those approaches included biofeedback, vegetarian food, meditation techniques, yoga, tai chi, astrology, massage, and herbal remedies.[2]

When it finally arrived, Comet Kohoutek failed to produce either visual spectacle or cataclysmic events. Glimpsed only occasionally as a dim speck in the morning sky, it passed silently without any accompanying earthquakes, floods, or extraterrestrial encounters. In hindsight, however, it did signal something of historical importance: the emergence of the New Age spiritual movement, which is defined by an interest in personal transformation and healing, the merging of science and spirituality, the exploration of levels of consciousness and diverse religious traditions, and a spiritual connection to the natural world.[3] The Kohoutek Celebration in the San Francisco Civic Auditorium was an early manifestation of the New Age movement, and it was also a showcase for a distinctive kind of music that would develop alongside that movement.

Attendees of the two-day event heard an alchemical mixture of consciousness-expanding music that included group chanting, a Sufi choir, and the otherworldly sounds of Francesco Lupica's thirteen-foot stringed instrument, the Cosmic Beam. Notably, there were two musicians in attendance who would each release their first albums the following year: Iasos performed his "Celestial Music" in the main auditorium, and Steven Halpern had a display to promote his music at the event. The release of debut albums by these two influential artists in 1975 was a milestone in the crystallization of New Age music.[4]

Iasos and Halpern were part of an eclectic cohort of musicians that includes Suzanne Doucet, Georgia Kelly, Laraaji, Constance Demby, Michael Stearns, Emerald Web, Peter Davison, Suzanne Ciani, Steve Roach, Kevin Braheny Fortune, Paul Winter, Edward Christmas, Deuter, Paul Horn, Don Slepian, and many others. All were active in the 1970s and early 1980s, and though they came from diverse musical backgrounds, they shared an approach to creating music that circulated on cassette tapes and could be found in spaces associated with the New Age movement such as metaphysical bookstores, health food outlets, and New Age fairs similar to the Kohoutek Celebration.

To one degree or another, the New Age musicians of this era were immersed in the kinds of spiritual practices and metaphysical philosophies that were on display at the San Francisco Civic Auditorium in January 1974, and several were theorist-practitioners who published books on music and spirituality. In fact, this cohort of New Age musicians is best understood as an artistic movement, a school of visionary art that manifested in the medium of recorded sound. This book is the first cultural history and scholarly analysis of this musical school of visionary art, drawing on extensive interviews with many of the musicians and situating their work within its wider historical and cultural context.

There has been surprisingly little scholarship on New Age music, and when the genre is discussed, it tends to be appreciated only in relation to the history of ambient music. Victor Szabo's *Turn On, Tune In, Drift Off* is the most expansive study of New Age music, but it presents it as part of "ambient music's psychedelic past," suggesting that it is significant primarily as an ancillary phenomenon to Brian Eno's more critically celebrated ambient releases and subsequent forms of electronic dance music.[5] I take a different approach, offering New Age music not as a quirky stepping stone to ambient music but as the audio component in a multimedia school of visionary art.[6]

Visionary art is art that emerges from and bears witness to non-ordinary states of consciousness as experienced through visions, near-death experiences, psychedelic drugs, and the meditative and ecstatic states induced by spiritual practices.[7] Carl Jung, whose transpersonal approach to psychology was an important influence on the New Age movement, made a distinction between psychological and visionary modes of artistic creation. The psychological mode deals with the emotional struggles that constitute the foreground of everyday life and is relatively easy to communicate and understand.[8] Visionary art, on the other hand, goes beyond the easily understandable foreground of life to enter territory that exceeds the grasp of purely rational comprehension.[9] With visionary art, Jung writes, we are not reminded of everyday waking reality but rather of "dreams, night-time fears and the dark recesses of the mind."[10] The topics that concern visionary artists can be apprehended only intuitively and are communicated with symbols that strive to express the unknown. Jung refers to such visionary symbols as "bridges thrown out towards an unseen shore."[11] The visionary school of New Age music created sonic bridges to an unseen shore, carrying listeners to dreamlike inner landscapes, forging sonic pathways to realms of cosmic awareness, and establishing modes of listening meant to integrate mind and body.

Visionary art provides a conceptual framework that is in harmony with the attitudes and statements of the originators of New Age music. Pioneering New Age musician Suzanne Doucet asserts that visionary experience defines New Age music: "Visionary art is art that makes it possible for the public to experience other-than-regular states of consciousness," she said. "You bring people to a different state through the music."[12] Harpist Georgia Kelly recalls a gathering that took place in 1980 that was attended by musicians like Steven Halpern, radio host Stephen Hill from *Music from the Hearts of Space*, and bookstore owners. The goal of the meeting was to come up with a name for the music they were creating and promoting. The final decision was to call it "New Age" music, but Kelly and others had been advocating for the term "visionary" music: "I think that's a very accurate word to describe it," Kelly said.[13] I agree with Kelly, and in this book, I reconsider New Age music of the 1970s and early '80s as a school of visionary art happening in audio.

The analysis of visionary art has typically focused on the work of visual artists such as William Blake, Ernst Fuchs, Alex and Allyson Grey, Robert Venosa, Martina Hoffmann, H. R. Giger, Amanda Sage, and Penny Slinger. The New Age musicians of the 1970s and '80s had much in common with these visual artists and brought a similar approach to the realm of recorded music. *Bridge to an Unseen Shore* expands the literature on visionary art by extending it into the domain of audio. That said, I take a multimedia approach that tracks New Age music as it intersects with a wide array of visual forms, including visionary painting, planetarium performances, laser lightshows, blacklight posters, album art, video art, and an avant-garde tradition of visual music. New Age music was at the forefront of multimedia experimentation in the 1970s and '80s and deserves wider recognition as a model for audiovisual experiments in the digital era. Several New Age musicians had successful careers composing music for film and television, and New Age music found a place on the soundtrack of television programs like *Cosmos* (1980) and experimental documentaries like *Chronos* (1985) and *Baraka* (1992).

Telling the story of this cohort of visionary musicians sheds new light on the art and media of the 1970s and '80s, and it also brings something new to scholarship on the New Age movement. Little attention has been paid to the music or the visual art associated with that movement.[14] When we encounter New Age spirituality through the music that emerged alongside it, we can newly grasp some of its characteristic ways of thinking. There is an intimate relationship between the New Age movement and New Age music, and the two will intersect and overlap many times in the pages ahead.[15]

Beyond a shared name, what is the relationship between the movement and the music? Scholars writing about subcultural music have used the concept of homology to refer to "the symbolic fit between the values and lifestyles of a group, its subjective experience and the musical forms it uses to express or reinforce its focal concerns."[16] There tends to be an organic relation between the central values of a subculture and the visual and musical styles it prefers. As we will see, New Age musical forms were in harmony with New Age practices and ways of thinking, and the music had an organic connection to cultural niches created by the New Age movement.

In an influential article written in 1972, the sociologist Colin Campbell described the emerging New Age movement as a "cultural underground" that included a host of "deviant belief systems and their associated practices" that were opposed to the mainstream.[17] Seen in this light, New Age music should be placed alongside other examples of subcultural music of the 1970s like punk and disco, and in the chapters that follow, we will consider similarities and differences among these outsider genres. That said, the New Age movement was not monolithic and was less a singular "cult" than what Campbell calls a "cultic milieu" that was "continually giving birth to new cults."[18] My goal in this book, then, is to note the homologies between New Age music and the New Age movement writ large while also acknowledging the movement's diversity through the consideration of particular embodiments of it, such as the Continuum school of movement and meditation and the "sound and light" theories of the Surat Shabd Yoga community.

The New Age movement dawned with the arrival of Comet Kohoutek in 1973 and became the fertile cultural ground in which the seeds of New Age music were planted. Fourteen years later, in 1987, New Age music had grown and flourished to become a marketable genre in the popular music industry. That year, another astronomical event inspired a cultural reaction that hearkens back to the Kohoutek Celebration of Consciousness. The Harmonic Convergence was a global celebration that took place in August 1987, prompted by an impressionistic interpretation of the Mayan calendar and a theory that astronomical alignments had opened a cosmic window that would allow for contact with "higher galactic intelligences."[19] Gatherings to celebrate the Harmonic Convergence took place all over the world and received extensive media coverage.

The Kohoutek Celebration of January 1974 garnered scant attention from the press, but the Harmonic Convergence brought New Age spirituality into the bright light of mainstream media coverage. Indeed, New Age spirituality crossed over from the cultural periphery to the mainstream of American culture in the late 1980s. The figurehead of that crossover moment was Shirley MacLaine, a film star in the early 1960s associated with Frank Sinatra's Rat Pack who expanded her influence in the 1970s to include television specials and best-selling memoirs. MacLaine's autobiographical book *Out on a Limb* (1983) charts her exploration of New Age practices like channeling and past-life regression and was made into a primetime network television miniseries in 1987. Along with the Harmonic Convergence and the publication of books like Marilyn Ferguson's *The Aquarian Conspiracy* (1980), MacLaine's multimedia celebrity brought more visibility to New Age ideas while also prompting considerable critique and ridicule.

New Age music had its own dramatic emergence on the public stage in 1986 and '87. During those years, it became a recognizable radio format and a category for Grammy Awards, gained the backing of major record labels, was the subject of a *Time* magazine feature story, and found a new visual outlet on the music video cable channel VH1. A cohort of New Age stars emerged at this time who had little in common with the visionary school pioneers, and the music's ties to alternative spirituality were starting to seem like a marketing problem. The visionary school's distinctive sonic aesthetic and theories about the healing functions of music fell out of step with the entertainment landscape of the MTV era. By the 1990s, New Age music was associated with aging baby boomers and had become the target of widespread critical vitriol. As one writer put it, it became popular to dislike New Age music.[20]

This book will chart New Age music from its crystallization in 1973 to its remarkable crossover moment in 1987, but the story does not end there. Since the 2010s, New Age music has been rediscovered and reconsidered by collectors, music journalists, reissue labels, and a new generation of listeners who have been introduced to once-obscure cassette-only releases via online streaming services. Practices that seemed exotic at the Kohoutek Celebration in 1974 like yoga, health food, alternative healing, and mindfulness are now accepted parts of the culture, albeit without many of the occult and mystical trappings of the 1970s. Recreational cannabis use is legal in many states, and psychedelic therapy is a rapidly growing industry. The approach to musical composition with modular synthesizers that was developed by key figures in the visionary school is still vital and influential fifty years later. New Age experiments in multimedia have new relevance in an era of immersive venues like Sphere in Las Vegas. Moreover, New Age musicians were creating environmental art in the 1970s and so are an important point of reference for discussions of art and media in an era of climate change and species extinction. *Bridge to an Unseen Shore* is a comprehensive overview of this fascinating musical movement and will provide cultural and historical context for a new generation of listeners who feel in tune with its orientation toward mindfulness and self-care.[21]

By choosing to approach New Age music as a school of visionary art, my book begs the question, Is New Age music a genre or a movement?

The ambiguity between these two ways of describing the music can be found in an essay titled "New Age Music Made Simple," written by Stephen Hill, the host of the radio show *Music from the Hearts of Space*. In the first two paragraphs of the essay, he describes the music as both a "nascent *genre*" and a "new international musical *movement*."[22] Which is it? In film studies, scholars make a distinction between film genres and film movements. A genre, they propose, is a group of films with shared characteristics, and a movement is a group of people, filmmakers who share a set of artistic and political goals.[23] Examples of film genres are horror, Western, musical, and science fiction. Examples of film movements are Soviet montage, the French new wave, cinema novo, and Italian neorealism. Movement and genre also have different implications about historical duration: a movement is more restricted in time and place (France in the 1950s and '60s, for example), while a genre can continue for decades or centuries.

Since the mid-1980s, New Age music has been recognized by the music industry as a genre, and there are times in my analysis when it's useful to talk about it in those terms, for example when I'm discussing its aesthetic traits or charting its evolution over time. What I'm calling the "visionary school of New Age music," however, is more like a movement, a cohort of people with a shared set of goals and aesthetic techniques who are active at a specific time. One result of making this distinction is that there could be music that fits in the New Age genre but not in the visionary school movement, and we will see some examples in chapter 6.

My decision to present New Age music as a movement is in part the result of my methodology. The history I present is drawn from in-depth interviews with many of the musicians from this era, as well as visual artists, filmmakers, writers, and record company executives. For me, these interviews were more than fact-finding missions. Because I was interested as much in the ecstasies of visionary art as in the practical concerns of independent artists working in the music business, my conversations with musicians and artists oscillated between their radiant spiritual insights and the ups and downs of their careers in the industry. It was a privilege to talk with my interviewees at this stage in their lives, when they could look back with a thoughtful and nuanced perspective on a chapter of cultural history that is both long past and utterly alive in the present. While I was working on the book, I often told friends that I was interviewing people in their seventies and eighties about the '70s and '80s. To be honest, these interviews helped me navigate my own spiritual and emotional crisis, brought on by the death of my parents, the chaos of a disorienting and troubling political landscape, and a middle-aged body beginning to show signs of wear and tear. I frequently found myself moved to tears by my interviews, and I felt a deep personal conviction that there was vital wisdom in their wordless music and luminous films.

One of my first interviews was with the musician Michael Stearns. At one point in the conversation, our discussion of synthesizers and sequencer patterns moved into heady topics like the role of language in the experience of time. Stearns locked eyes with me through the Zoom call interface and said, "I'm calling you Jacob, but who is Jacob? That name was given to you, but who was Jacob before you were given that name? To me, the possibility that is presented with this music is to lose your sense of self within it, and there's a chance of discovery there, whatever that discovery might be."[24] Maybe it was the fact that Stearns and his cohort are roughly the same age as my parents, or maybe it was because of the uncanny resonance of some of his statements with things I had been thinking about, but I was choking back tears, trying to keep my composure, and feeling like this project was not going to be anything like I had expected.

Writing this book has personal resonance for me, but I didn't write it just for myself. In fact, I have a definite readership in mind: my students. I've spent the past fifteen years teaching courses about the history of the music industry at Northwestern University, and I thought a lot about my undergraduate students as I worked on this book. Teaching through the Trump years and the COVID lockdown, I saw more and more students struggling with mental health issues. I wanted them to know about the visionary school of New Age music, both as an uplifting and centering listening alternative and as a different model of what it means to be an artist in the modern world. The more I learned about New Age music and the spiritual and artistic practices in its orbit, the more I wanted my students to know about it. The artists of the visionary school were deeply spiritual without rejecting science; they were savvy do-it-yourself entrepreneurs making subcultural music that was meant to heal and uplift listeners. They were successful artists who maintained long careers without having to sell themselves as online celebrities. And they were environmental artists before it was fashionable. Perhaps most important, they had lived through the rise and fall of the New Age movement's utopian dreams and still had a sense of hard-won optimism. I thought my students should give them a listen. To borrow the words of the great visionary artist William Blake, I felt that if I could convey what was special about the New Age music scene, I'd be giving my students the end of a golden string, which, if they followed it, might lead them to heaven's gate.[25]

That said, *Bridge to an Unseen Shore* is not a classroom textbook, and the history I present will have something to offer scholars of sound and popular music as well as readers who are curious about topics like ambient and environmental sound, modular synthesizers, electronic music, music therapy, and alternative spirituality.[26] Scholars in film and media studies will connect with the book's case studies on the history of visual music, including musical performances in the planetarium, the Laserium light show, and experiments in visual music during the era of home video. Finally, art historians interested in visionary art will respond to the book's comparison between audio aesthetics and visual forms such as 1960s poster art, psychedelic light shows, and the paintings of the California visionary school.

The first in-depth study of an important but critically neglected musical movement, *Bridge to an Unseen Shore* features voices of the artists who defined it and situates it within a cultural and multimedia context. The first five chapters in the book each take as their organizing framework a particular defining characteristic of the music. Within that framework, each chapter charts the music's history between 1973 and 1987, introduces a cohort of musicians and fellow travelers, and provides analysis of their visionary works. Chapter 1, "Visionary Sounds," makes the case for the originators of New Age music as a school of visionary art.

We learn about New Age music's ties to various visionary experiences—communication with channeled entities, near-death experiences, and psychedelic epiphanies—as well as its do-it-yourself approach to musical creation as facilitated by modular synthesizers and home recording equipment. One of the distinctive characteristics of the visionary school is the location in which it was often created: a home studio that served both as a laboratory for creating new sounds and a site for inner spiritual growth. A visionary sensibility guided the use of the latest audio tools toward the creation of a distinctive sound, and in this chapter, we immerse ourselves in the warm bath of New Age musical aesthetics.

It wasn't just the music that made New Age music distinctive; it also had its own alternative network of distribution. Chapter 2, "Holistic Sounds," moves out of the New Age home studio to chart the ways in which New Age music circulated as self-produced recordings that were released on cassette and distributed in retail locations like metaphysical bookstores and health food stores. Radio programs like *Music from the Hearts of Space*, based out of San Francisco, helped codify the genre, create community among the musicians, and reach listeners.[27] Independent record companies like Ethan Edgecombe's Fortuna Records, an underappreciated example of a Black-owned record label, developed innovative approaches to marketing and distributing the music.

The New Age emphasis on healing allowed New Age music to move into sites not typically associated with music distribution, such as yoga studios, wellness centers, spas, doctor's offices, and hospitals.[28] New Age musicians pioneered the guided meditation cassette, which became a prevalent form of self-therapy and established the blueprint for current mindfulness apps like Calm, Headspace, and Insight Timer. Guided meditation tapes are key texts in this chapter and provide rich documents both of the New Age movement's holistic aspirations and the ways in which it failed to live up to them.

In a photo from the Kohoutek Celebration of Consciousness in 1974, we see a young woman at a biofeedback display wearing a headset while looking at a mandala-like pattern on a screen. Biofeedback is a procedure whereby physiological variables are connected to light and sound

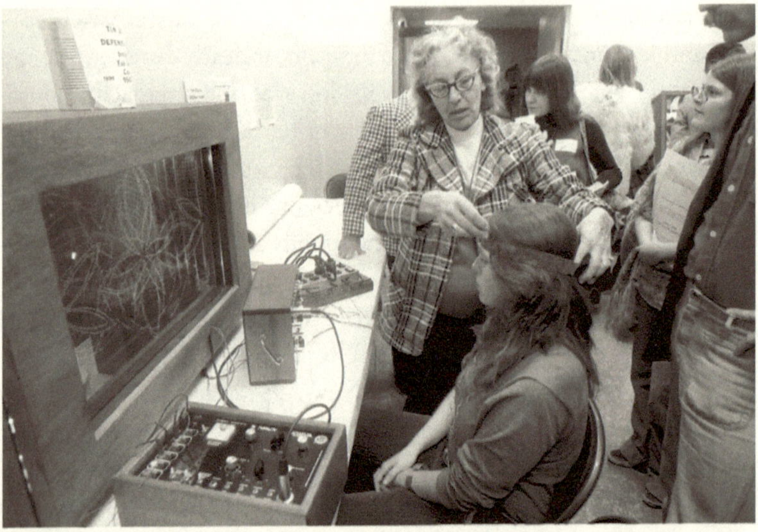

Demonstration of a biofeedback device at the Kohoutek Celebration of Consciousness, January 1974. Photo by Peter Simon, from the Peter Simon Collection, Special Collections and University Archives, University of Massachusetts Amherst Libraries.

displays and is emblematic of a New Age desire for multisensory experiences that could harmonize bodily sensation, mental perception, and spiritual growth.[29] That multisensory impulse was mobilized by the visionary school in a flowering of multimedia collaboration, and in chapter 3, "Luminous Sounds," I describe how New Age music became the catalyst for a host of multimedia experiments that constitute what I call "New Age audiovision."

New Age music was paired with a wide spectrum of visual forms, both avant-garde and popular. In that regard, it was typical of visionary art, which emerges from both the avant-garde and what scholar Erik Davis calls "our collective landscape of commercial dream-making."[30] The visionary school's New Age music was combined with color organs, poster art, album art, planetarium concerts, and laser light shows. Alongside these popular and commercial forms, New Age music was the common ingredient in a little-known history of visual music that stretches from experimental filmmaker Jordan Belson's Vortex concerts in the late 1950s to video releases by New Age musicians in the 1980s. A central theme in chapter 3 is luminosity, and across the diverse manifestations of New Age audiovision we find a unifying aesthetic of crystalline, gemlike light that is characteristic of the visionary experience. New Age music expressed that experience in sound, expanding the canon of visionary art and acknowledging the multisensory aspect of numinous states.

Chapter 4, "Cosmic Sounds," continues the investigation of New Age music's multimedia manifestations but shifts the focus from abstract visual music to the soundtrack for more mainstream film and television productions. The 1970s were a time when Hollywood producers were experimenting with new musical idioms, and New Age music became part of the mix. On television, Carl Sagan's PBS series *Cosmos* (1980) introduced many listeners to New Age music—which was also known as "space music"—and demonstrates the genre's close connection to space art, science illustration, and airbrush art of the 1970s. New Age music moved onto the cinematic soundtrack as well, with Michael Stearns's scores for Ron Fricke's experimental documentaries, which built on Fricke's groundbreaking work on *Koyaanisqatsi* (1982). Stearns began releasing New Age music as part of a vibrant scene of musicians, artists, and dancers at the Continuum studio in Los Angeles, and chapter 4 tells the story of that scene and its manifestation of New Age music's cosmic overtones. New Age music is "cosmic" in its ambitions to represent multiple scales of space and time, from inner consciousness to distant galaxies and from pulsating intercellular processes to the deep time of the universe. That interest in calibrating microcosm and macrocosm, inner and outer experience, made New Age music the ideal sonic accompaniment to similarly expansive film and TV productions that, in turn, provided new methods of distributing New Age music.

The 1970s have been called the Green Decade, and the New Age movement shared the ecological orientation of the nascent environmental movement of that time. In chapter 5, "Environmental Sounds," I consider New Age music's innovative use of wildlife field recordings and its engagements with ecological sciences like cybernetics, systems theory, acoustic ecology, bioacoustics, and biosemiotics. This chapter traces the web of interactions and alliances between New Age music and Greenpeace's Save the Whales movement, which gained international momentum in 1975, just as Iasos and Steven Halpern released their debut albums. Greenpeace's historic mission to confront whalers in 1975 was one of several attempts from that period to use modular synths to communicate with whales, and whale vocalization can be heard on New Age albums by Paul Horn and Paul Winter, among others. New Age music's environmental collaborations also resulted in other manifestations of New Age audiovision in the form of innovative multimedia album packaging and documentaries about human/animal encounters with a New Age soundtrack.

Though critics may differ about the start date of New Age music, most agree that its original manifestation came to an end around 1987. The final chapter, "Now Age," begins by describing New Age music's remarkable transformation into a category of mainstream popular music in the mid-1980s. As noted above, 1986–87 was a time when several major media events raised the profile of the New Age movement while also spurring considerable backlash against it. It would be easy to end the story in the late 1980s, and in so doing, present a familiar narrative of decline from authentic outsider art to co-optation and corruption by mainstream popular culture. Chapter 6 takes a different approach, and while acknowledging 1986–87 as a significant turning point, I continue beyond it to chart the experiences of the visionary school artists into the new millennium. Chapter 6 charts New Age music's reboot in the era of streaming services and smartphone apps. In my interviews, I was curious to ask the visionary school cohort about the optimistic outlook of the New Age movement that had greeted the arrival of Comet Kohoutek as a hopeful starseed and was still present during the Harmonic Convergence. Like any artistic movement, their attitudes and opinions about the present are not monolithic and provide a fascinating barometer for how their broader generational cohort have navigated the recent cultural and political landscape.

Some of the most inspiring conversations I had with my interviewees were prompted by questions about their outlook on the future. The future orientation of visionary art and its resilient optimism are boons that New Age music of the '70s and '80s can bestow on the present.[31] The visionary artist Ernst Fuchs argued that the function of art is to provide society with utopian ideas and impulses that are not typical of the world we inhabit but that may be typical in the future.[32] The resilient optimism of the visionary school of New Age music is extremely valuable now as a way to foster hope and imagine possible futures during uncertain and troubling times. *Bridge to an Unseen Shore* concludes, then, by arguing that the history of visionary music has a role to play in a future age that may still be made new.

ONE

Visionary Sounds

AN ILLUSTRATION IN A BOOK by the German philosopher Heinrich Khunrath (1560–1605) depicts an alchemist's *lab-oratorium*. This spacious chamber is divided in two, with a tent labeled "oratorium" on the left side and pillars enclosing a workspace designated "laboratorium" on the right. We see the alchemist kneeling in the oratorium, facing an altar on which can be seen a book on sacred geometry. In the laboratorium on the other side of the room, we see the tools of hands-on alchemical practice: bellows and coal to tend the furnace and beakers and bottles for mixing chemical compounds. In the center of the room, midway between the laboratorium and the oratorium, as if negotiating the realms of spirit and matter, is a table labeled "*musica sancta*" (sacred music) that is laden with musical instruments: a lute, violin, harp, and bell.[1]

The alchemical tradition depicted in this illustration was an important influence on the New Age movement of the 1970s, and the New Age musicians who were aligned with that movement created their own musica sancta that balanced spiritual and technological pursuits. The alchemist's *lab-oratorium* is a fitting emblem for a new kind of home studio that became feasible in the 1970s, one that was the site of both visionary illumination and state-of-the-art audio science. Compare the Khunrath image to a scene from a 1979 documentary on the New Age musician Iasos. Iasos stands in his home studio, a crowded space packed with reel-to-reel tape recorders, cassette tape decks, graphic equalizers, and an ARP synthesizer. The walls of the studio are covered with images that one journalist described as "spacey, otherworldly pictures of inner

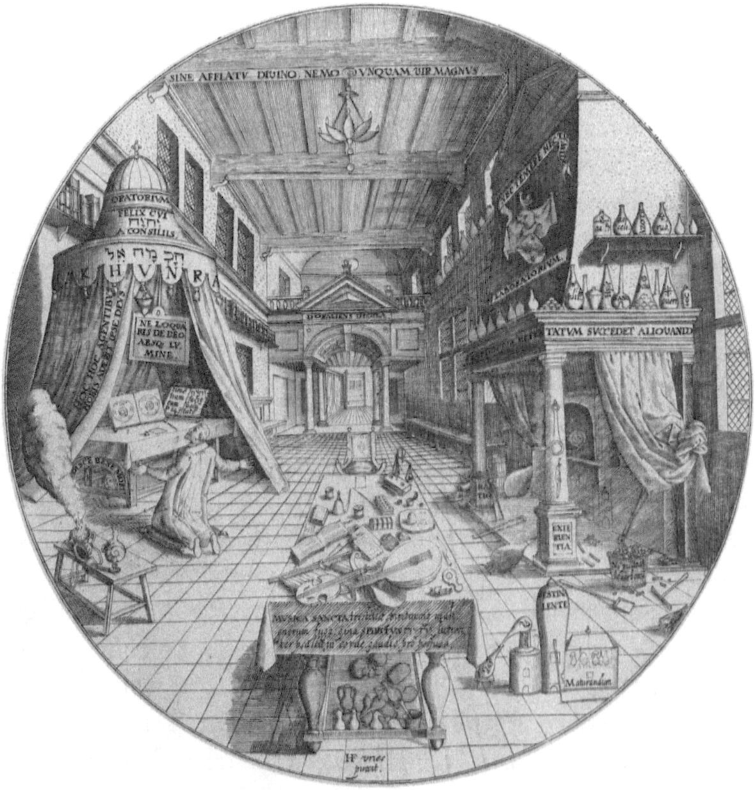

Illustration from Heinrich Khunrath's *Amphiteatrum sapientiae aeternae.*

vistas and etheric delights."[2] We glimpse a trippy painting by visionary artist Joseph Parker, photographs of natural landscapes, and images of blissful spiritual teachers. In interviews, Iasos made clear that his home studio was the site of spiritual as well as musical labor. "I call this my electric altar," he said to one visitor, and he described his studio as a "sacred temple" dedicated to receiving musical ideas from higher dimensions.[3]

Look again at the alchemist in the oratorium. Though he appears to be studying geometry, he is clearly not a dispassionate scientist. His body language, with arms outstretched and head raised to the heavens, suggests a state of ecstatic prayer or epiphany. An inscription beneath the canopy of the Oratorium reads, "Do not speak of God without illumination."[4] Substitute the word "art" for "God," and that statement would be an apt motto for visionary art, which is centrally concerned with numinous experiences of ecstatic illumination in both the creation and reception of artistic works.[5] Deriving from the work of Carl Jung, the term "numinous" was taken up by psychologists who were interested in non-ordinary states of mind. Stanislav Grof, a pioneer of the transpersonal psychology that flowered at the same time as the New Age movement, describes numinous experiences as those that are felt to be encounters with an order of reality that is radically different from the everyday material world. Numinous was a useful analytic category for Grof because it was more neutral than alternative terms like "religious," "mystical," "holy," or "sacred."[6] Visionary art draws upon and celebrates numinous experiences and non-ordinary states, and it is often received by audiences who acknowledge or replicate those experiences and states, which can result in a therapeutic or spiritual function for the artwork.

Numinous experiences may involve seeing images but they might also involve hearing otherworldly music or voices. The numinous experiences of the pioneers of New Age music often took sonic form and were communicated in audio. They were visionaries, but they were also "auditives," who used their studio art to hear the unheard, just as visionary painters have sought to "see the unseen."[7] New Age musicians saw themselves in these terms. Iasos stated that a shared impulse had fostered both the creation of a new style of visual art—visionary painting—and a new style of music—New Age music.[8] Including New Age music in the category of visionary art not only clarifies the motivations of the music, it also broadens the scope of visionary art to acknowledge that numinous experiences are not just perceptual and intellectual experiences; they are also powerfully emotional ones. The originators of what became known as New Age music were a school of visionary artists whose work in audio bears witness to the mood, atmosphere, and emotional tone of non-ordinary states and experiences as well as to their forms and shapes.

The visionary sounds created by the pioneers of New Age music had their roots in numinous experience and were cultivated in a distinctive kind of studio space. For perhaps the first time in history, artists working in sound could find the same sanctuary in a home studio that painters had enjoyed for centuries, a place where they had the time and the tools to translate their other-worldly experiences into self-contained works of single-authored audio. The image of the alchemist's lab-oratorium that begins this chapter provides a framework for understanding the spiritual and material dimensions of making music for the visionary school. In what follows, we will step into the oratorium to learn about the visionary aspects of New Age music. Then we cross over to the laboratorium to investigate the audio technologies and techniques that made those visionary experiences audible. Finally, we move to the center of the room to listen to the *musica sancta* that reverberates throughout the space.

ORATORIUM

The best way to orient ourselves to the visionary landscape of New Age music is to start with one of the featured performers at the Kohoutek Celebration of Consciousness in 1974. Iasos was born Joseph Benardot in Alexandroupolis, Greece, in 1947. He moved with his family to New York when he was four years old, and in the mid-1960s, he studied anthropology at Cornell University, where he also played flute in a smooth jazz band called the Nova-Shadow Quartet. Turning his back on a career in anthropology, he moved to California in 1968 to focus on his music. Around this time, he began to have an inner experience of "heavenly music." "It was like having a radio on in my head," he told an interviewer in 1977. "I used to listen to it and dance."[9] Auditory illuminations also resulted in his new name, which came to him one day when he heard an inner voice address him as "Iasos."[10]

The heavenly music he was hearing was not made by conventional instruments, and he didn't know how to create it. Nonetheless, he felt the encouragement of an inner voice, and in 1973, he had a life-changing experience during a session of automatic writing when he made contact with a spiritual being he referred to as Vista. This was the entity who had

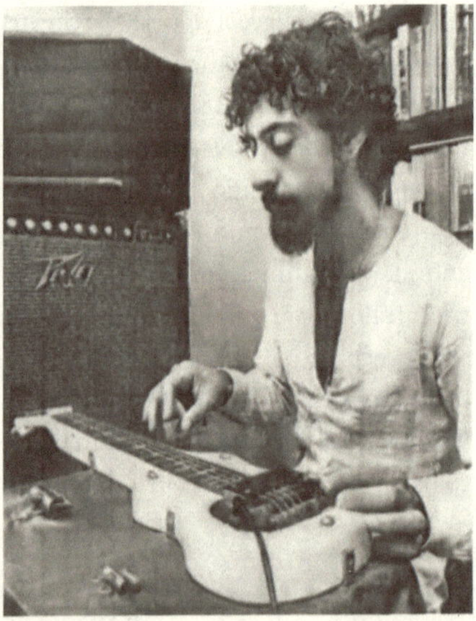

Iasos playing a lap steel guitar, circa 1976. © 2026. Photo courtesy of Iasos Beyond Editions.

been transmitting the mysterious music into his mind, and Iasos believed that he and Vista had made an agreement to work together before he was born.[11] Vista became the source for many musical ideas, which Iasos kept in a thick notebook he called *Sound Alchemy: Cookbook for Unusual Sounds.*[12] Iasos spoke openly about his collaborative creative process with entities like Vista, and his first album, *Inter-Dimensional Music* (1975), is credited as having been created not *by* Iasos, but *through* Iasos.[13]

Iasos's "heavenly music" is a good example of how visionary experience can take sonic form, and we find a similar dynamic with other pioneers of New Age music. Steven Halpern was born in Manhattan the same year as Iasos. He grew up on Long Island and felt at an early age that he was particularly sensitive to sound in the environment. A jazz trumpet player in high school, he attended the State University of New York at Buffalo in the mid-1960s, where he became interested in radical politics and spirituality. Around this time, he began to wonder about combining his interests by creating music for meditation. In 1969, with a post-graduation job lined up in Buffalo, Halpern decided to take a few weeks off to check out the music scene in San Francisco. On his way, he traveled to the University of Santa Cruz to see the manuscripts of visionary artist William Blake. While meditating on a bench in the redwoods outside of Santa Cruz, he heard "tinkling, crystalline sounds" and a voice saying, "This is the music that you've been praying to hear. Your job is to bring it out to the world."[14] This numinous experience of sound spurred the creation of the music on his debut album, *Spectrum Suite* (1975).

Just as Iasos and Halpern were preparing to release their debut albums, another pioneer of New Age music, Laraaji, had a life-changing sonic experience. Laraaji was born in 1943 in Philadelphia with the name Edward Larry Gordon, or "Larry G.," which he morphed into his New Age moniker. He studied music at Howard University and pursued a career in comedy at the Apollo Theatre in New York. He was also an actor and appeared in the 1969 film *Putney Swope*. Around this time, he was performing on the Fender Rhodes electric piano with an improvisational jazz-rock ensemble called Winds of Change. Then, in 1974, after long hours of intense meditation, he took a walk, and upon returning home, he happened to make eye contact with himself in a mirror. He abruptly fell into a deep meditative state as "a soundtrack for eternal time" became audible to him, taking the form of "multiple layers of brass instruments weaving and jamming and exploring space timelessness as sound." Laraaji felt this numinous experience to be "a cosmic homecoming," and it inspired him to embark on an extensive study of the spiritual dimension of sound and reshape his musical practice around a new instrument, the thirty-six-string autoharp.[15]

The examples of Iasos, Halpern, and Laraaji demonstrate how numinous experiences could take sonic form and inspire a new kind of visionary music. Visionary painters of the era had similar experiences, as we can see with Robert Venosa's epiphany in 1971, which he described as visions of a "dynamic energy in high-velocity motion, crystallizing and manifesting in a form that can only be described as angelic." Venosa felt compelled to translate those visions to his canvases, and he stated that it was only when he allowed the creative process to "work its way through me, instead of from me," that he was able to accomplish the task.[16] An example of Venosa's artistic translation can be seen in *Angelic Manifestation* (1974). Venosa's angelic manifestations and Iasos's heavenly music are two branches on the same visionary tree.

There are many routes leading to the numinous, and for several New Age musicians, it was a near-death experience that set them on the path. Steve Roach had such an experience in 1973, when he was eighteen years old. Roach was born outside San Diego and enjoyed what he called a typical Southern California teenage lifestyle, which included motocross racing. In 1973, Roach suffered life-threatening injuries when he was thrown end over end from a motorized off-road vehicle he was riding in the desert. He woke up in the hospital, feeling that he was outside of his body, floating in a corner of the room, looking down. The room was saturated in white light, and he felt his consciousness vibrating and scintillating in a way that he described as being "a sound that was not music" and unlike anything he had ever heard. He speculated that perhaps this was the sound of his consciousness dying, but whatever it was, it was intensely visceral. Roach recovered, but the experience forever changed his life. "I got completely infused," he said, "and I brought that back." Soon after this, he bought his first synthesizers. "The whole community around me thought I'd completely lost my mind," he said, "which was great because I had. I'd lost my mind and found the ultra-mind."[17]

Kat Epple of Emerald Web experienced a similarly profound and visceral near-death experience as a child. Epple was born in the small town of Peebles, Ohio, outside Columbus. "It's part of Appalachia," she said, "a very poor area. Some of the folks even spoke the old language, a mixture of Gaelic and Appalachian."[18] She learned to play piano when she was six years old, but finding herself drawn to the flute, she began serious study of that instrument in her teens. When she was nine years old, she and her brother were walking home from the store. "It was almost sunset," she recalled. "It looked like it might rain soon, but it wasn't raining yet, so we were talking and walking. I heard a big train go by in the trees nearby, and then we both realized that there's no train track there."

What she was hearing was the sound of a rapidly approaching tornado. They ran as fast as they could toward home, but Kat fell behind.

> I could hear the train coming closer, and the wind picked up, and then, as I'm still running with all my might, everything got really quiet and there was this beautiful sound. It was almost like being inside of a huge flute that was playing a chord. It was so beautiful that it was completely paralyzing. I just stopped and it was a spiritual feeling, because I'm sure it was going all through my body. People might describe it as angels or something, because it felt so good and it was so beautiful. It was so beautiful that it made me cry. I was standing there, and then I suddenly felt my body being pulled up off the ground. My feet were being pulled off the ground, and I grabbed a tree and held on as I was being pulled up into this tornado. . . . I could see big trees that were being picked up and moved around like they were doing a dance. . . . Then I heard the train again, and I was able to get off the tree and run inside.[19]

"That was a very spiritual experience," she said. "The feeling of that music playing. I've never been able to equal the music I heard that day."[20]

Epple's near-death experience had a powerful sonic component, and it helped orient her music to the cosmic and elemental concerns of visionary art. When I asked Epple if she saw a connection between her spiritual experience of the tornado and later experiences with psychedelic drugs, she replied, "Absolutely. . . . The two are very connected."[21] Indeed, coming of age in the 1960s, most of the pioneer New Age musicians had formative experiences with psychedelic drugs.

The German New Age musician Deuter spoke about the profound effects of hallucinogenic drugs, especially LSD. Georg Deuter was born in Falkenhagen, Germany, in 1945. Growing up in what he called a "tiny village amongst trees," he developed an early affinity with the woods and the silences of nature. He taught himself to play flute and guitar, and as a young man, he became part of a vibrant music scene in Munich. It was there that he had his first experiences with LSD. "It was incredible," he told the music journalist Lee Underwood, "such an opening of the mind. . . . For me, the experiences were very strong, very enriching, very meaningful. They gave me a totally different vision of life, a completely different perspective from a different standpoint." Deuter compared the experience to living in a cave and suddenly seeing the sun: "I saw that there was a blue sky outside, and it was much bigger than I had ever thought. It was like seeing a movie of how it is outside the cave. . . . I wanted to *live* those things I saw in the movie," he said.[22] These insights helped to transform him into a spiritual seeker, and he travelled to India several times in the 1960s, eventually living for five years at Bhagwan Shree Rajneesh's ashram in Puna, composing and recording music as part of the ashram's communal meditation practice.[23]

Deuter's trajectory from LSD to ashram is typical of many New Age musicians, who felt the consciousness-altering potential of the psychedelic revolution of the 1960s and wanted to find ways to continue, extend, and deepen it. As Deuter put it, they wanted to *live* the movie. Peter Michael Hamel, a composer who was part of the same Munich music scene as Deuter, published a book titled *Through Music to the Self* (1978). In it, Hamel writes that music could provide what drugs had failed to achieve; the creation of "a genuine, lasting intensification of awareness."[24] For these New Age musicians, as for the countercultural generation more broadly, psychedelics, spiritual awakening, and music were intimately intertwined.[25] In his book *Psychedelic Information Theory*, James L. Kent argues that music can be a bridge between psychedelic intoxication and everyday states of consciousness, serving both as a soundtrack to mind-altering trips and as a way to encode the drug experience so that it can be relived after the fact.[26] As we will see, some of the distinctive characteristics of New Age music can be understood as the encoding of psychedelic experience.

Non-ordinary states of consciousness and moments of numinous illumination are a common thread that runs through the lives of the New Age musicians of this era, be they visions, near-death experiences, psychedelic drugs, or spiritual and meditative practices. These musicians did not regard such events as fleeting novelties but as pivotal and deeply meaningful episodes in their lives, and they translated them into music saturated with their sublime emotional qualities.[27] Like the alchemist in the oratorium, they did their work with the gestures of ecstatic illumination.

Visionary experience became a defining characteristic of New Age music, setting it apart from the mainstream of popular music. This is not to say that musicians working in other genres couldn't be inspired by numinous experiences but rather that they became a defining characteristic of New Age music, and the embrace of such experiences helped to make the visionary school a musical underground, just as the New Age movement was a "spiritual subculture."[28] Without the support system of established musical institutions, these musicians relied on a self-sufficient, do-it-yourself approach to creating their recordings. To explore their audio alchemy, we need to move from the oratorium to the laboratorium.

LABORATORIUM

The New Age home studio was a sacred altar, but it was also a workspace where the latest audio technology allowed musicians to become remarkably self-sufficient as composers, recording artists, and producers. New Age music emerged during the era of multi-track magnetic tape recording, and the visionary school were early adopters of newly affordable tape recording systems that allowed them to avoid paying expensive fees for studio time and session musicians.

"I'm very much a loner," Iasos said in an interview. "I do it all myself. . . . In the old days, before multitrack recording, you needed to have multiple musicians to have music that had more than one instrument, but nowadays, with multitrack recording, one guy can do it all." Iasos had difficulty manifesting the sounds he heard in his head when he relied on other musicians, who tended to make his music "more normal, earthly, and conventional." A friend suggested that he try doing it all himself at home. When he did, he finally felt satisfied with the results and his career began to blossom. Iasos avoided working with engineers and producers as well. "If you have engineers then the result becomes a blurred compromise," he said. "I'm always 100 percent in control of what I'm manifesting."[29]

Steve Roach noted that the mainstream music industry operated in $200-an-hour professional recording studios. "It would be like if you had a history of painting where painters were only allowed to work in that kind of commercial, institutional environment," he said. What kind of paintings would have been created in such a pay-by-the-hour context? Early in his career, Roach decided that he wanted to find an alternative way to make recordings, and he set about acquiring the tools to create his own "sacred, quiet, controlled space."[30] Roach refers to his self-contained sonic sanctuary as the "timeroom."[31]

The New Age laboratorium was made possible by new audio technologies, not only affordable multitrack recorders, but also modular synthesizers. The modular synth is an instrument comprising separate components (or modules) such as oscillators, filters, sequencers, and amplifiers that are contained in a box or rack and connected to each other with patch cables, making it highly flexible and customizable.[32] Modular synths designed by Robert Moog and Don Buchla became available in the late 1960s, and a third synth developer, Serge Tcherepnin, played a significant role in the visionary school of New Age music when he launched his company in the 1970s.[33] Tcherepnin studied composition at Harvard University and then taught at CalArts in the 1960s, where he encountered Don Buchla's synths. He left CalArts to become a freelance synthesizer manufacturer in the early 1970s, with the goal of creating "the complete home studio" that would "function for the composer much like the painting studio functions for the painter."[34]

New Age musician Kevin Braheny Fortune said that Tcherepnin wanted to make "the Volkswagen of synthesizers," that is, a "people's synth" that was affordable and accessible.[35] Braheny Fortune was born in Elgin, Illinois, and studied saxophone in high school, but became a multi-instrumentalist while at VanderCook College of Music in Chicago. Trained in classical music and jazz, Braheny Fortune was motivated to explore new musical horizons by psychedelic experiences with mescaline and LSD in the late 1960s and early 1970s. "I did it in a very intentional, almost sacred way," he said. "I wanted to learn something about myself, about consciousness." Braheny Fortune said that New Age

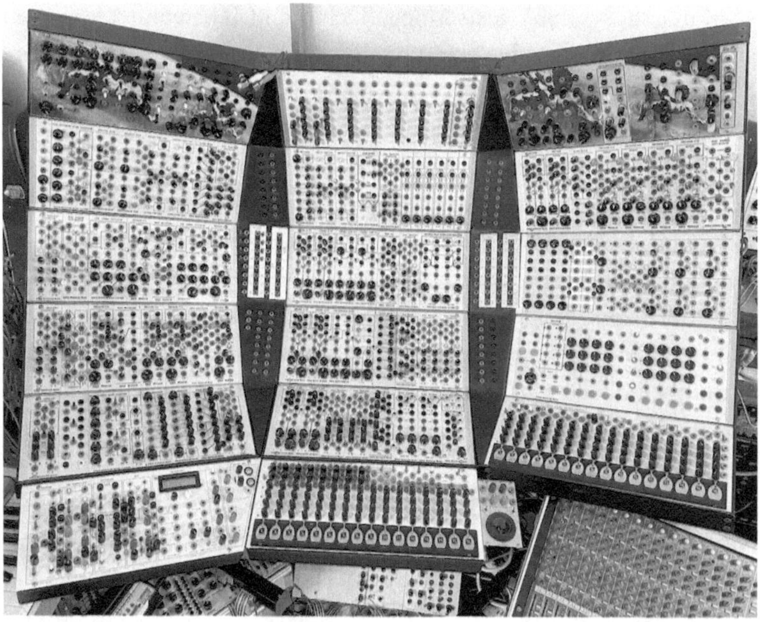

Kevin Braheny Fortune's Mighty Serge synthesizer. Photo courtesy of Kevin Braheny Fortune.

music had its origins in this desire for mind expansion, and that psychedelics helped him to move beyond his habitual ways of thinking about music to create something new.[36]

He purchased his first synthesizer around this time and moved to Los Angeles in 1975, where he met two important figures in the emerging world of analog synths: Malcolm Cecil, a musician and producer who cocreated the "TONTO" synthesizer, and, via Cecil, Serge Tcherepnin, who had designed an oscillator for Cecil's TONTO system.[37] Braheny Fortune began working with Tcherepnin on his "Serge" modular system, and by 1977, he had constructed an impressive modular synth setup that rivaled TONTO. Braheny Fortune called his synth "The Mighty Serge." Using this system, along with his expertise on instruments like saxophone and flute, he created seminal New Age tracks like "Lullaby for the Hearts of Space" and "Perelandra."

While the synth pioneers Moog, Buchla, and Tcherepnin are all men and audio technology has traditionally been a field dominated by men, New Age music became a space where a number of female synth pioneers could use that technology to gain access to a male-dominated culture of studio recording and electronic music. Suzanne Ciani, who released popular New Age albums in the 1980s, discovered that there were "no women" in behind-the-scenes music production during that era. "There were no engineers, no assistant engineers. Maybe there was somebody out in the front desk that was female," she recalled. That exclusionary culture only heightened the appeal of getting in on the ground floor with new modular synth technology, and Ciani was soon mastering the Buchla synth.[38] Kat Epple learned to operate early Moog and Buchla units while she was at the University of South Florida. "As soon as we started studying the synthesizers, we fell in love with them," she said. Modular synths appealed to Epple for several reasons. "I love the concept of molding the sound and having it evolve as it plays," she said. That allowed her to emulate the sounds that she heard in her dreams. Moreover, synths also gave her a sense of controlling the musical experience above and beyond playing her flute parts in symphonic music. When someone asked her, "What instrument do you want to play in an orchestra?," she replied, "I want to play an orchestra."[39]

New Age music was a haven for a number of female synth pioneers, not only Ciani and Epple but also Suzanne Doucet, Joanna Brouk, and Pauline Anna Strom.[40] These female artists enrich the history of electronic music as well as the canon of visionary art, another domain, like electronic music, that has tended to be male dominated.[41] Modular synths spurred the development of sonic visionary art in part because they prompted new ways to think about creating music. As Kat Epple put it, synths made her realize that making music was more than just playing the notes that you or somebody else wrote; instead, it was "creating whole new sounds." With synths, "I could see the music as sound waves," she said. "I loved that."[42]

In a typical modular synth circuit, or "patch," an oscillator produces a continuous sound wave, which is then modified using filters to change

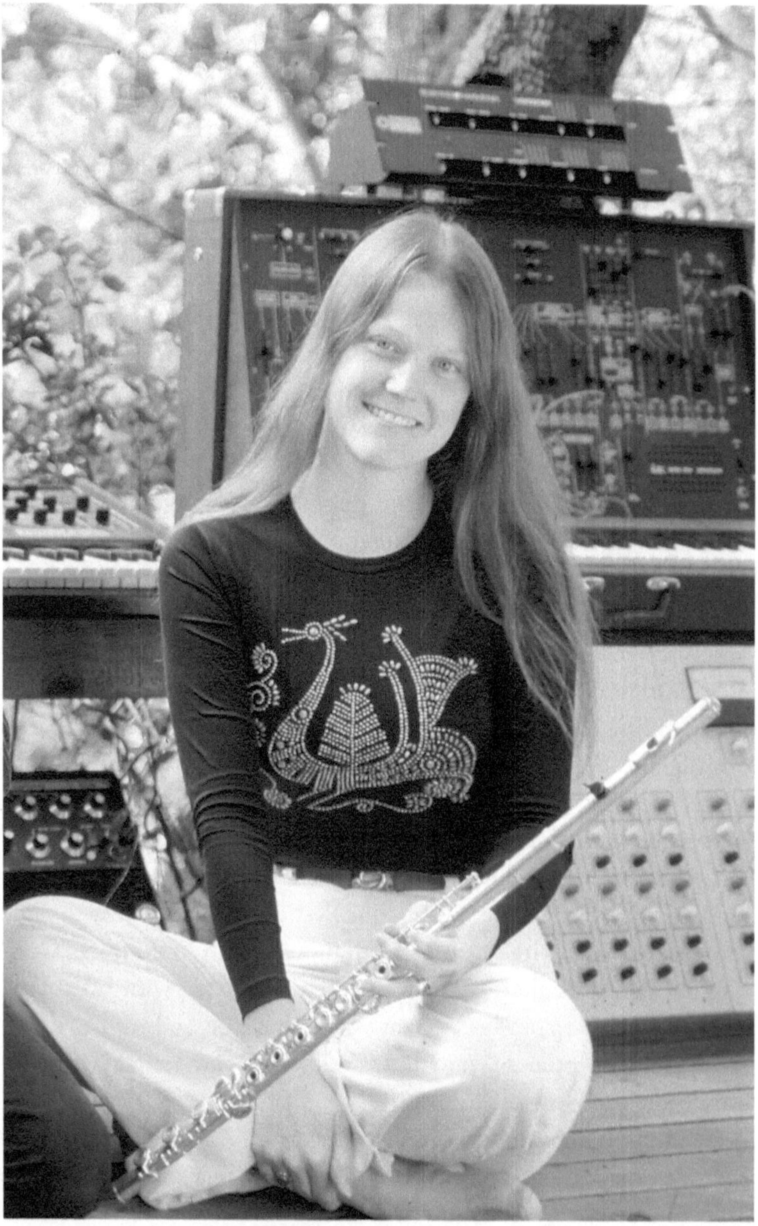

Kat Epple of Emerald Web, circa 1980. Photo by Bjorn Kartomten.

the timbre, amplifiers to adjust the volume, envelopes to shape the attack and decay, and a sequencer to organize the sound into a repeating pattern.[43] This kind of "subtractive synthesis" is often compared to a sculptor chipping away at a block of stone to reveal a statue.[44] This approach to making music is quite distinct from a more traditional approach to composing with a piano or guitar, which starts with a repertoire of chord progressions and melodies rather than raw electrical oscillations. In another type of musical synthesis, new sounds are constructed by blending the tones created by different oscillators on the modular rack.[45] The result of this kind of "additive synthesis" is that the composer can create a new musical instrument with each session. In fact, a modular synth is not an instrument that produces melodies, but an instrument that produces musical instruments.

Modular synths were important tools in the New Age laboratorium, allowing for a new conceptual framework for making music.[46] The liberating audio science of the laboratorium meshed well with the visionary impulse to manifest new levels of consciousness in the Oratorium. Modular synths were not the only New Age instruments on the laboratorium table, however. The Fender Rhodes electric piano provided the sparkling tones that are the signature sound on Steven Halpern's early albums.[47] The harp is another prominent instrument in New Age music, with Gail Laughton's album *Harps of the Ancient Temples* (1969) often cited as one of the prototypes for the genre. Georgia Kelly and Joel Andrews were influential New Age harpists of this era, and Iasos not only played the zither but used a plastic yogurt container to glide across a keyboard to imitate the strumming of a harp on the track "Crystal Fountain of Light."[48] Laraaji is closely associated with his thirty-six-string autoharp, an instrument whose name he finds to be rich in metaphysical overtones: "Auto means 'self.' Harp of the self. Harp of the universally complete self."[49]

The flute is another favorite instrument; Iasos and Kevin Braheny Fortune play the flute, as do the two members of Emerald Web, and the list of other notable New Age flutists includes Paul Horn, Peter Davison, Larkin, James Newton, Kitaro, R. Carlos Nakai, and Schawkie Roth.

The flute can be credited with forging the musical and romantic partnership of Kat Epple and Bob Stohl of Emerald Web. After a long day being a student at the University of South Florida, Epple went outside to unwind. She was sitting under a tree playing her flute when Bob walked by and heard the music wafting in the breeze. He had his own flute with him and began to play along. Epple had her eyes shut as she was playing and so did not know the origin of this mysterious second flute. Both continued to play and harmonize with each other. When they finished this impromptu duet, Epple opened her eyes to find that a crowd of people had gathered to listen. Epple and Stohl were soon working together, though they realized they needed to expand their instrumental palette. ("What the heck are you gonna do with two flute players?") That's when they discovered synthesizers.

The combination of flute and synthesizer heard on Emerald Web recordings is a signature sound of the visionary school of New Age music, and it is a sound that shows how these artists slipped between musical categories. Epple recalled that there were times when the flute seemed to be an affront to electronic musicians, who would say, "Why the hell are you bringing flutes into an electronic music studio?" At the same time, she recalled playing at a New Age event where another performer on the bill asked, "What the hell are you doing bringing a synthesizer to a New Age festival?"[50] R. Carlos Nakai, the most renowned practitioner of the Native American flute in the New Age style, made several albums that combine synths with the flute: *Cycles* (1985) and the debut album by the group Jackalope, released in 1986. "The synthesizer was very intriguing to me," Nakai said, because of the range of sounds it could produce. "I can make ocean sounds. I can make bird sounds. I can make sounds like there's a pipe organ near me."[51] Nakai was working with the independent label Canyon Records, which suggested marketing his records as "New Age." Nakai liked the label because he felt that it allowed him a high degree of creative freedom. "It allows me to dream as much as I want to, to combine electronics with my voice, with natural sounds, with everything." His music is "Old/New Age" he said, because it combines old and new, past and future.[52] The visionary school of New

Age music developed an orientation that allowed these instruments to happily coexist where others saw them as incompatible.

The Fender Rhodes, harp, and flute are all instruments with clear, pure tones in a high register, and part of their appeal for visionary music can be explained by the way they serve as sonic metaphors for a transcendent, spiritual, "high" state of consciousness. The flute and the harp are also instruments that suggest ancient and even prehistoric sounds. Gail Laughton's proto-New Age album *Harps of the Ancient Temples* has tracks with titles like "Stonehenge 1600 B.C.," "Greece 300 B.C.," and "Pompeii 76 A.D." In the guide to New Age music made by the radio program *Music from the Hearts of Space*, there is a subcategory of "Contemporary Ancient" music, defined as "music made today with awareness of the sounds and expressions of the deep past."[53] Flutes and harps worked well to communicate that kind of contemporary ancient awareness.

An appeal to ancient or primordial sounds is characteristic of New Age music and of the New Age movement as well. New Age philosophies tend to believe that all religious traditions and spiritual practices lead to the same perennial, essential, esoteric core.[54] At its worst, this kind of perennialized outlook can result in a facile hodgepodge of cultural appropriation and stereotyping.[55] By and large, the pioneers of New Age music avoided that pitfall. They were careful to credit their sources of inspiration, earnest in their study of non-Western musical traditions, and developed their own distinctive alchemical mix of old and new rather than appropriating traditional styles wholesale. The impulse to find connections across temporal, geographical, and cultural gulfs led to some stunning innovations in the New Age musical palette: the trademark combination of modular synths and acoustic instruments like the flute and harp, for example, or Steve Roach's blend of synths and didgeridoo drones. Indeed, where other listeners at the time viewed synthesizers as diametrically opposed to more traditional, "organic" sounds, the New Age cohort saw both as equally natural and spiritual. Iasos saw a unity where other people saw a dichotomy between electronic music and the organicism of the New Age movement. "What could be more organic than electrons?" he asked. "What do you think a flower is made of? I think of electrons as these very, very tiny God-beings that are extremely sensitive to consciousness and are just rushing—literally at the speed of light—to fulfill your will."[56]

Iasos's comments illustrate how work in the New Age laboratorium was shaped by the spiritual outlook of the oratorium. It's time now to listen to the distinctive blend of musical currents pulsing through modular synths and ethereal melodies emanating from flutes and harps as we step away from the laboratorium and walk to the table at the center of the alchemist's lab-oratorium. What did New Age *musica sancta* sound like?

MUSICA SANCTA

Peter Michael Hamel recounts an Armenian folk legend about an old man who spent hours playing a cello that had only one string. Holding his finger at the same place on the string, he would earnestly bow the same note for hours on end. One evening his wife gently observed that other cello players had four strings and moved their fingers up and down its neck. The old man shook his head and said, "Of course the others move their fingers up and down. They are looking for the right place. I have found it."[57]

As Hamel's anecdote indicates, the minimalist music of composers like Philip Glass, Terry Riley, La Monte Young, and Steve Reich was a major influence on the visionary school of New Age music.[58] New Age musicians were interested in minimalism as a model for what Peter Michael Hamel called "meditative music," music that could remove one's "inner restlessness" and quiet the ceaseless thrum of "reasoning and cogitating."[59] Hamel wrote that minimal music worked to dissolve the distinction between movement and non-movement, resulting in a "deep self-experience."[60] In addition to being meditative, the minimalist drone could be experienced as deeply psychedelic, rhyming with the ways in which drugs like LSD and psilocybin destabilize the linear perception of time.[61] James L. Kent writes that psychedelics create a sense of timelessness in which an object of attention, even one as mundane as a rock or as unchanging as a musical drone, will "be amplified with increasing salient complexity the longer it is held in focus."[62]

The influence of minimalism was something New Age music shared with another outsider music of the 1970s: disco. Hit records by Donna Summer and Giorgio Moroder used repeating synth lines to create sleek, propulsive dance music, mobilizing minimalist techniques to get bodies moving. Musicologists like Robert Fink have described the links between disco and minimalism but tend to present this history strictly as a dialogue between the classical concert hall and the disco dancefloor. New Age music brings another perspective to accounts of minimalism's cultural resonance and reveals how that musical idiom moved into another set of contexts and functions.[63]

The influence of minimalism can be heard on New Age's many soothing, gently pulsating drones. Notably, these long, sustained tones tend to be in the familiar and comforting tonality of a major scale and so fall within traditional notions of Western harmony. In their *Music from the Hearts of Space* guide book, Anna Turner and Stephen Hill write that the music they played on their influential radio show was based in harmony. "Sounds which are harmonic with one another give a sense of completion and completeness," they explain.[64] The repetitive, droning, harmonic sounds characteristic of the minimalist composers of the 1960s had a liberating effect on soon-to-be New Age musicians who felt confined by their academic musical training. Several New Age pioneers studied composition in universities but left because they found the dominant style of atonal music to be restrictive.[65] They may not have been fully integrated into the world of contemporary classical music, but New Age musicians often had considerable musical training.

Peter Davison studied music composition at Cal State Northridge and UC San Diego. The model of composition being taught there was dissonant and arhythmic. "That's what I was supposed to do," he said. "I remember the first time in one of my classes that I used a major third, and I got an F!" Davison appreciated the atonal style but felt that it was held up as the only viable or valid approach.[66] The message he received

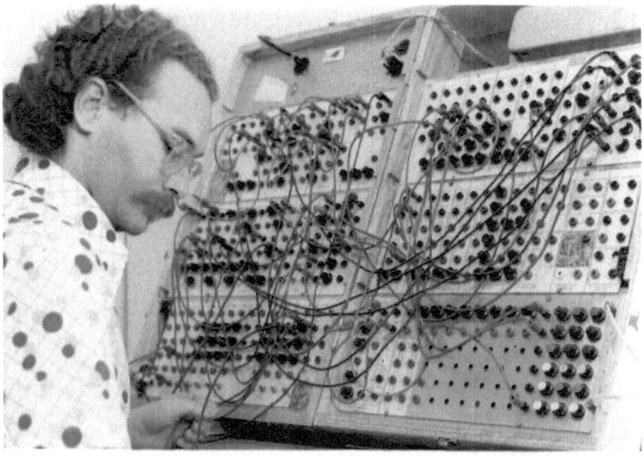

Peter Davison working with his Serge synthesizer. Photo courtesy of Peter Davison.

from his teachers and peers was that he had to reject the rules of harmony and "break out from the prison of going from a one chord to a five chord. I finally said, 'You know something, I love chords. I love harmony. I like going from a one chord to a five chord.'" Such was his frame of mind in 1979, when he began recording the tracks that would comprise his first New Age album. "It was so freeing," he said.[67] Davison also wanted his music to reach an audience, and he felt a certain responsibility to make music that was "more healing, soothing, uplifting, relaxing, pleasant to listen to and easier to understand" than what was happening in university composition programs.[68]

Davison set up a home studio that included a Serge synthesizer. He had been introduced to modular synths in the late 1960s and learned to operate them so well that he was asked by his instructor to teach the electronic music section of his Twentieth Century Music class at Cal State.[69] In 1975, Davison was working for Serge Tcherepnin, building the first synths for his new company. Tcherepnin made Davison an offer: if he built the first eighteen synths, he could keep the nineteenth. Davison's custom-designed Serge unit can be seen on the original cover of his first LP, *Selamat Siang: Music on the Way* (1980).[70]

Another New Age composer who rejected academic training in favor of a more harmonic approach is Don Robertson. Born in Denver, Colorado, in 1942, Robertson was drawn to music as a child but was discouraged by his father, who forced him to join the Navy in 1960. After his discharge in 1964, he studied music at the University of Colorado and the Juilliard School in New York and also learned to play traditional Indian instruments like sitar and tabla. In the late 1960s, he studied composition with avant-garde composer Morton Feldman and absorbed the work of contemporary composers like Anton Webern and Arnold Schoenberg. He came to reject this approach when he realized that this kind of music "did not elevate me. It did not make me feel good. I would play Schoenberg's music on dark, gloomy days and enter a depressed mental fog."[71]

Realizing that modern avant-garde music contributed to his feelings of confusion and pain, he decided to pursue a different, more tonal and uplifting style. Robertson's first album, *Dawn* (1969), is an early entry in the New Age genre and features his more positive approach to music. On the opening track, we hear a hypnotic performance by Robertson on the zither, which creates swirling sonic patterns like eddies in a river. His cassette release *Celestial Ascent* (1980) developed this style, with side one exploring variations on a single minor chord, and side two a fifteen-minute exploration of a sunny major chord.[72]

The two tracks on Robertson's *Celestial Ascent* resolutely remain on a single chord, abandoning the verse-chorus-bridge song structure typically heard on popular music. Steven Halpern said that he rejected chord progressions built on patterns of dissonance and resolution because he wanted to encourage listeners to remain in the present moment, which he referred to as the "hear-and-now."[73] Halpern wrote that most musical compositions use chord progressions to create a sense of anticipation followed by a sense of relief, and "as long as the listener's mind keeps anticipating the final resolution of the music, the listener is not truly at rest."[74] Halpern marketed his New Age releases as an "anti-frantic alternative," and on the debut record in this style, *Spectrum Suite* (1975), we hear the warm, bell-like tones of the Fender Rhodes in gently cascading arpeggios that glide across a major chord.[75]

New Age music tends to eschew the tension and release of harmonic development as well as standard verse-chorus song structure. In popular music, the goal is usually to create big, memorable choruses and melodic "hooks" that get stuck in the listener's head.[76] In New Age music, by contrast, melody takes a backseat to musical timbre, as indicated by Hamel's anecdote about the old man playing a single note on the cello. That anecdote is also emblematic of the fact that New Age music tends to downplay instrumental virtuosity, setting it apart from one of its important precursors: progressive rock. The heyday of progressive or "prog" rock was the early 1970s, with releases by bands like Genesis, Yes, Pink Floyd, King Crimson, Jethro Tull, and Emerson, Lake, and Palmer. Visionary school musicians were inspired by bands like these, and there are several ways we can hear the influence. Prog and New Age were "post-hippie" extensions of the 1960s counterculture. Both combined traditional acoustic instruments with modern amplified and electronic sounds, deployed musical forms of longer duration than the standard three minute pop song, and explored sci-fi and fantasy themes.[77]

Visionary school musicians were selective in their borrowing from prog, however, and New Age music is different in several respects. While both prog and New Age combined acoustic and electric sounds, the prog approach emphasized contrast through the alternation of loud electric and soft acoustic sections. New Age music emphasizes a harmonious blend of acoustic and electric and avoids jarring section transitions. Prog rock was also much more geared to live performance in the rock style, with extended solos that bombastically showcase instrumental virtuosity.[78] New Age musicians had the same synths and flutes as Yes and Emerson, Lake, and Palmer, but instead of producing long, intricate solos, they produced meditative drones and cosmic atmospheres. In this regard, New Age music is a stripped down, back-to-basics response to progressive rock that parallels punk's similar rejection of prog's self-indulgent posturing.

A nice example of how prog rock influenced the visionary school, albeit in circumscribed ways, can be found in Steve Roach's mention of the Yes album *Close to the Edge* (1972) as an influence. Roach is quick to clarify that it was really just the first fifty seconds of the album that caught his ear: a long fade-in that creates a beguiling and mysterious atmosphere from recordings of birds, rushing streams, diaphanous keyboards, and tinkling bells before the bombastic entrance of the band, all simultaneously playing a thousand notes a minute. Roach said that he wanted to hear that opening minute extended to an hour. Roach's interest in the quiet, textually rich opening of the album indicates how New Age musicians approached the home studio as a laboratory for timbral alchemy—recall Iasos's *Cookbook for Unusual Sounds*—with modular synthesis as a means to invent novel tones and textures. A track on Iasos's debut album, *Inter-Dimensional Music* (1975), shows the New Age preference for timbre over melody and harmonic development. "Bubble Massage" is four minutes of hyper-real bubble sounds created by recording dry ice being dropped into a large coffee pot filled with hot water. Iasos altered the speed of the recording to create layers of "bubble harmonics." Iasos's low-budget, DIY studio art was guided by spiritual and therapeutic goals; he was interested in water's resonance with the "emotional body," and that motivated him to create a track that would wash or purify that aspect of the self.[79] "Bubble Massage" shows us how the priorities of the oratorium could inspire novel musical timbres in the New Age home studio.

Perhaps the most distinctive textural characteristic of New Age music is its sense of space, created by reverberation and echo effects. New Age music was also known as "space music," and references to wide open spaces and heavenly vistas permeate the genre—note the New Age radio show *Music from the Hearts of Space*, for example, or the New Age record label Celestial Harmonies. Steven Halpern claimed that a sonic representation of space was a "vital dimension" of New Age music, linking the music to the sounds heard in prehistoric caves and cathedrals, where "echo and reverberation carry strong religious and otherworldly symbolism."[80] The visionary school of New Age musicians may have been working in small home studios, but their recordings brought listeners to vast, sublime spaces.

Reverberation became a central aspect of Kevin Braheny Fortune's musical practice while he was studying music at VanderCook College of Music. Spending long hours in a tiny, cinderblock practice room equipped with an old upright piano, Braheny Fortune would use a heavy brick to hold down the piano's damper pedal and then play his saxophone to make the piano's strings reverberate. Thus began his compositional investigation of what he thought of as "space music." "There's a contemplative aspect to the duration and spaciousness of sounds," he said.[81] Braheny Fortune was creating a do-it-yourself version of the music that would manifest on the influential albums of Paul Horn, *Inside the Taj Mahal* (1968) and *Inside the Great Pyramid* (1976). On the former album, Horn recorded his flute melodies as they interacted with the twenty-eight-second delay time created by the acoustics of the marble dome in the Taj Mahal.

Horn's "Inside" albums were rereleased on Eckart Rahn's Celestial Harmonies record label, which made the intersection of music and architecture a central aspect of their catalog. Rahn said that professional recording studios were "one of the worst places to record," since they lacked reverberation and so provided no inspiration to the musicians.[82] In addition to Horn's albums, Rahn released two on-location albums by the flutist James Newton. Newton, born in 1953, was deeply influenced by the African American spirituality and music that surrounded him. His mother was very religious, and she poured that spiritual outlook into him. "My mother sang all day when she was at home," he said. "That's a real Black American Southern rural tradition. People coming up out of the church, and they're singing spirituals and gospel music all day while they're working, or while they're sitting down. That had a major impact on me."[83] Newton played with Stanley Crouch's jazz group in the 1970s and then made a series of solo albums in the 1980s on New Age record labels. *Axum* (1981), released by the ECM label, was inspired by Newton's research into the history and theology of Ethiopian mysticism.

Newton said that Paul Horn's "inside" recordings hit him "like a ton of bricks," spurring him to think about making his own recordings outside the studio. While teaching a flute master class in New Mexico, he encountered Echo Canyon in the Carson National Forest and was overwhelmed by the visual beauty of the place and how his flute sound bounced off the canyon walls and swirled in different directions. Newton set up a recording session there, working with Stephen Hill of *Music from the Hearts of Space* as engineer. Hill used a car battery for power and set up a number of mics, some pointed toward the flute and others toward the canyon. They recorded in the middle of the night to avoid the sounds of passing trucks.[84] The result was the Celestial Harmonies release *Echo Canyon* (1984). Newton worked with Rahn on another album, *In Venice* (1987), recorded in the Armenian Catholic monastery San Lazzaro degli Armeni in Venice, Italy. Stephen Hill was also the engineer on Jordan De La Sierra's *Gymnosphere: Song of the Rose* (1977), which was tracked in a studio and then replayed in San Francisco's Grace Cathedral to provide a sense of space.[85]

Paul Horn's approach to space and echo also influenced R. Carlos Nakai. In 1988, Nakai attended a workshop with Horn, who gave him a digital delay unit and suggested he experiment with it. Nakai said that when he tried it, he said, "Oh my God! The Grand Canyon is in there. Canyon de Chelly is in there. These places that I've been to, they're in this box."[86] Nakai incorporated the long echo of the delay unit on his album *Canyon Trilogy* (1989), which went on to sell over one million copies. Nakai and Horn eventually collaborated on two albums, *Inside Canyon de Chelly* (1997) and *Inside Monument Valley* (1999).

For the visionary school, reverb and echo were audio techniques that linked the science of the laboratorium with the ecstasy of the oratorium to become a sonic shorthand for spiritual illumination. The suggestion of music emanating from pyramids, cathedrals, or temples has a parallel in the iconography of visionary art from this period, in particular the work of Gilbert Williams, where we often see crystalline temple spaces. Where visionary painting shows us temple exteriors, New Age music takes us inside those spaces and, by extension, to similar spaces in our heads.

Visionary imperatives shaped the New Age approach to musical time as well as musical space. Iasos stated on several occasions that "musicians are time architects." "A normal architect creates structures in space," he explained. "I create structures in time."[87] New Age music takes two parallel but related approaches to time.[88] One approach to New Age music

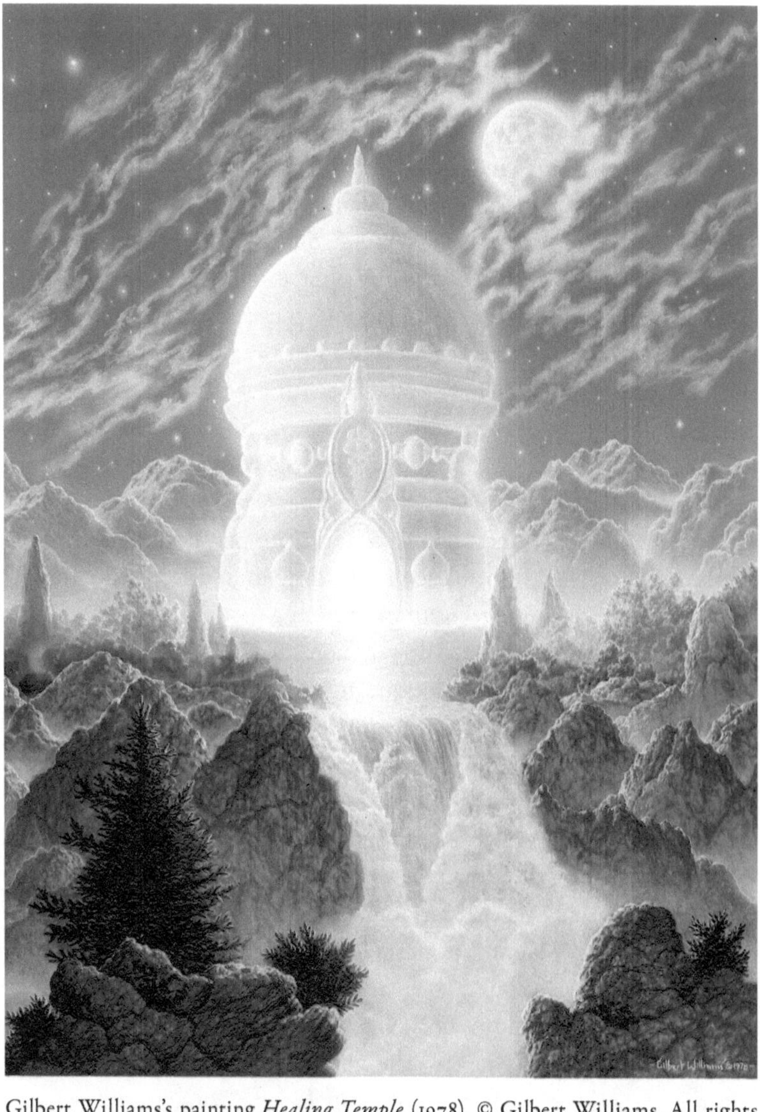

Gilbert Williams's painting *Healing Temple* (1978).

slows the perception of time by creating few sonic events of long duration: think minimalist drone music. This kind of music can serve as an aid to relaxation and meditation, mirroring visionary experiences that are powerful in part because they give one the sense of stepping out of linear everyday time to make contact with eternity.[89]

Steve Roach's "Structures from Silence," the title track from his 1984 album, is a sublime example of New Age music's ability to suggest timelessness. Over the course of twenty-eight minutes, elegant tissues of sound float past the listener before fading gracefully back into silence.[90] Iasos's track "Cloud Prayer" (1975) is another composition of this type, with smokey, rumbling chords played on an echo-drenched lap guitar rising and falling like slow-motion ocean waves. Joanna Brouk's cassette releases "Healing Music" (1981) and "The Space Between" (1981) both feature remarkable solo piano performances that spiral around simple chord patterns that alternately float and shimmer, finding an infinite plenitude of melodic information in the simplest musical structures.

All of these New Age recordings embody a model of visionary music that guides the listener toward slower, more meditative and relaxed states of mind. There is a second technique in which, instead of slowing down the perception of sound events to create a meditative state, the music presents a rapid stream of events against a steady beat, creating a trance state in the listener.[91] In the domain of New Age music, this is not created by long, majestic clouds of sound but by pulsating, mandala-like patterns created on the sequencer units of modular synths.

The most influential practitioner of sequencer-based music for the visionary school of New Age music is Klaus Schulze, who got his start playing with the influential German group Tangerine Dream. Schulze began releasing solo albums in the early 1970s that have a darkly beautiful gothic aesthetic that suggests the work of visionary artist H. R. Giger. On the track "Totem" from the album *Picture Music* (1975), we hear the hallmarks of the trance style: a relentless sequencer pattern etches musical figures of sacred geometry while spectral synths fill in the vistas of a surreal landscape. Steve Roach is the key figure in the visionary school who continued this approach, though it can be heard throughout

New Age releases of the era. Suzanne Doucet's "Shiva's Dance" from the album *Transmission* (1983) creates a hypnotic structure using a drum machine, and J D Emmanuel's album *Wizards* (1982) features tracks like "Expanding into the Universe" and "Movement III" that have a nonstop synthesizer groove and laid-back improvised keyboard accompaniment that pull the listener into a dreamy trance.

Sequencer grooves can be used to create dance music (see disco), and while tracks like "Shiva's Dance" can get your toes tapping, it was the spiritual imperatives of the oratorium that guided the use of this sonic tool. For Kevin Braheny Fortune, sequencers were like the mantras used in meditation, repeated words or phrases used by the meditator to attain a meditative state. Braheny Fortune explained that the brain stops paying attention to the meaning of the repeated mantra, which then "turns into something else," allowing the mind to move to different realms. "Sequencers can do that same thing," he said.[92] Mantras provide a verbal analogy to New Age sequencer patterns, and a visual analogy can be found in the grid-like patterns of visionary art. The visionary artists Alex and Allyson Grey talk about a numinous experience they had together when, after taking "heroic doses" of LSD and lying in bed wearing blindfolds, they felt that they had "dissolved into a lattice realm." As with many visionary experiences, this was felt to be both deeply beautiful and profoundly real. "This was the true reality," Grey stated. "This interconnectedness is the subtle body of the cosmos—and we are each an important node in that infinite network."[93] The Greys refer to this realm as the "universal mind lattice," and it is rendered in Alex Grey's work of the same title. The grids and lattices found in the work of Grey and other visionary painters come from the same numinous sources as the sonic mantras and mandalas of New Age music.[94]

The techniques used by the visionary school of New Age music—drones, sequencer patterns, echo and reverb, modular synthesis—were mobilized to bear witness to mystical experiences and non-ordinary states of consciousness.[95] This is *musica sancta* forged in the New Age laboratorium. The pioneers of New Age music were visionary artists working in sound, sharing much in common with visual art counterparts like Robert Venosa, Gilbert Williams, and Alex and Allyson Grey. The painters of the California visionary school, contemporaries of the first New Age musicians, frequently constructed their works so that they would function as meditational instruments that could, in the words of curator Walter Hopps, "lead the mind's eye along with the optic eye toward a new birth of awareness." Hopps notes that these works often depict figures in the landscape that invite the viewer to "re-live the painter's contemplational adventure."[96] In Gage Taylor's "South Aquaria" (1973) for example, we see a person seated in meditation in the midst of a trippy, hyper-real, Edenic landscape. Recordings by the visionary school of New Age music functioned as meditational instruments as well but in a sonic register, leading the mind's ear toward a new birth of awareness and inviting the listener to relive the musician's numinous experiences.

Let's return to the image of the alchemist at work in their lab-oratorium that began this chapter. Though unquestionably a sacred space, the New Age lab-oratorium was not an isolated monastic retreat. New Age musicians provided sonic tools for their fellow spiritual seekers, who would put them to use far from the confines of their solitary home studios. As a result, the pioneers of New Age music became innovators not only in their approach to making music but in their approach to distributing it. The New Age home studio was a node in an alternative distribution network that allowed visionary music to travel to places and contexts that were not on the map for other genres of recorded music in the 1970s and '80s. In the next chapter, we depart from the instrument-laden table at the center of the lab-oratorium,and head to the middle distance in Khunrath's image, to where we see an open doorway. What lay beyond that door?

TWO

Holistic Sounds

YOU ARE LISTENING to a harp playing slow, delicate musical patterns that shimmer like sunlight reflected on the surface of a tranquil lake. After a few minutes, the harp is joined by a man's calm, gentle voice, asking you to rest your body and become aware of the thoughts passing through your mind. Now become aware of the emotions you are feeling, he says, and then move your awareness to the sensations in your body. Letting go of mental, emotional, and physical tensions, send relaxation from the top of your head to the tip of your toes. This process is facilitated by a particular kind of listening. "Imagine your entire body is like an ear," the man suggests, "every surface of your body hearing the music and my voice."

This is the start of a cassette released in 1979 titled *Rainbow Butterfly*, by harpist Georgia Kelly and therapist Emmett Miller. *Rainbow Butterfly* was the first guided meditation cassette with New Age musical accompaniment, a format that proliferated as part of the New Age genre. Kelly was one of the founders of New Age music and, as we've seen, she and her visionary school peers shared a distinctive approach to creating music. They also had a distinctive approach to distributing it, and when their music left the New Age lab-oratorium, it wound up in spaces that were not typically associated with music retailing, such as metaphysical bookstores, health food outlets, yoga and dance studios, clinics, and wellness centers.

There is a technological explanation for New Age music's alternative distribution network, which coincided with the era of compact cassette tapes, a format that gave recorded sound a new degree of mobility and portability. Music producer and filmmaker Douglas Mcgowan asserts that "probably more than any other type of music," New Age lived on cassette tape. "It's a field dominated by self-publishers," he writes, "and its rise coincided with the rise of the cassette."[1] The independent record labels that came to specialize in New Age music sold considerably more cassettes than vinyl LPs; Fortuna Records sold four times as many cassettes as LPs, and Celestial Harmonies' cassettes outsold albums ten to one.[2] Small, lightweight, durable cassettes helped New Age music become the soundtrack for yoga classes and meditation sessions and were easily displayed in bookstores and health food groceries.

New Age musicians were early adopters of the cassette as a means to distribute their innovative recordings, but technology is only part of the story. New Age's alternative distribution network developed in close connection to spaces and ideas associated with the New Age movement. Not only were cassettes of New Age music found in places specific to the New Age movement, but the theory of music that motivated New Age musicians was shot through with the New Age concept of holism. For historian Wouter Hanegraaff, New Age holism is defined in opposition to dualism and reductionism; it is a rejection of both dualistic oppositions (between mind and body for example) and the reductionist tendency to break phenomena into component parts, something often associated with scientific rationalism. New Age practices are holistic to the extent that they seek to overcome dualism and reductionism.[3] As a result, the goal of many New Age therapies is to restore a sense of wholeness to people's lives through an address to mind, body, and spirit.[4] Kelly and Miller's *Rainbow Butterfly* took part in the New Age movement's holistic mission. Notice how it begins by aligning the listener's thoughts, emotions, and bodily sensations.

When music was brought under the sign of New Age holism, its mandate expanded to include the body as well as the mind, such that it could resemble a form of medicine as much as a form of art. In a guide to New Age music published in 1989, PJ Birosik writes that massage therapists, doctors, and nurses had all discovered New Age music's capacity to foster physical relaxation. "No other music has had this kind of wide-reaching effect on mental and physical health," she writes, concluding that New Age music is "the ultimate blend of art and science."[5]

Holistic currents propelled New Age music as it traveled out into the world from its sources in the lab-oratorium. This was music that circulated as a curious blend of art, science, and spirituality, and that was meant to be listened to with the entire being, not just the ear. Cassettes made the music mobile, like dandelion seeds blown in the wind, and the New Age movement's holistic outlook provided niches where those musical seeds could take root. In this chapter, we map the spaces of New Age music's alternative circulation, with each section considering a node in the New Age distribution network and an aspect of New Age holism that shaped the visionary school's theory of music.

VIBRATION

"In the beginning was the Word, and the Word was with God, and the Word was God." This famous passage from the Gospel of John was often quoted in New Age discussions of sound. Kirpal Singh, a spiritual teacher who influenced several New Age musicians, talked about the "sound current or sound principle," which he held to be the underlying force in the universe. Singh writes that the primordial sound current is "at once the beginning and the end of all that exists." He connects this idea to the opening lines of the Gospel of John cited above. The "word of God" that existed in the beginning was not spoken language, Singh asserts, but "vital vibrations."[6]

Singh's school of Surat Shabd Yoga illustrates a common expression of New Age holism: the belief in the universe's essential reality as energy or vibration. This is what the musicologist Victor Szabo calls the "vibrational ontology of the universe," which was foundational to New Age spiritualities and philosophies of sound.[7] Because sound is the result of vibrating air molecules, it is a handy metaphor for other kinds of periodic or vibratory phenomena, from the movements of subatomic particles, to the breath and heartbeat of the body, to radiation from the Big Bang that created the universe. New Age flutist Paul Horn gave a concise encapsulation of the vibrational ontology when he wrote, "We *are* sound, that is what we are made of. Sound is vibration. Human beings are vibrations, solidified in human form. . . . All of existence is vibration." As Horn's comments show, sound was good for holistic thinking, and by extension, so was music. "Sound is fundamental to our physical constitutions," Horn wrote, "and music is the universal language precisely because it touches us at that deep, essential, universal level."[8]

One of the fullest elaborations of the New Age vibrational ontology was crafted by the scholar and musician Randall McClellan. McClellan got his PhD in music at the Eastman School of Music in Rochester, New York. In the 1970s, he taught music at Hampshire College in Massachusetts and Combs College of Music in Pennsylvania. Like many of the visionary school, his approach to composition was influenced by the American minimalists and classical Indian music, and he was a dedicated student of esoteric theories of sound and music. McClellan released a series of cassette tapes between 1979 and 1985 titled *The Healing Music of Rana*. Liner notes explain that the project emerged from a philosophical tradition that recognizes "vibration as the fundamental creative force."

The fourth cassette of the series includes a lecture titled "Music as a Healing Force," delivered by McClellan over his own musical accompaniment.[9] McClellan explains that sound is a holistic phenomenon that affects us on the mental, spiritual, and physical plane. "Sound is not only heard," he says. "It is also felt in every portion of our body, not just the ears." Listening to music becomes a route to holistic health since the body is understood as a series of "interlocking and interdependent vibrational systems" that seek to find a state of balance and equilibrium.[10] "The value of music as a healing agent," he concludes, "is that it unifies mind and body, spirit and matter through its vibrational patterns."

McClellan's lecture shows how the vibrational ontology lays a foundation for a view of music as a healing force. If vibration was the fundamental reality underlying material and mental systems, then it made sense for musical vibration to be the best tool for integrating and balancing those systems. Side one of Georgia Kelly's *Rainbow Butterfly* is a case in point; it presents a guided meditation that interweaves two vibrational channels of communication—sound and light—to integrate the mental and physical systems of the body. Miller's voiceover takes the listener through the color spectrum while Kelly's harp explores a different key and musical mode for each color. The frequency of sonic vibrations (pitch) aligns with the vibrations of light (color) to integrate the listener's emotional, mental, and physical life.

The cassette that included McClellan's lecture is a good example of New Age music's quirky blend of art and science; it is simultaneously musical entertainment and a scholarly disquisition on music theory. Cassette tapes were a common accompaniment to mind-body practices during the 1970s, providing meditations as well as guided yoga classes and lectures by spiritual teachers. The pages of *Yoga Journal* in the 1970s and '80s are full of advertisements for yoga classes on cassette, as well as music by New Age artists. *New Age Journal* had a regular column on cassette tapes in 1982 and asserted that "these days thousands of tapes of all types—music, readings, lectures, guided imagery—offer a vital new means of self-help and self-education."[11] An illustration for one of the columns shows a meditator sitting on an enormous cassette tape in the lotus position with eyes shut, wearing headphones plugged into the title of the column: "Aural Samadhi."[12]

The content of Randall McClellan's lecture material was developed in his book *The Healing Forces of Music* (1987), one of several treatises on music and healing to be published by New Age musicians of this era. It is fitting, then, that metaphysical bookstores were some of the first places to retail New Age music.[13] One bookstore was particularly important as a distribution outlet for New Age music: the Bodhi Tree, a metaphysical bookstore founded in 1970 on Melrose Avenue in Los Angeles. A 1987 article in the *Los Angeles Times* described its displays of bodywork supplies, fragrant soaps, and books on topics such as acupuncture, Buddhism, homeopathy, hypnosis, meditation, the occult, psychotherapy, tantra, and yoga.[14] The Hollywood star and New Age spokesperson

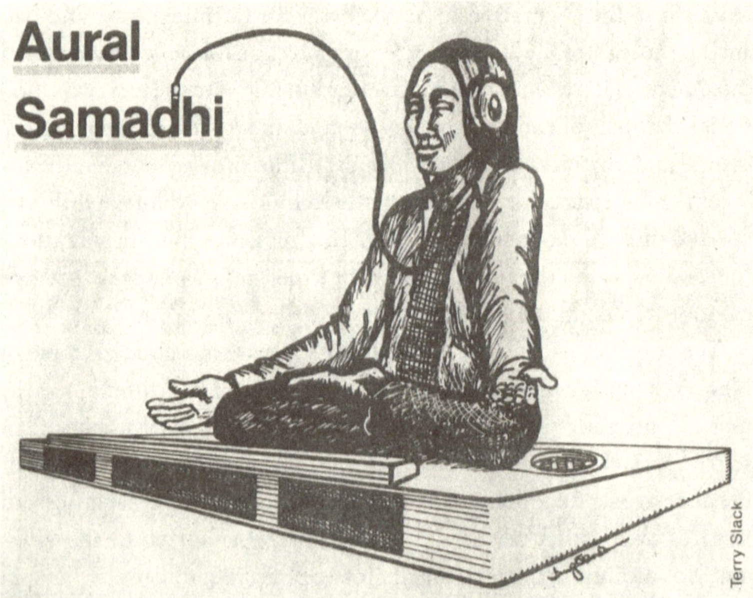

Illustration for a 1982 article on cassette tapes in *New Age Journal*.

Shirley MacLaine described her first visit to the Bodhi Tree. "I smelled sandalwood incense filtering faintly through the rooms of the cluttered bookstore," she writes. "Posters of Buddha and of yogis I had never heard of smiled down from the walls. Customers with books in their hands stood about drinking herb teas and talking in soft voices."[15] Behind the cashier's counter, customers could find stacks of cassettes. Cassette tapes were well suited to retail spaces like the Bodhi Tree because they were small and easy to display.

The Bodhi Tree was the launching pad for a number of New Age musicians. Georgia Kelly recorded her first album of original harp solos, *Seapeace*, in 1978. Born in San Francisco in 1941, Kelly learned to play the harp as a student in the 1950s. She studied music in college but dropped out because she felt boxed in by the way that music was being taught. Working at Stanford University during the 1960s, she became involved in the campus peace movement. She returned to the harp after moving to Big Sur and took classes on film scoring at UCLA, which gave her new motivation to play her own compositions. These were the compositions that she recorded for *Seapeace*.[16]

Kelly's album was completely self-funded. "I knew I couldn't go to a record company," she said. "I'd have to do it myself, and I did." With little money for studio time, she recorded the entire album in one night. When it came to distribution, she created her own record company, Heru Records, and took her first release to the Bodhi Tree. "I went there with my album," she recalled, "not knowing if they would be interested in it or not. They said, 'We'll get back to you.'" A week and a half later, Kelly received a letter ordering ten albums. "I was so excited," she said, "I delivered them myself." After selling the first ten albums, the bookstore ordered another twenty-five, and then another fifty. Kelly reasoned that if the Bodhi Tree was selling the album, other metaphysical bookstores might be interested as well. She went to the Santa Monica Library, which had phone books from all over the country, and wrote down the contact information for all the metaphysical bookstores she could find. She called each one to see if they would carry the album and estimated that 85 percent of the stores ordered it over the phone. As a result, her career took off. "They played it in the stores," she said, "and that made it happen."[17]

Like Georgia Kelly, Peter Davison recorded his first New Age album and then wondered what to do with it. Recall from the previous chapter that Davison abandoned the atonal music he had been taught in college for a more harmonic and uplifting alternative. In 1979, Davison was living in Santa Monica, recording new compositions in his home studio. One night, some friends came over for dinner, saw his Serge synthesizer, and heard some of his new tracks. "Wow," they told him. "You're making New Age music!" "What is *that*?" Davison asked. "I didn't know there was such a thing as New Age music." His friends told him about New Age ideas concerning music and healing, and Davison realized, "I love New Age music! I'm going to make New Age music!"[18]

When his album was finished, he looked up "New Age" in the business section of his local phone book and found a company called Pyramid

Distributors. "At the time, everything was about pyramids," he recalled.[19] Davison is referring to a widespread interest in "pyramid power" during the 1970s, which was the belief that spiritual energy resided in the geometry of the Egyptian pyramids. Davison recalled that people were buying miniature pyramids, pyramid-shaped candles, pyramid energy kits, and even sleeping under pyramid-shaped structures. Pyramid Distributors was run by Michael Anderson, who distributed pyramid products to metaphysical bookshops and health food stores around Los Angeles. Davison told Anderson he was making an album of New Age music and asked if he'd be interested in distributing it. Anderson agreed and took some of Davison's albums to his biggest customer: the Bodhi Tree. The album was soon selling well at the Bodhi Tree and other metaphysical bookshops in the area, which gave Anderson and Davison the leverage they needed to expand, working with distributors across the country who handled similar retail outlets.[20] Though Davison's first two albums were pressed on LP records, he soon realized that cassettes were less expensive to make and sold better. His subsequent four albums were released on cassette only.[21]

While Michael Anderson was establishing his distribution circuit in Southern California, Ethan Edgecombe was developing a similar circuit in Northern California. Born in 1951, Edgecombe's parents had emigrated to Florida from the Bahamas.[22] Edgecombe developed an entrepreneurial spirit when he was very young, working for his father's summer business on Mackinac Island in Michigan starting when he was ten years old and selling a Black community newspaper in Fort Lauderdale.[23] His summers on Mackinac Island in the 1960s and early '70s exposed him to countercultural college students who had summer jobs on the island.[24] "My whole perspective and mindset changed as a result of being up there," he said. For one thing, he discovered marijuana and psychedelics, which he said was "transformational." "I started experiencing something beyond the physical," he said, "and beyond the mental."[25]

Edgecombe brought this new sensibility back to Florida, where he became part of a countercultural scene, attending concerts in Miami by artists like Led Zeppelin, Jimi Hendrix, and Buddy Miles.[26] Edgecombe described himself as "a child of psychedelia," but that lifestyle began to take a toll on his nervous system, and he decided he needed a change. After discovering macrobiotics, vegetarianism, and yoga, he started a business growing sprouts and selling them to local health food stores.[27] Around this time, Edgecombe noticed a new kind of music being sold in a few of the health food stores and metaphysical bookstores he frequented: early albums by Steven Halpern and the harpist Joel Andrews's *Locrian Invocation* (1975). These records, he said, became "part of my healing."[28]

As fate would have it, Edgecombe soon found himself at the epicenter of this new music when he moved to the San Francisco Bay Area.[29] Finding that stores didn't stock the Joel Andrews LP, he decided to do it himself. Making use of a closet in his house as storage space, he bought some of the albums at wholesale price and formed a distribution company that he named Fortuna.[30] Fortuna began as a one-man operation, and Edgecombe would drive a circuit around the Bay Area twice a week, supplying a network of bookstores, health food stores, and head shops that stocked his music. "It was a great sideline for these stores," he said, "because they could play the music and people would be interested . . . and they'd have it right there to sell on cassette."[31] Fortuna soon grew beyond Edgecombe's closet, first taking over his garage, then moving to a warehouse. He began signing artists in 1980, and Fortuna Records became a seminal record label in the New Age scene, releasing albums by Emerald Web, Steve Roach, Don Slepian, William Aura, Edward Christmas (who recorded under the name Swami Kriya Ramananda), David Parsons, and many others.[32] Fortuna played a pivotal role in fostering and advancing New Age music, and stands as an underappreciated Black-owned independent record company that should be added to a list that includes Black Swan, Vee Jay, Motown, Philadelphia International, Sugar Hill, and Def Jam Records.

The fact that Edgecombe sold homegrown sprouts before he sold homebrew cassettes indicates that health food stores were a node in the New Age alternative distribution network.[33] Kat Epple remembered that Edgecombe supplied health food stores with a cassette display so that shoppers could pick them up and add them to their groceries.[34] In fact, New Age music was emerging at the same time as the health food movement (Erewhon, one of the first health food store chains, opened its first West Coast store in Los Angeles in 1969), and the two embody a similar brand of New Age holism; note the health food movement's interest in the larger systems that link farm and table and its view of diet in relation to mental, physical, and environmental well-being.

Health food provided not only a site for distributing New Age music but a metaphor for describing it.[35] Steven Halpern compared the growing popularity of health food to the emergence of New Age music, which he saw as an alternative to "sonic junk food."[36] Anna Turner, one of the hosts of KPFA's *Music from the Hearts of Space*, also made the food/music comparison, writing that music has "as great an effect on the subtler levels of our organisms as food does on the physical." Just as different foods generate different energies in the mind and body, so different kinds of music "alter our emotional fields with their refined, electromagnetic energies."[37] Turner's reference to energy as an underlying link between the domains of food and music brings us full circle, back to the vibrational ontology. New Age cassettes could sit comfortably next to the bookshelves in the Bodhi Tree and the bulk bins at Erewhon because of their portable, low-cost form but also because of their embodiment of a New Age holism based on a belief in the universe's essential reality as energy or vibration. The vibrational ontology set the stage for New Age music's blend of art and science, and it also shaped how musicians thought about their audience.

INTENTION

As we saw in the previous chapter, New Age music was often made in home studios using four-track recorders and modular synths. This technology was empowering for independent artists who lacked record company backing, but it posed a challenge: isolated in their home studios, and without the emphasis on touring and live performance found in other musical genres, how could New Age musicians reach and connect with an audience? One answer to that question was radio.[38]

Regional radio airplay of New Age music began in the early 1970s, most notably on Stephen Hill and Anna Turner's *Music from the Hearts of Space* program on KPFA in Berkeley, which went on the air in 1973 and was nationally syndicated on National Public Radio (NPR) in 1983. Many of the same cassettes that were displayed at places like the Bodhi Tree also made it to Hill and Turner's *Music from the Hearts of Space*. Douglas Mcgowan cataloged Stephen Hill's music collection and found that there were three times as many cassettes as there were records.[39] Hill referred to the cassette format as a "revolution": "The cassette changes the whole game for everybody," he said in a 1984 interview. "One ounce of a plastic cassette can create an entire cultural moment, and be shipped anywhere, and cheaply."[40] Many New Age musicians sent their self-produced cassettes to Hill and Turner and got a boost in their career from the airplay.[41] *Music from the Hearts of Space* was the most prominent—but not the only—New Age or "space music" radio show. *Musical Starstreams* from San Francisco went on the air in 1981, and *Star's End* from WXPN in Philadelphia was launched in 1976 by the music writer John Diliberto, who later hosted the syndicated ambient music program *Echoes*.[42]

Radio shows like *Music from the Hearts of Space* expanded the reach of the New Age alternative distribution network, and radio technology provided a metaphor for a holistic model of artistic intention.[43] In radio broadcasting, electromagnetic waves function as a carrier wave for sound, that is, the contours of the sound wave are mapped onto an electromagnetic wave, which then travels over space to be converted back into sound by a receiving set. The carrier wave fit nicely with a holistic view that the universe is, at root, composed of various kinds of interacting vibrations, and it became a metaphor for the creation and reception of New Age music.

"Sound is a carrier wave of consciousness," writes the New Age musician Jonathan Goldman, author of the book *Healing Sounds* (1992). His point was that sounds carry information about the state of awareness of the person who created them. If you are angry and create a sound, "even though it may be a pleasant sound, you will be sending anger that is incorporated into that sound," Goldman writes. "This will be perceived on some subtle level by those receiving the sound."[44] For some musicians, intention was the defining characteristic of the New Age genre. Paul Horn, for example, stated that New Age was defined by "the quality of the person playing it"; if the musician is "of higher consciousness," then whatever music comes through that person is New Age music.[45]

The carrier wave metaphor gives expression to a holistic model of musical circulation in which the New Age home studio—and the inner, spiritual work that took place there—is connected to the spaces where the music was heard. It also encouraged the performance of devotional acts as part of the recording process in order to establish the correct intention. Paul Horn performed a religious ceremony before recording his album in the Great Pyramid.[46] Steven Halpern told an interviewer that he meditates and does yoga, tai chi, or reiki before recording to get his "human instrument in tune." He talked about the "Halpern Hippocratic Oath": "Composer, compose thyself. A musician must be calm to play calming music."[47]

There is a certain irony to this model of artistic intention, as it exhibits a form of reductionism that is at odds with New Age holism. Musical experience is held to be determined by one part of the system—the artist's inner state—which operates in an automatic way: higher consciousness equals New Age music. Many other variables, such as the features of the music itself, the listener's state of mind, the particular qualities of the instruments or studio gear, are subordinated to one determining element: the musician's inner experience. When taken too literally, the result is an insufficiently holistic holism.

In her book *Music: The New Age Elixir* (1996), a trenchant critique of music healers, the music therapist Lisa Summer argues that an emphasis on artistic intention tends to ignore the labor of musical composition.[48] According to Summer, composers usually want to eliminate traces of their compositional process in order to create a seamless experience in which the listener remains ignorant of the arduous task of creating the composition.[49] In other words, a composer might have been in a peevish and frustrated state of mind while crafting calm and soothing music. Summer's book is an important critique of the claims of music healers, some of whom were New Age musicians.

Her analogy to the composition of classical music is not a perfect fit, however. After all, New Age musicians were not just composers of musical scores; they were also performers and recording artists. Arguably, recording captures certain sonic nuances that a written score does not, and while audiences have no way of perceiving the countless revisions that lay behind a finished written score, they may well respond to subtle indications of the emotional or mental state of a musician during a performance.[50] The New Age emphasis on artistic intention makes more sense in an era of home studios and composer-performers. Moreover, much of New Age music has an improvised component, which makes it even more reliant on the moment-to-moment state of the composer-performer. Finally, the determinative effects of intention were clearly not automatic or all-determining, otherwise, why would musicians have to work so hard to establish the right mental state through pre-session ceremonies? More than anything, the New Age emphasis on intention was an aspirational goal that both spurred the artist's spiritual work and connected that work to an imagined listening public.

Regardless of the extent to which an artist's intention can ride on the sound waves of a recording, these ideas about intention can tell us something about New Age attitudes toward musical authorship and authenticity. As a school of visionary art, New Age music deemphasizes individual authorship by making the musician a kind of mediator or channel.[51] The ultimate creator of the album is not Iasos, for example, but an interdimensional being named Vista. The music comes not from Paul Horn but from a transpersonal state of consciousness produced through meditation and ritual. Individual authorship is also downplayed by the music's functional utility as a tool for mind-body practice, which shifts the emphasis to the music's effects. According to Suzanne Doucet, the focus of New Age music is not on the artist but on the listener. "The market is not looking for stars," she said in a 1987 interview. "It's the total opposite. They want to find themselves."[52] The reduced prominence of New Age artists relative to other musical genres can be seen by the general absence of artist photographs on New Age album covers and marketing materials.[53]

New Age artists of the visionary school were not promoted in the ways typical of the popular music industry, and a high premium was placed on their spiritual life. In other musical genres, authenticity might be established through the details of the star's biography, the hard work of paying their dues on the ladder of success, or their organic connection to a particular scene, identity, or tradition. New Age music derives authenticity from the artist's spiritual credentials, a dynamic that is similar to New Age healers who lack the authority of the science-informed medical establishment and so must rely on their "claims to be spiritual."[54] Discourses surrounding New Age music—interviews about tai chi sessions in the studio, liner notes, and song titles—function to assert those spiritual credentials. One ramification of New Age's blend of art and science then, is that artists could resemble healers, mystics, or gurus as much as pop stars.

HARMONY

Though they weren't known for touring or marketing themselves as celebrities, New Age musicians did make personal appearances at another venue where New Age music was sold: New Age fairs. These were gatherings of practitioners, merchants, and speakers who shared an interest in New Age paradigms of spirituality and healing. The Kohoutek Celebration of Consciousness of 1974, described in the introduction, is an early example that foreshadowed similar gatherings throughout the 1970s and '80s.

The Festival for Mind-Body-Spirit was first held in 1977 and attracted sixty thousand visitors over five days.[55] That same year, the Rainbow Rose Festival was held in Pasadena and featured talks by New Age luminaries like Buckminster Fuller, Elisabeth Kubler-Ross, John Lilly, Fritjof

Capra, and Swami Satchidananda, along with workshops, musical performances, and a screening of a documentary film about ancient Mayan culture.[56] In a 1982 essay on the Whole Life Expo, the writer Bill McKibben described exhibits promoting crystals, reflexology, health food products like barley grass juice and garlic tablets, and fringe religious groups like Eckankar.[57]

For musicians who lacked the promotional clout of a major record label, New Age fairs offered an opportunity to promote their releases to a receptive audience. Michael Stearns remembers attending these fairs to set up a booth with large pillows where people could sit and listen to his cassettes through headphones. He could sell a few hundred cassettes that way, enough to cover two or three months of food and rent. "That was how a lot of us supported ourselves," he recalled.[58] Georgia Kelly promoted her music at New Age fairs and remembered that some of them had a stage where New Age musicians would perform. The fairs "did a lot of good for us," she said, and helped to spread the word about their music.[59] Ethan Edgecombe worked a booth for Fortuna Records at New Age fairs in Los Angeles, the Bay Area, New York, Chicago, Oregon, and Washington state.[60]

New Age fairs provided a venue where musicians could encounter a large number of like-minded seekers and distribute their music outside the usual channels of the mainstream music industry. When musicians occupied a booth between a reflexologist and a merchant selling healing crystals they demonstrated that they shared with the New Age movement an outsider status with regard to prevailing religious and scientific orthodoxies. In his influential 1972 article, sociologist Colin Campbell wrote that the emerging New Age milieu featured a host of "deviant" belief systems and practices, foremost among which was a rejection of orthodox scientific beliefs and an associated "deviant medicine."[61] The New Age music scene was immersed in the New Age movement's implicit critique of the dominant Western traditions of science, philosophy, and medicine.[62]

One way to register New Age music's deviant status is through the moral panic it inspired among some fundamentalist Christians. In a book titled *Straight Answers on the New Age* (1989), radio talk show host Bob Larson wrote that New Age musicians "indulge in various forms of occult meditation and cosmic awareness philosophies." Perhaps Larson had Iasos in mind when he wrote that "some of them freely admit using trance channeling as a source of inspiration." A biblical perspective, he asserted, would define such music as "satanically inspired."[63] A few years later, a newspaper in Calgary published an article with the memorable headline, "New Age Music: Does It Soothe the Soul or Summon Satan?"[64] We find another manifestation of New Age's deviant status in the stigma surrounding New Age fairs. Georgia Kelly remembered that New Age gatherings were derisively referred to as "fruit and nut fairs." From this perspective, New Age fairs were a place to sell albums, but they also served to strengthen a sense of participation in a subcultural community.[65]

Recognizing New Age as a subcultural music of the 1970s puts it in the same category as other outsider genres of this era like punk and disco.[66] New Age music appears at first glance to be the antithesis of punk, and yet the two share a scrappy, do-it-yourself ethos of self-production and distribution, often on cassettes. *Hearts of Space* cohost Stephen Hill praised New Age artists for demonstrating how new recording technologies had made it possible for one musician to not only write and perform music but to record and release it. "Essentially it's like creating your own record company," he said.[67] Similar statements could be made about the early punk scene.

New Age music may have had a similar DIY ethos as punk, but it certainly didn't sound like it. Unlike other subcultural genres of the period like punk, heavy metal, and hip hop, New Age music's deviant status did not result in a dark, aggressive, or pessimistic emotional tone. New Age music foregoes sonic dissonance and distortion in favor of harmony and tonality.[68] Birosik writes that "feeling good is the key to New Age music," and it was created to be "a positive force in your life," evoking feelings of peacefulness, joy, relaxation, intimacy, and bliss.[69] Iasos was adamant that his music would never include negative emotional qualities. "Earth is so filled with music with dark emotions and dark intentions, it doesn't need any more," he said.[70] Iasos refused to put sonic distortion on his recordings ("In heaven there's no distortion") and even objected to audiences clapping at his concerts, which he felt was an act of sonic violence, a "waterfall of random explosions" that had a shattering effect on the musical structures he had created in the air. "Leave it to Earth to come up with a destructive sound to signify beautiful meanings of appreciation and gratitude," he complained.[71]

Iasos is just one case, of course, and his exclusive focus on positive emotions was not a position shared by all of the visionary school of New Age musicians. There is a darker strain of New Age music influenced by German synth pioneers like Klaus Schulze and Tangerine Dream that has affinities with the surrealist painting of H. R. Giger and Yves Tanguy.[72] Surrealism and visionary art are, in fact, closely related but distinct. Both share an interest in exploring unconscious and nonrational mental states, but surrealism's understanding of the unconscious is decidedly Freudian. For Freud, the unconscious was a site of repressed desires, mostly dark impulses towards sex and violence, and when surrealist artists dive into non-ordinary states of mind, they tend to find dark, disturbing, and transgressive images. Visionary art draws on another model of the unconscious, one with affinities to Carl Jung rather than Freud, that understands the unconscious as the source of sublime and life-affirming archetypal images of wholeness and growth rather than simply being a trash can for repressed sexual and murderous drives.[73]

It is under the sign of Jung and the transpersonal psychology he helped establish that the visionary school of New Age music developed its positive emotional palette, which was easily aligned with New Age mind-body holism, self-growth, and healing techniques.[74] Those techniques are often based on an assumption that positive thinking, perhaps bolstered by positive music, produces therapeutic change and can even cure chronic diseases.[75] Iasos asserted that "all diseases are really psychosomatic."[76] This belief in the healing power of mind over matter can be heard on a guided meditation cassette by Laraaji and Kristina Nomeika, *The BodyMind Energizer* (1987). Nomeika guides listeners through a body scan meditation that involves visualizing the "energy body that surrounds us." Nomeika asks the listener to identify with this glistening energy body and to notice any locations where its color or energy pattern is out of balance. "Change it now, cut it out remove it," she says. The efficacy of this kind of "aetheric surgery" is based on the assertion that all matter has intelligence and responds to thought such that meditative practices can, over time, heal illnesses as serious as cancer.[77] "At this time, you are choosing health," Nomeika says. "You are choosing to become enlightened through the positive. You are choosing to evolve through a healthy perfection."

Assertions that disease is ultimately psychosomatic or a matter of conscious choice are a clear indication of how the New Age movement's deviant science grew from soil prepared by earlier currents of "New Thought," from Christian Science to Dale Carnegie's *How to Win Friends and Influence People* (1936) and Norman Vincent Peale's *The Power of Positive Thinking* (1952).[78] We are moving into problematic territory here, and critics like Barbara Ehrenreich have argued that a blind faith in the "power of positive thinking" can mislead people who are unwell and even add to their suffering by placing the blame for an illness on their own failure to smile their way out of it. The reduction of illness to patterns of thought is another example of an insufficient holism, since it collapses the systemic nature of mind-body to the determinative effects of mind.[79] In this model, positive music creates positive thoughts, which can cure the body. Another model of healing music removes thought from the equation altogether.

RESONANCE

Resonance is the ability of sound to affect matter at a distance. You've experienced sonic resonance if you've ever noticed that a specific musical note will make a light fixture rattle or if you've seen a singer shatter a wine glass with the power of their voice. The resonant affordance of sound became the basis for claims about music's health benefits.[80] New Age musician and author Jonathan Goldman argues that music affects

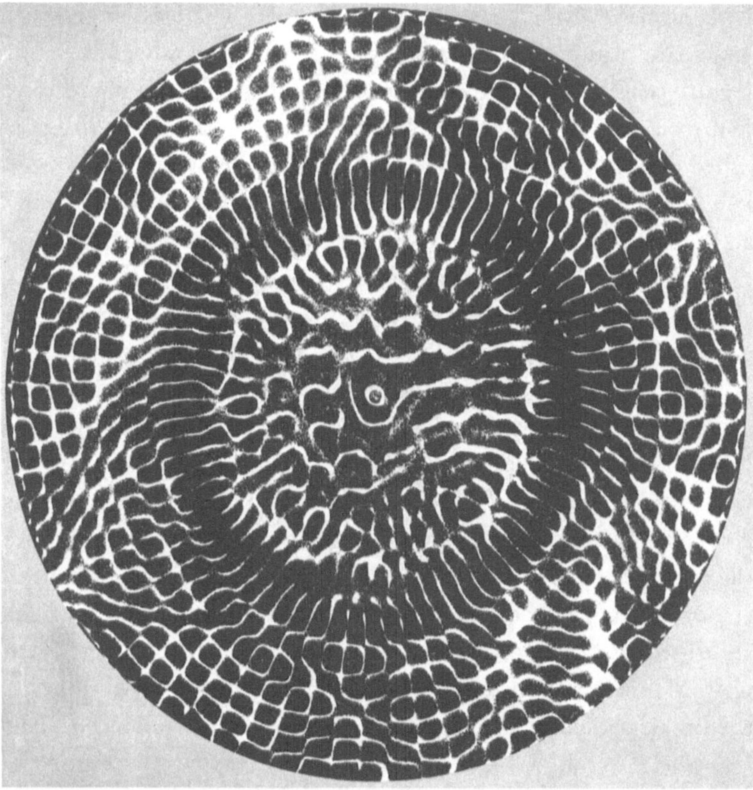

Illustration from Hans Jenny's book *Cymatics* (1967). © 2025 MACROmedia Publishing. Used by permission (www.cymaticsource.com).

the "resonating systems within the human body. Just as it is possible to set an object into its own natural motion through resonance, so it is possible to restore the natural vibratory frequencies of an object that may be out of tune or harmony."[81]

Goldman and other New Age musicians often supported their claims about resonance by reference to "cymatics," the study of how sound waves affect physical matter.[82] Cymatics was the invention of the Swiss physician Hans Jenny, who investigated how sound waves create patterns in fluids and powders. Inspired by the work of the physicist Ernst

Chladni, Jenny would cover a metal plate with fine powder and then vibrate the plate at a particular sonic frequency. The powder settled into regular geometric patterns determined by the frequency of the tone. Jenny was a visual artist as much as a laboratory scientist, and he published a book of photographs titled *Cymatics: The Study of Wave Phenomena* (1967).[83] Jenny's fascinating images are, like New Age music, an idiosyncratic blend of art and science, and capture the imagination through their mandala-like symmetries. For some New Age musicians, this was evidence that sound can influence matter, with potential healing benefits for the body.

Therapeutic claims were made for cymatics by Peter Guy Manners, an osteopath from Worcestershire, England. Manners developed a sound-based healing technique that he explained in a 1986 interview with musician Jonathan Goldman.[84] "Every part of the human anatomy gives off a signal," Manners says. When those signals are "in line with the general harmonic of the whole body, then you are in good health." If, however, any of those frequencies "fall out of alignment, then you are dis-eased or out of harmony; dis-harmonic." Later in the interview, Manners demonstrates his cymatic instrument, which is about the size of a briefcase and contains a cassette player to produce specific frequencies of sound. He turns on the device, and we hear the soothing hum of harmonious tones coming out of a handheld applicator. He places the sound-producing applicator on the back and shoulders of a volunteer, explaining that the applied frequencies make the patient relax automatically, because they are "entirely in relation to the natural frequency there."[85]

Manners's cymatic treatment reduces the listening experience to a prescribed set of frequencies thought to determine automatic outcomes—another example of an insufficient holism. The New Age approach to holistic listening generally involved making the entire body into an ear, but for Manners, the ear and the mind of the listener become superfluous; sound bypasses them and goes directly from the applicator into the body. Manners's cymatic applicator was not the only sonic healing device on the market. Several companies made beds equipped with speakers that bathed the body in healing frequencies while the owner slept.[86] In his essay on the 1982 Whole Life Expo, Bill McKibben described another product that was meant to bypass the conscious mind.

McKibben found that one of the busiest booths at the Expo was run by Potentials Unlimited, a company founded by Barrie Konicov, a professional hypnotist who made self-hypnosis cassette tapes that combined New Age music with subliminal messages.[87] The company's *Subliminal Persuasion* series of cassettes featured ocean sounds and soothing music, while below the level of conscious awareness, there were "carefully researched and tested words and phrases designed to encourage the behavioral change you desire." Other companies producing cassettes of this kind included Valley of the Sun and Consciousness Tapes. New Age pioneer Steven Halpern released his own series of subliminal cassettes with titles like *Accelerating Learning*, *Effortless Relaxation*, *Listen and Lose Weight*, and *Enhancing Success*. "No special effort or concentration is involved," Halpern's liner notes explain. "Simply listen to this tape as soothing background."

There is little evidence that subliminal messages on audio recordings have any measurable effects, but these tapes are notable in the context of New Age music's holistic blend of art and science.[88] As with cymatic applicators and sound therapy beds, subliminal tapes enact an insufficient holism by disregarding the active, conscious component of listening. Steven Halpern's subliminal cassettes indicate that he was a visionary school musician who was willing to explore the murky terrain of sound healing. In a 1981 ad for his music, we see his cassettes alongside a doctor's black bag and stethoscope with the copy, "When tension strikes, take two Halpern."[89] Halpern's career shows that one of the dangers of combining art and science in this way was that one could end up being shot by both sides, that is, simultaneously ostracized by the music industry as insufficiently entertaining and rejected by the medical community as being insufficiently scientific. Halpern recalled music industry people telling him that they didn't want artists talking about health and relaxation. "We're about entertainment," they told him. In defiant response, he started using the promotional catchphrase, "entrainment, not entertainment."[90] Halpern ran into trouble on the other side of the art/science spectrum when the FDA pursued him for making unsubstantiated health claims about his music.[91] It is difficult to imagine this scenario playing out in a genre other than New Age music.

Cymatic sound applicators, sound therapy beds, and subliminal cassettes grew out of the deviant science of the New Age movement and its vibrational ontology. Music healers and companies like Potentials Unlimited and Valley of the Sun enacted an insufficient holism by reducing or even eliminating the active role of the listener in the holistic system of music's production, distribution, and consumption. For a more promising blend of art and science, we return to where we began: Georgia Kelly's *Rainbow Butterfly*.

TRANSFORMATION

A personal crisis in Kelly's life led to the invention of the guided meditation cassette. Kelly had given up the harp entirely for a period in the 1960s but began to perform again in the 1970s. At that time, she experienced intense stage fright while playing classical music. "I would just freeze, and I didn't know where I was in the piece," she recalled. "It scared me." Kelly had been playing regularly at the Esalen Institute in Big Sur, California, a center of the Human Potential movement (a subset of the New Age movement that stressed transformation, growth, and self-actualization).[92] During a break in one of her performances, she ran into the therapist Emmett Miller and told him about her stage fright. Miller made her a recording of his affirmations on a cassette, and she added calming music as an accompaniment to his voice. Sessions with the cassette led to the realization that her stage fright was a manifestation of a thwarted desire to write and perform her own music. "My career came out of that revelation" she said.[93] Her first album came out in 1978, and *Rainbow Butterfly* was released in 1979. Miller went on to release a series of meditation cassettes, collaborating with New Age musicians like Steven Halpern and Raphael.[94]

Though she pioneered the guided meditation format, Kelly was cautious about making health claims and made a clear distinction between "healing music" and "therapeutic music." "Healing implies that something works virtually every time," she said, while "therapeutic implies tools and methods that are used to aid healing. It is unlikely that music can heal something like cancer, but people have often gotten rid of things like emotional tension, muscle aches and migraine headaches" by listening to New Age music.[95] Kelly's therapeutic approach was well suited to clinics and wellness centers, and her tapes were used in the stress management division of the Kaiser Permanente Medical Center, as well as in drug abuse programs, prisons, and private therapy practices.[96]

Jon Kabat-Zinn, director of the Stress Reduction and Relaxation Clinic at the University of Massachusetts Medical Center, collaborated with Kelly on a meditation tape and video, which was broadcast on the center's in-house television channel. *The World of Relaxation* aimed to help listeners develop relaxation skills to further the process of healing and recovery. Kabat-Zinn told a writer for the *New Age Journal* that the initial goal was to teach people to handle the stress of being in the hospital, but they soon discovered that these skills applied at home as well. Kabat-Zinn was enthusiastic about music as a means to teach people to listen in a nonjudgmental way, which he felt was crucial to self-healing. Learning to hear each note as it comes, to "hear the space in between the notes," could help a person to calm down and become more attentive to the moment-to-moment changes in their body and so deal more effectively with pain.[97]

Like many guided meditation cassettes, *The World of Relaxation* leads the listener through breath awareness and a body scan meditation with music.[98] At one point, Kabat-Zinn asks you to imagine a hole on the top of your head where you are breathing in and out, much as a whale breathes in and out of its blowhole. Allow the air—and the music of Kelly's harp—to move in and out, freely and unimpeded through your entire body, he says.[99] Here again we find that holistic listening means transforming the entire body into an ear, with music integrating and aligning the mind-body system.

The World of Relaxation ends with a statement about creating "new options, new alternatives, new ways of looking at old problems" as part of growth toward greater wholeness.[100] In this culminating moment, healing is understood as transformation, not only of the body but of other components of the holistic self as well. Transformation was an important concept in the New Age movement as indicated by its central role in Marilyn Ferguson's popular book about the movement, *The Aquarian Conspiracy* (1980). A faith in transformation of both self and society was what linked the various manifestations of the New Age movement, Ferguson wrote. "You can break through old limits, past inertia and fear, to levels of fulfillment that once seemed impossible," she writes. "It can all be otherwise."[101]

Transformation is the dominant theme on side two of *Rainbow Butterfly*, where Miller prompts the listener to use Kelly's music as a mental vehicle to travel to a special place and then imagine being inside a cocoon. The meditation ends with the listener emerging from the cocoon transformed into the eponymous rainbow-colored butterfly. Similar dynamics of virtual travel and transformation can be heard on many New Age guided meditation cassettes. In Iasos's *A Drop of Light* (1987), we journey inside a crystal and visit a crystal healing garden, and in Michael Stearns and Carolyn Conger's *Sacred Pool* (1988), the listener visits a mystical garden and hears a narrative about a "shape-shifting" king. The title track of Smith and Erickson's *Blue Skies* (1985) takes the listener for a ride on a cloud before diving to the bottom of the ocean to reemerge from the water transformed. "If you were going to come out of the ocean as a strange and unusual creature, what would that be?" KZ Smith asks. "Would you come out as a great big, tough turtle? A delicate salamander? An invulnerable reptile? A pink flamingo? How about a white egret? You can slink, claw, fly out of that ocean. How do you like being a different shape? Does it bring out a sense of humor in you? You can be as colorful, imaginative, crazy as you want."

There is a certain tension on these cassettes between restoring the body to its original, "natural" state on the one hand and transforming the body into something new on the other. These two imperatives can be mapped onto two forms of spiritual experience described by psychiatrist Stanislav Grof. The first he calls the "immanent divine," which is characterized by a subtle but profound transformation in the perception of everyday reality. Grof compared this experience to a black and white television set that was suddenly changed to vivid, living color.[102] The body scan meditations on New Age cassettes work in this manner, bringing the listener back to the reality of one's mind and body but from a more integrated and holistic perspective. Grof referred to a second form of spiritual experience as the "transcendent divine." This involves an encounter with realities or beings that are unavailable to everyday perception. To return to the television analogy, this is like discovering that there are multiple channels on a TV set that we believed had only one option.[103] Guided meditation cassettes that feature virtual travel and body transformation work in this register, recalibrating the holistic self and changing the channel of consciousness to colorful butterflies, shapeshifting archetypal entities, or delicate salamanders.

The tension between immanent and transcendent divine shows the complexity that exists within New Age guided meditations, which were, in turn, shaped by a set of New Age ideas about vibration, intention, harmony, resonance, and transformation. The circulation of New Age music in the 1970s and '80s relied on a genre-specific network of distribution and a genre-specific set of ideas. New Age musicians did not always live up to their holistic aspirations. But how could they? Bridging the gap between art and science, mind and body, music and medicine, is a very tall order. Their attempts are historically significant despite their shortcomings, constituting a multi-faceted investigation of the role of sound in mind-body dynamics.[104] Moreover, the books, lectures, and spoken-word cassettes produced by this cohort of musicians stand as underappreciated works of vernacular sound theory. Indeed, these grassroots theorist-practitioners were asking questions about sound and vibration that would be taken up by the discipline of sound studies twenty years later.

The New Age blend of art and science is worth revisiting for scholars of sound studies as a means to take up musicologist Nina Eidsheim's call for a re-conception of "sound as event through the practice of vibration."

Eidsheim recognizes that this would mean embracing what is commonly ignored by academics, specifically, music therapy.[105] Furthermore, New Age guided meditation cassettes are valuable sonic documents that outline a culturally specific form of listening, what sound studies scholar call an "audile technique."[106] As we have seen, the New Age audile technique was shaped by New Age holism and involved listening with the entire body, imagining one's entire self to be an ear. When appreciated as vernacular sound studies, a cassette like *Rainbow Butterfly* is not only a New Age blend of art and science, it is a blend of multiple arts and multiple sciences.

My reference to an insufficient holism throughout this chapter comes from the anthropologist Gregory Bateson. Bateson and his daughter Mary Catherine defined holism in cybernetic terms, as a tendency to produce complex wholes from the ordered grouping of parts, such that the whole had properties that were not present in the separate parts. To be holistic in this definition means being attentive to emergent, system-wide properties.[107] To focus too narrowly on the parts and fail to see the characteristics of the whole was to fall into an insufficient holism, but there was also the danger of fetishizing the phenomena that emerged from wholeness and ascribing to them supernatural agency.[108] Mind-body problems give rise to two problematic reductions, Bateson wrote. Mind-body could be reduced to mind, ascribing power to supernatural entities outside the body, or it could be reduced to body in a mechanistic manner that viewed people as biological machines. Both options fed each other in an amplifying cybernetic feedback loop whereby the supernatural premise of external mind invites charlatanism, which spurs a retreat to a materialism that becomes intolerably narrow. We are forced to choose between one unsatisfactory position or another.[109]

Bateson had firsthand knowledge of the New Age milieu and the Human Potential movement, having taught at Esalen in the 1970s. In fact, he was at Esalen at the same time as Georgia Kelly, and the two met there.[110] Bateson felt trapped between the Scylla of scientific materialism and the Charybdis of romantic supernaturalism. In the end, he chose to live at Esalen, "with its incantations, its astrological searching for truth, its divination by yarrow root, its herbal medicines, its diets, its yoga, and all the rest." "I am appalled by my scientific colleagues," he wrote, "and while I disbelieve almost everything that is believed by the counterculture, I find it more comfortable to live with that disbelief than with the dehumanizing disgust and horror that conventional occidental themes and ways of life inspire in me. They are so successful and their beliefs are so heartless."[111]

In the last years of his life, Bateson wanted to find a place for what he called the sacred, which he hoped would provide a third option besides the supernatural and the mechanical. He hoped that a combination of art and science could be the basis for knowledge to support a sacred celebration of "natural unity."[112] In its own way, New Age music was on a similar mission, and its network of insufficient holism remains a tantalizing bridge to unseen sacred shores.

THREE

Luminous Sounds

"WHY ARE PRECIOUS STONES PRECIOUS?" begins Aldous Huxley's famous essay "Visionary Experience." Huxley was curious about the fact that again and again, accounts of such experiences contained descriptions of "luminous landscapes and architectures encrusted with gems."[1] Huxley answered his own question by positing that precious stones remind us of a latent potential in our minds, a luminous, "more-than-real" world that we glimpse only occasionally in moments of visionary illumination. The existence of this luminous inner world helps to explain our fascination with fire as well as precious stones, and Huxley referred to gems as "crystallized fire."[2]

New Age music of the visionary school sparkled with its own sonic luminosity created by the crystalline and ethereal sounds of synths, flutes, and harps, and it became a catalyzing ingredient in multimedia experiments with sound and light during the 1970s and '80s. Aldous Huxley found the luminous quality of visionary experiences in artforms like stained glass windows, fireworks, magic lantern shows, and the cinema.[3] This chapter updates Huxley's list through an examination of a host of New Age music's visual partners: color organs, Day-Glo pigments, blacklight posters, psychedelic light shows, planetarium presentations, video art, and laser shows. New Age music paired well with these gleaming visual forms because of its spacey expansiveness and lack of lyrics, which left plenty of room for complementary sensory information.

In the previous chapter we explored New Age music's alternative distribution network, which encompassed cultural niches associated with the New Age movement. In this chapter we examine another set of cultural niches where New Age music took root, a constellation of intermedia musical forms I'm calling *New Age audiovision*. New Age audiovision is an underappreciated part of the history of abstract, non-narrative visual music that stretches from the geometrical abstractions of experimental animation and Busby Berkeley musical sequences to the latest pop music videos.[4] Blossoming in the period after the peak of the Hollywood musical and before the debut of MTV, New Age audiovision was an outgrowth of the wave of intermedia experimentation documented by Gene Youngblood in his book *Expanded Cinema* (1970). Youngblood describes intermedia experiments involving film, television, radio, magazines, books and newspapers.[5] He doesn't mention it, but music, and New Age music in particular, was a vital part of the intermedia mix during the decade after the publication of his book.

One of the distinguishing characteristics of New Age audiovision is that it emanates the warm glow of New Age spirituality. As we have seen, sound and light had a mystical function in Kirpal Singh's school of Surat Shabd Yoga, which influenced several New Age musicians of the visionary school. Sound and light are "guides to a weary traveler on a lonesome journey in a pitch dark night," Singh writes. "The two together have been described as Flaming Sound or Sounding Flame."[6] For musicians inspired by philosophies like Singh's, sound and light were vehicles for spiritual insights and ecstatic illumination. New Age musician Constance Demby, whom we will meet in this chapter, studied Singh's school of the "eternal sound current" in 1977. "I love light and sound together," she said. "In fact, there is nothing in the Universe that is not light and sound. Everything vibrates. All of matter is coalesced light and coalesced sound, and together they go back to the very beginning of Creation. . . . When we put sound and light together in music and colors, they can have a tremendous impact. Our soul responds on a very deep level."[7]

This chapter proceeds under the sign of Huxley's crystalized fire and Singh's sounding flame, as well as the philosopher Gaston Bachelard's investigation of "the delirium of excessive expression" that he found in poetic reveries about precious stones. Bachelard called this delirious poetics "the will to shine."[8] Our primary guide to the "New Age will to shine" is Ken Jenkins, whom we meet in the late 1960s, when he was an engineering student at Carnegie Mellon University in Pittsburgh.

PSYCHEDELIC SHOWCASE

Like many college students in the late 1960s, Ken Jenkins was growing out his hair, experimenting with mind-altering drugs, and listening to the progressive rock music of the era. He spent a considerable amount of time smoking marijuana and listening to records on headphones, since loudspeakers would disturb his Carnegie Mellon dorm mates. Listening to progressive rock on headphones, he would "trip out," losing himself in the music for hours. The more he listened, the more he wished there was an equally compelling visual experience to pair with his records. Putting his engineering studies to use, Jenkins decided to build a "color organ," a simple electronic device with colored lights that were triggered by the volume and frequency of recorded music. His color organ became a fixture at social gatherings during his senior year.[9]

Jenkins's color organ, working in tandem with trippy progressive rock of the 1960s, is a preview of New Age audiovision, but the color organ itself had been around since the radio era. An article in *Popular Science* from 1936 describes a color organ that could be connected to a radio set to produce colored lights as an accompaniment to radio programs. The screen was said to produce "dancing hues as pleasing to the eye as music is to the ear," with low notes bathing the screen in deep red, notes in the middle register appearing in shades of green, and high notes in a brilliant blue.[10] Color organs moved from the radio to the hi-fi stereo in the 1960s. In 1969, *Popular Electronics* provided instructions on how to build a color organ and encouraged readers to turn their living room or den into a "psychedelic showcase."[11]

The color organ was not the only luminous entertainment paired with the hi-fi stereo. Blacklight posters were closely tied to contemporary records, and they adorned the walls of many dorm rooms like Ken's. Like color organs, ultraviolent "blacklight" devices had been around since the 1930s but took on new cultural significance in the 1960s.[12] Two young boys in Berkeley, California, Joe and Bob Switzer, read an article on blacklights in the December 1932 edition of *Popular Science* and created iridescent paints from substances they found in their father's drugstore.[13] The two boys formed a company in the 1940s, Switzer Brothers, and their Day-Glo pigments were soon being used on military signal panels, airfields, buoys, clothing, and product packaging.[14]

In the mid-1960s, the Switzer Brothers' Day-Glo colors were appropriated by the counterculture as an accompaniment to the psychedelic drug experience. The prismatic culture that emerged around the use of psychedelics like LSD corroborates Huxley's theory that there is a connection between luminosity and visionary states of consciousness. In *Psychedelic Information Theory*, James L. Kent writes that subjects on psychedelics often report "increased luminosity and saturation of colors," as well as "halos or auras of light surrounding objects" and "geometric matrices rendered in swirling palettes of fluorescent purple and neon green."[15] Albert Hofmann, the Swiss chemist who synthesized LSD, described his first experience of accidentally ingesting it in 1943 as a dreamlike state in which he perceived "an uninterrupted stream of fantastic pictures, extraordinary shapes with intense, kaleidoscopic play of colors."[16] In his personal account of psychedelic exploration, John C. Lilly associated the LSD experience with "the sudden enhancement and deepening of all color and form."[17] Day-Glo colors became emblems of the psychedelic experience, decorating the iconic bus used by Ken Kesey and the Merry Pranksters on their LSD-fueled exploits.

By 1970, a journalist had declared that "the great color revolution is here" and that "freaks" were applying Day-Glo pigments onto "walls, floors, faces, Volkswagen buses, vests, arms, robes and World War I flier helmets."[18] Day-Glo colors were used in the marketing of psychedelic rock albums of the late 1960s, as can be seen on cover art for Cream's *Disraeli Gears* (1967). Posters for rock concerts also manifested the psychedelic will to shine, as can be seen in Robert Fried's eye-popping technicolor vortex *The High Mass Is Coming* (1967); Wilfried Satty's *The Inner Eye* (1968), *Meditation* (1969), and *Fool on the Hill* (1967), which feature a high-octane color palette and references to spiritual transcendence; and Rick Griffin's cover design for the Grateful Dead's album *Aoxomoxoa* (1969).

Blacklight posters were a radiant subset of the psychedelic poster market, and many blacklight poster designs of the 1960s and '70s depict images of popular rock groups like the Beatles and Led Zeppelin, revealing their close connection to the music of the era. Blacklight posters were also part of the live music scene. In the late 1960s, New Age musician J D Emmanuel worked for a company that made and distributed blacklight posters based in Houston, Texas.[19] Emmanuel recalled that blacklights were part of the decor of a music venue in downtown Houston, Love Street Light Circus, which had a row of pallets in front of the stage where people could lay down and listen to the music if they were in an altered state. The balcony was equipped with a bank of overhead projectors for light shows as well as blacklight posters. The total experience, he said, was about "blending the music and the visuals together."[20]

Blacklight posters were doing more than simply promoting contemporary pop records. They had a spiritual function as well. Blacklight posters often functioned as tools for meditation or accompaniments to psychedelic journeys and were sold in head shops and metaphysical bookstores where New Age cassettes could also be found. Joseph Parker, one of the artists associated with the California visionary school of painting, designed a number of popular blacklight posters oriented to the spiritual seeker.[21] In the words of one collector, by the end of the 1960s, the blacklight poster was "the premier freak flag to hang at the front door to a new consciousness."[22]

Color organs and blacklight posters were luminous media that developed alongside the psychedelic and progressive rock of the late 1960s and early '70s. Ken Jenkins was part of the psychedelic will to shine, but he took his passion for sound and light further than most. After making his color organ, he built more complex luminous devices that produced shifting patterns of light.[23] A friend recommended that Jenkins check out the work of the artist Thomas Wilfred. When he did, Jenkins took an important step in developing the vocabulary of New Age audiovision.[24]

LUMIA

The Danish-born artist Thomas Wilfred moved to the United States in 1916, where he earned his living for a time as a professional musician. His passion, however, was to develop an art form that used light as an expressive medium. In 1922, he gave the public debut of a device he called the Clavilux, which used a keyboard to control the placement of prisms in front of a light source to create shifting colors and geometric patterns.[25] He called this approach the art of light, and the mobile forms it produced, "lumia." Wilfred's colorful lumia are a stunning manifestation of the will to shine, and resemble multicolored flames, luminous clouds, or the lights of the aurora borealis.[26] Most of Wilfred's performances took place in silence, but his lumia sometimes accompanied musical performances, as when he collaborated with Leopold Stokowski and the Philadelphia orchestra in 1926.[27]

Wilfred's art was deeply mystical in orientation. He described light as the "universal expression of the greatest force our senses can grasp," and he wanted lumia art to express "a greater reality, a cosmic consciousness, that we may balance the human entity against the great common denominator—the universal rhythmic flow."[28] The cosmic scope of Wilfred's vision is indicated by his advice to would-be lumia artists, who he said should work as if they were seated at the controls of an imaginary space liner in deep space, looking through a large window at the nose of the spacecraft. Imagining this window as a stage, the lumia artist could create "a fantastic and radiant realm, a celestial architecture of lightyear dimensions."[29]

Trippy light shows, cosmic consciousness, epic sci-fi drama. There was much for multimedia artists of the 1960s and '70s to appreciate in Wilfred as an artistic predecessor. Wilfred's lumia became a point of reference for the live light shows of the 1960s, as performed by Joshua White's Joshua Light Show in New York City and the Heavy Water Light Show in San Francisco (more on Heavy Water below).[30] Wilfred also had an influence on Ken Jenkins, who developed his own system for creating Wilfred-esque lumia. "Picture a flashlight," Jenkins says. If you want to make something interesting out of the light it produces, you have two options. You can "put stuff between that flashlight and the screen to modulate the light, to warp it or change it," as with the prisms in Wilfred's Clavilux. Your second option is to "bounce the light off of something shiny that reflects it." When you move the reflective material you get a dynamic lumia.[31]

In pursuit of materials to produce lumia in these ways, Jenkins traveled to a store called Edmund Scientific in Barrington, New Jersey. Founded in 1942 to sell products like lenses for telescopes and microscopes, Edmund Scientific embraced the countercultural will to shine and advertised items like color organs and blacklights. A 1970 ad for Edmund Scientific has a banner that announces, "Special Unique Psychedelic Lighting," under which can be found descriptions of several color organs, a blacklight fixture, a kaleidoscopic projector, a "visual effects projector set," and a "Psychedelic Lighting Handbook."[32] For Jenkins, the big draw of Edmund Scientific was that they sold irregular pieces of optical glass that resulted from mistakes in the manufacturing process. These rejected pieces were particularly good at producing lumia. Jenkins also purchased slide projectors and kaleidoscopic lenses at Edmund Scientific.[33] With this new toolset and a conceptual framework for creating lumia, Jenkins began doing live performances with his company, Immediate Future: Kinetic Light Art.

One of the first events he did was a light show for the conference Transpersonal Frontiers: Harmony in Mind, Body and Spirit, hosted by Jim Fadiman's California Institute of Transpersonal Psychology. Along with Stanislav Grof, Fadiman was one of the founders of transpersonal psychology, and he had also been a speaker at the Kohoutek Celebration of Consciousness in 1974. The Transpersonal Frontiers conference was held in February 1977 at the San Francisco Airport Hilton, and

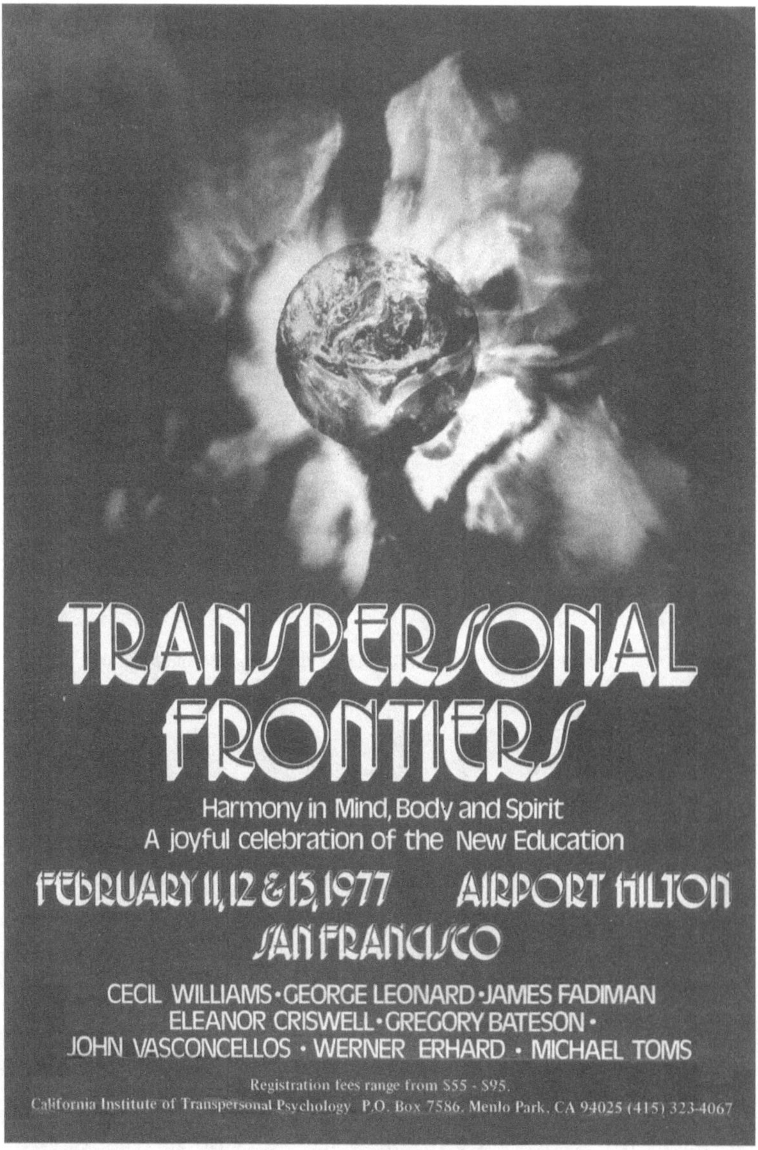

Poster for the Transpersonal Frontiers conference of February 1977. Image courtesy of Ken Jenkins.

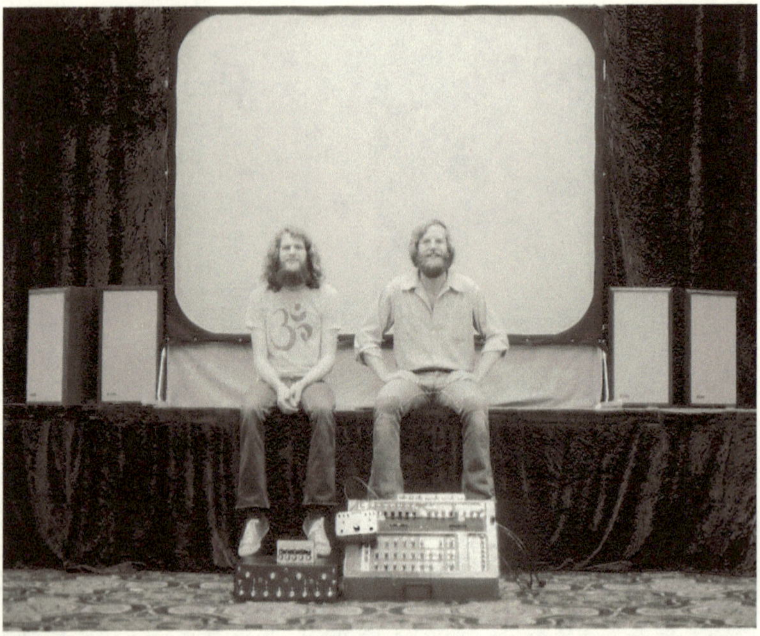

Ken Jenkins (*left*) and his partner Dean Cutler at the Transpersonal Frontiers conference. Photo courtesy of Ken Jenkins.

Immediate Future presented a "visual meditation" featuring music by Iasos, Vangelis, Geoffrey Chandler, and Tangerine Dream. As this playlist indicates, Jenkins had by this time switched from the progressive rock of his college days to what would become known as New Age music. "When the New Age stuff came out with no words, it was more suitable for the soundtrack to my visuals," Jenkins said. "That's where I went."[34]

One person attending the Transpersonal Frontiers conference was Dorothy Fadiman, Jim Fadiman's wife, who was working on an audiovisual presentation about an LSD session during which she had an epiphany about the spiritual dimension of light.[35] Fadiman tried to write about her experience but couldn't capture its spirit and power in words. At first she created a slide presentation, but she began to conceive of the project as a film, working with the filmmaker Michael Wiese. Fadiman

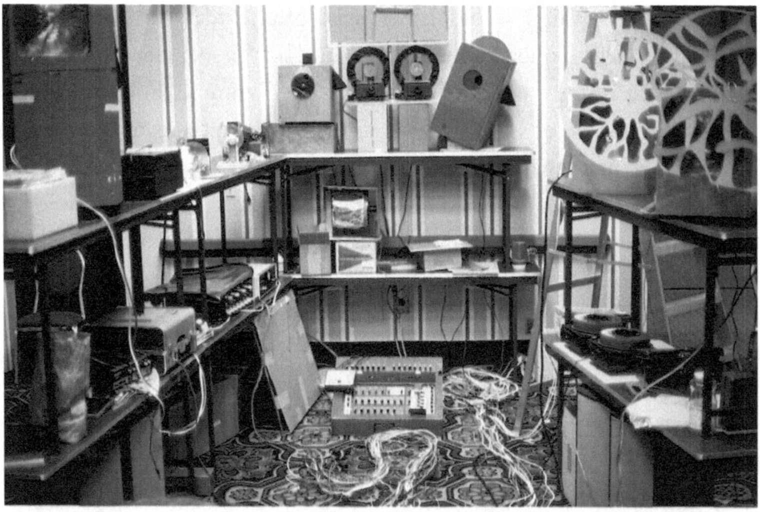

Lumia projectors, kaleidoscopic mandala projectors, laser projectors, and slide projectors used by Ken Jenkins at the Transpersonal Frontiers conference performance. Photo courtesy of Ken Jenkins.

saw Jenkins's visual meditation at the conference and asked him to participate in her project, which at the time was called *Do Saints Really Glow?* Jenkins accepted the invitation and remembered it as his first step into filmmaking.[36] Fadiman's film was eventually given a title that signals its wholehearted embodiment of a New Age will to shine: *Radiance* (1978). Fadiman worked with Stephen Hill on the soundtrack for *Radiance*, which features New Age music by Iasos, Geoffrey Chandler, and Klaus Schulze and stands as the first fully fledged example of New Age audiovision.[37]

Radiance begins with colorful lumia created by Ken Jenkins, as Fadiman narrates the experience of feeling her body filled with light and the sense of a profound connection to the entire universe. Fadiman describes how she became conscious of "an exquisite radiance permeating the fabric of all life." As Fadiman explains that every living thing has its own luminous quality, we see a jellyfish pulsing gracefully through the water. The next sequence, which describes fire as a primal force, is followed by a discussion of holy light in Judaism, Christianity, Buddhism, and Hinduism. Subsequent sequences deal with celestial cycles, ancient landmarks linked to the heavens like Stonehenge and the Pyramids, and the human body as a "temple of light." *Radiance* ends with reports of near-death experiences that describe entering a tunnel of light. Iasos's majestic track "The Angles of Comfort" and ravishing mandala-like images created by Ken Jenkins accompany a final invocation to the Great Mother's "blinding light of love."[38]

Radiance marks the crystallization of New Age audiovision in terms of both form and content, and it exudes central themes of the New Age movement such as perennialism, holism, the vibrational ontology, and sound and light as the medium of spiritual experience. *New Age Journal* published an article on the film, reporting that five hundred people packed into the New Varsity Theater in Palo Alto, California, to see it, with hundreds more turned away at the door.[39] Jenkins was not the only visual artist who collaborated with Fadiman on *Radiance.* The film also contains mandala paintings created by Jeanette Stobie, whose work had been included in the visionary art exhibit at the Kohoutek Celebration in 1974 and who later collaborated with New Age musician Michael Stearns (more on Stobie below). *Radiance* also features images made by the filmmaker Jordan Belson. Often included in histories of experimental film, Belson had ties to New Age music that are less well known. We begin this overlooked aspect of Belson's career at a venue that was a crucial showcase for New Age audiovision: the planetarium.

PLANETARIUM

In his book *Expanded Cinema*, Gene Youngblood writes that Jordan Belson's abstract films create a state of "nonordinary reality" for the viewer that is similar to the experience of hallucinogenic drugs. Belson, Youngblood writes, brought together Eastern theology, Western science, and consciousness-expanding drug experiences, and was, "like the ancient alchemists . . . a true visionary."[40] As Youngblood's comments indicate, Belson had much in common with the visionary school of New Age music, and so it is not surprising to find that he inspired and collaborated with them.

Belson found a venue for his visionary combination of theology, science, and consciousness expansion at the Morrison Planetarium in San Francisco.[41] The Morrison opened in 1952, during a boom in planetarium construction that was driven by the Cold War space race, government funding policies, and an increase in the school population.[42] The baby-boom generation grew up attending school field trips to see planetarium lectures, and a new labor force of planetarium staff sought to spice up their programming with drama and entertainment to keep audiences engaged.[43]

Born in Chicago in 1926, Belson studied art at the University of California, Berkeley, where he became interested in abstract film. Music was an important part of his filmmaking, as he explained to an interviewer: "I don't think I would be interested in film if it didn't have sound."[44] It was Belson's collaborator, the sound artist Henry Jacobs, who first attended a show at the Morrison Planetarium and recognized the space's potential for multimedia art experiences. Jacobs teamed up with Belson to put on the legendary Vortex Concerts at the Morrison from 1957 to 1960, which featured Belson's abstract imagery projected on the planetarium's dome while Jacobs played recorded music by composers such as Karlheinz Stockhausen, Toshiro Mayuzumi, and Luc Ferrari. The planetarium's sound system boasted thirty-eight speakers in a circular configuration, and Jacobs oversaw the creation of a special rotary handle that allowed him to "swing the sound through the whole circle of speakers at any desired tempo."[45] This produced the "vortex effect" that gave the concerts their name.[46]

Belson's contribution was to create abstract images that were projected onto the dome. Belson combined these projections with in-house planetarium effects that simulated stars and meteors. He also used a set of paired projectors to create overlapping grid patterns. One reviewer wrote that these interference or moiré effects turned the dome into "a cosmic merry-go-round," showering the audience with "vast, flaky blips" and sending "light-shapes chasing each other across the sidereal ceiling."[47] We can get a sense of the kinds of images Belson projected by watching his film *Raga* (1958), some of which was used in the Vortex program. Closely synchronized to a soundtrack of classical Indian music, stunning kaleidoscopic patterns shimmer in and out of existence around a central point. Belson described the film as a mandala in cinematic form that was meant to be an object for meditation.[48] Belson described one particularly dramatic moment in the Vortex program: "We made the whole dome very dark red and then we introduced the full starfield into the dark red and gradually faded the red out, leaving only the bright stars against absolute black. . . . The audience would always break into spontaneous applause when they saw it."[49] One attendee of a 1958 Vortex Concert remembered the show ending with a sparkler descending on a wire "like a comet."[50]

By all accounts, the Vortex Concerts were visceral and deeply trippy experiences, and they were successful enough to continue for three years.[51] For one reviewer, the concert provided "the closest approximation to a sense of absolute infinity which I have ever experienced."[52] The Vortex Concerts set a high bar for planetarium sound and light shows, but they were not alone. In fact, recorded music became an increasingly important part of the planetarium experience during the 1960s.[53] Although planetarium musical programs initially featured Western classical music, that began to change in the 1970s. An important figure in that transformation is the New Age musician Tim Clark.

Clark was a composition major at Eastman School of Music in Rochester in the late 1960s, a time when the school was building its first electronic music studio. As with other New Age musicians, Clark had mixed feelings about the kind of music that was emphasized by the composition program. "I got locked into writing the kind of music that everybody else was writing at the time in the universities, which was mostly atonal serial music. I hated it, but I did it," he said. "Every time I would put in some little major chord or something they would say, 'No, you can't do that.'" In 1970, after one year in a PhD program, he dropped out.[54]

When Clark was a student at Eastman, the Strasenburgh Planetarium in Rochester used one of his compositions, "Starburst," in a show. After leaving the PhD program, Clark landed a job as the planetarium's composer in residence. He couldn't believe his good luck. "I was an employed electronic music composer with a paycheck," he chuckled. "It was just totally ridiculous!" The gig at the Strasenburgh provided Clark with his own sonic lab-oratorium: an entire electronic music studio at his disposal, which included a mixing board, multitrack recorders with adjustable speeds, and a Moog synthesizer donated by Robert Moog himself.[55]

In a 1974 article in the trade journal *The Planetarian*, Clark is described as the only planetarium composer in residence in the country, and he gives advice about using turntables and tape recorders to match music with the dramatic peaks of a planetarium show. "Don't be afraid to mix two pieces together," he advises, and gives the example of blending the "Venus" movement from Gustav Holst's *The Planets* with Terry Riley's minimal classic "Poppy Nogood and the Phantom Band," which would create "a wispy, mysterious sound dramatically unlike either of the pieces taken individually."[56] This alchemical blend of minimal electronic music and mystical classical music is a blueprint for the New Age music that would soon find a prominent place in the planetarium repertoire.

During Tim Clark's tenure there, the Strasenburgh became a leader in experimentation in sound and image at planetariums. In 1972, the experimental filmmaker Stan VanDerBeek put on *Cine Dreams: Cinema of the Mind* at the Strasenburgh. This was an all-night, multimedia event in which planetarium visitors were encouraged to sleep as VanDerBeek's kaleidoscopic images swarmed overhead.[57] Robert Moog made a public appearance to demonstrate his synthesizer at a 1973 event called *Moog Universe*, which was billed as a "one hour electronic music concert and light show extravaganza."[58]

The psychedelic light shows inspired by Thomas Wilfred's lumia also found a home at the Strasenburgh in the form of the Heavy Water Light Show from San Francisco, which was operated by the wife-and-husband team of Joan Chase and John Hardham.[59] Heavy Water had toured with San Francisco rock bands like Jefferson Airplane, Santana, and the

Grateful Dead and designed the album cover for *Santana III* (1971) and the interior art for Jefferson Starship's *Sunfighter* (1971). Their live concert projections can be seen on the back cover of Jefferson Airplane's *30 Seconds over Winterland* (1973).[60]

While on tour with the Grateful Dead in 1973, several members of Heavy Water visited a planetarium in Salt Lake City and struck up a conversation with the director about doing a light show with recordings by the rock bands with whom they'd been working. These initial shows were a success, and Heavy Water found that they preferred the planetarium to the large arenas where rock concerts were starting to be held. "We really liked the planetarium because it was a small, controlled environment where we could control the light and the sound," Hardham said. "It was intimate, like performing in a club, and we had the stars as a background. What more could you ask for?"[61] Heavy Water began to book their performances in planetariums, and their favorite venue was the Strasenburgh in Rochester, where they worked with Tim Clark several times. In 1975, Heavy Water and Clark collaborated on a show called *Moog Light*, which featured slides, overhead projectors, lumia projections, and film footage, while Clark played the Moog synthesizer.[62]

Moog Light joins Dorothy Fadiman's *Radiance* as an early manifestation of New Age audiovision. Another event at the Strasenburgh featured a musician who would become a major figure in New Age music. Constance Demby studied sculpture and painting at the University of Michigan and moved to New York City in the early 1960s. Working with steel sculptures in 1966, she discovered that they produced unusual sounds when they were made to vibrate. She proceeded to create several unique musical instruments, the "Space Bass" and the "Whale Sail." In 1968, she performed with these musical sculptures at a New York City gallery owned by Robert Rutman. Demby and Rutman collaborated on a multimedia event called *Space Mass* in 1970, which incorporated environmental sculptures, visual projections, synthesizer music, and video displays.[63]

Demby and Rutman moved to Maine in the early 1970s and formed a multimedia performance group called Central Maine Power Sound &

Light. This group toured the East Coast during the early 1970s and frequently appeared at planetariums.[64] In 1974, Central Maine Power Sound & Light brought their show *Astral Projections: A Polyfusion of Media* to the Strasenburgh. In addition to Demby's steel creations and traditional instruments like the dulcimer, tamboura, zither, and flute, the group was joined by the video artist Bill Etra, who had developed the Rutt-Etra video synthesizer. Etra manipulated the input from three video cameras in real time and projected the results on the planetarium dome.[65]

Accounts of the *Astral Projections* show describe the lights dimming as the planetarium dome took on the appearance of an evening sky with drifting clouds that slowly changed color from white to gold to crimson. The musicians entered the planetarium in a solemn procession, wearing loose fitting garments and blowing conch shells. As they took their places and began to play, the dome transformed into a night sky full of stars. The music rose in intensity as video images erupted into view and then took on a gentle softness as video images of the musicians' hands and faces floated on a background of stars. As the performance came to an end, the night sky on the dome gave way to morning sunlight with clouds drifting across the sky.[66]

Astral Projections was one of a host of events at the Strasenburgh that reveal the planetarium to be a vibrant site of audiovisual experimentation at this time. New Age music became a key ingredient in that experience, and reciprocally, the planetarium shaped New Age music. Tim Clark began using tape loops and multitracking in his planetarium studio to generate sonic textures that would match lectures about stars, planets, and clouds. In one case, Clark sang a note and then looped it, altering the speed and layering tracks to construct a massive tone. Running that recording through the Moog's filters, he created atmospheres that he felt resembled clouds, which were then added to the planetarium show.[67] Though he took a different route, Clark arrived at the same musical destination as New Age tracks like Steve Roach's "Structures from Silence" and Iasos's "Cloud Prayer," which have a slow, stately pace that suggest clouds drifting lazily across a widescreen sky. In a 1979 documentary, we see Iasos performing "Cloud Prayer" on an echo-drenched lap guitar over superimposed images of cloud-strewn skies; a performance that would have fit right in at the Strasenburgh during the 1970s.

Iasos performed in planetariums on multiple occasions during his career, as did other visionary school artists, such as Steve Roach, Michael Stearns, and Kevin Braheny Fortune.[68] Emerald Web played their first planetarium concerts in 1974–75.[69] At that time, the band was based in Hartford, Connecticut, and they crossed paths with another musician who would go to have a long career at the intersection of New Age music and the planetarium: Jonn Serrie. Born in 1951 in Waterford, Connecticut, Serrie would attend church with his grandmother, a church organist. He was captivated as a child by the otherworldly quality of the organ as it filled the space of the church and fascinated by the fact that the organ could produce more than one kind of sound. His childhood familiarity with the organ served as a template for his later introduction to electronic synthesizers in the 1960s. What the organ was doing with air, the synthesizer was doing with electrons running through circuit boards. "I saw them as identical," he said.[70]

Serrie took a job demonstrating synthesizers made by Electronic Music Laboratories (EML) in Connecticut. The job at EML provided Serrie with a well-rounded education in audio, enabling him to develop the skills he needed to set up his own home studio.[71] While working at EML, he also played gigs in clubs in the Hartford area, which is how he met Emerald Web, whom he sometimes joined onstage. Around 1977, a friend asked Serrie if he had ever considered presenting his music at the planetarium in West Hartford. "The light bulbs really went off," he said. "Here was this wide-open market that no one else was looking at. Electronic music and planetarians go together like soup and a sandwich. . . . This is a way I can bring my music to a wide audience."[72]

In a variation on the do-it-yourself cassette ethos we discussed in the previous chapter, Serrie began sending cassettes to planetariums, and he placed a small ad in the back of *Astronomy Magazine* in 1984 with information about obtaining his cassettes of "Real Space Music." In a parallel to the New Age fair scene, Serrie went to planetarium conventions and got to know the key players in the field. As a result of all this legwork, Serrie ended up landing a job as composer in residence at the Alice G. Wallace Planetarium in Fitchburg, Massachusetts. Serrie went on to develop a catalog of music that has been heard both at planetariums and on New Age radio shows like *Music from the Hearts of Space.*

By 1980, more and more people were recognizing that New Age music and planetariums went together like soup and a sandwich. In 1984, *The Planetarian* published an article in which a planetarium staff member recounted flipping through the radio dial and hearing music that "seemed to be not of this Earth": "Its ambience, its ethereal sound, slowly carried me from my desk out into the universe. As I listened, I saw stars streaming by as I floated among them. I saw planets, moons, wispy nebulae, and slowly rotating galaxies. 'What great music for a planetarium show,' I thought."[73] The author had stumbled onto *Music from the Hearts of Space*, which only the year before was syndicated on eighty NPR stations across the country.

It was not only planetarium professionals who were seeing a connection between New Age "space music" and planetarium shows. If you were someone interested in experimental sound and image like Ken Jenkins, you'd have planetarium schedules on your radar. Indeed, the next phase of our investigation of New Age audiovision begins at the Minolta Planetarium in Cupertino, California. It was there that Ken Jenkins ran into an old acquaintance, Geoffrey Chandler. Both were at the planetarium to attend a light and sound event, and during a break in the program, the two struck up a conversation. Chandler was a visual artist and musician, and he had become immersed in the California New Age music scene. He invited Jenkins to attend a concert by Iasos. Jenkins was dazzled by Iasos's performance, not just because of the music but because of his stunning use of visuals. Iasos's live show at this time featured two slide projectors showing visionary paintings by artists like Gilbert Williams.[74] Before long, Jenkins met Iasos and began a collaboration with him. Through that work, Jenkins brought New Age audiovision into the domain of home video.

At the same time that Jenkins was doing live light shows in the San Francisco Bay Area, he also had a job as a technician at a company that made video equipment. After working on Dorothy Fadiman's *Radiance*, he was interested in making his own experimental films. He tried filming some of his light projections with a super-8 camera but became intrigued by the high-end video cameras at his workplace. "I should be doing video," he decided. "I'm an electronics guy."[75]

There was a broken camera sitting in the corner of the camera department, and his boss said he could have it. Collecting scrap parts from different models, he constructed a working camera. By accumulating more discarded parts, he assembled a remarkably high-tech video studio in his garage for a total cash investment of only $1,000.[76] Jenkins's do-it-yourself operation got another upgrade with his next job at Hewlett Packard (HP) in Palo Alto. HP's policy allowed employees to use the company's facilities for their own personal projects, which meant that for seven years, he had after-hours access to state-of-the-art video cameras, recorders, and special effects. "Back then, studio time was incredibly expensive. Hundreds and hundreds of dollars per hour," he said. This was a major barrier since his intricate visualizations required many hours of editing to perfect.[77]

As with New Age musicians and planetarium composers in residence, Jenkins had access to his own lab-oratorium where he could develop his skills outside of prohibitively expensive professional studios. As was the case with New Age musicians, audiovisual work for Jenkins was a spiritual as well as a technological endeavor. "I experience color in a spiritual way," he said. "There is a path of spirituality that has sound and light as a medium. I had experience of that and knew it was transcendent. It was something indescribably wonderful, uplifting, inspiring, healing and refreshing."[78]

Jenkins also resembles the visionary school of New Age music in the way he distributed his work. New Age musicians had mobilized the cassette format to circulate their sounds, and Jenkins mobilized the VHS videotape to circulate his luminous visual music. Working with Michael Wiese, who had collaborated on Fadiman's *Radiance*, Jenkins produced his first video release, *Beauty* (1978). He was not happy with the results of the video transfer, however, and continued to perfect his process, expanding *Beauty* for the collection *Illumination* (1989). *Illumination* is a culmination of Jenkins's work throughout the 1970s and '80s and features New Age music by Iasos, Constance Demby, Jonn Serrie, Suzanne Ciani, Michael Diamond, and Steven Halpern. As the title indicates, *Illumination* manifests the New Age will to shine, and the content of the video illustrates how New Age music and visionary painting were branches on the same tree: classic New Age sounds are paired with images that resemble Joseph Parker's ultraviolet skies and Robert Venosa's angelic forms.

Jenkins's trademark visual image shows the influence of his trips to Edmund Scientific; a kaleidoscopic mandala that grows outward or inward from a central point to create ravishing prismatic patterns. When those patterns move inward, one gets the sense of perpetual forward movement through a tunnel or wormhole. Such moments resemble the genre of early cinema known as the "ride film," which was made by placing a camera at the front of a moving train or other vehicle to provide a captivating sense of propulsive forward motion. For home viewers of *Illumination*, the television screen opens onto an abstract inner journey through myriad evanescent environments of color and shape, inspiring a sense of boundless plenitude. When Jenkins's mandalas move outward, one gets a similar feeling of plenitude as from a flower endlessly blossoming forth. There are moments in the video when centripetal and centrifugal movement pause, providing a blissful sense of repose and equilibrium.

Nonverbal, nonnarrative techniques like centripetal and centrifugal movement convey the meaning in Jenkins's work, and like New Age music, his is an aesthetics of texture. Jenkins's images speak in an elemental language, resembling crystals, liquid, ice, or the alchemical substance par excellence: liquid mercury, which is simultaneously liquid and metal. Watching Jenkins's visual music, one gets the impression that light is a *prima materia*, a philosopher's stone that can manifest any other kind of substance. Jenkins's ever-flowing elemental images are a visual analog for the transformation heard on the New Age guided meditation tapes described in the previous chapter. It is as though we were inside the caterpillar's chrysalis seeing the protean dynamics of liquid transformation before the emergence of a butterfly.

The comparison to *Rainbow Butterfly* is useful here, given that the elemental textures of *Illumination* are brought to life by vivid, hyperreal colors. In his cascading kaleidoscopic mandalas, one encounters one arresting color palette after another, like myriad musical chords created by the wind blowing across the strings of an aeolian harp.[79] This approach required Jenkins to think carefully about avoiding "color fatigue," which is when your eyes see one color so long that it loses its impact and eventually you hardly perceive it at all. Jenkins's perpetually blossoming mandalas are like color fountains continually renewing themselves, enlivening, refreshing, and prolonging our perception of color. As a result, watching *Illumination* is a powerfully visceral experience, the visual equivalent of a full-body massage.

Illumination is a key work in New Age audiovision, extending a tradition of experimental visual music by artists like Thomas Wilfred and Jordan Belson into the VHS era. In fact, Belson was a fan of *Illumination*. Jenkins met Belson through their work on Dorothy Fadiman's *Radiance* and later sent him a copy of *Illumination*. Belson replied with an enthusiastic letter in which he wrote of his "great pleasure of visiting the many truly divine places you have revealed. The gorgeous, glowing colors, potent and mysterious events, and the high moral and aesthetic plane leave me feeling spiritually cleansed after every viewing. More than anything else I've seen so far, this new work of yours is very close to my own ideals."[80]

Not only did Belson and Jenkins have similar ideals, they had some of the same collaborators as well. In fact, Belson made several films with music by New Age musicians of the visionary school. *Music of the Spheres* (1977) uses the solar system as an organizational principle and features music from Iasos's first album, *Inter-Dimensional Music* (1975).[81] Belson's images have the elemental intensity of Jenkins's work and tend toward a similar set of mandala-esque, kaleidoscopic forms—glowing, glassy orbs, smokey nebulae, humanoid figures composed of sparkling light, pulsating cellular spheres, light sparkling on watery surfaces, ocean waves moving in reverse. All these luminous images are harmonized with excerpts from Iasos's ecstatic tracks. Belson's *Infinity* (1979) features Iasos's track "Angel Play" and combines abstract shapes with footage of cathedrals and an incandescent sun rising over the ocean. Another Belson film from this period, *Apollo's Lyre* (1980), features the track "Apollo's Lyre" from Steven Halpern and Georgia Kelly's album *Ancient Echoes* (1978).[82]

These three Belson films, along with Ken Jenkins's VHS releases, are sublime examples of New Age audiovision and set the stage for subsequent visionary work on video. Jenkins helped Iasos on his first video release, *Crystal Vista* (1981). Iasos spoke about the spiritual power of combining music and image, stating that while music is capable of inducing "divine feelings," images are capable of inducing "divine thought-forms. Using them together," he said, "it becomes possible to induce the experience of states of heightened consciousness."[83] *Crystal Vista* approximates a live performance by Iasos in the late 1970s, with tracks from his catalog paired with slideshow-like displays of visionary art by the likes of Gilbert Williams and Joseph Parker and video sequences by Ken Jenkins. At times, *Crystal Vista* can feel like an animated blacklight poster display, and at one point, the screen becomes a porthole-like window on the planet Jupiter, recalling Wilfred's model of lumia art as the view from a spacecraft.

Iasos worked for over two decades to produce his follow-up video album, *Realms of Light* (2011), which builds on the style he and Jenkins had developed in the 1980s. *Realms of Light* features animated patterns that resemble earlier manifestations of luminous art like fireworks and fountains. Alchemical overtones are manifested here as well, with light patterns taking on plasmatic shapes that resemble a range of elemental substances, from bubbles to dewdrops. *Realms of Light* also features live-action footage, given surreal overtones with visual effects. For example, images of natural landscapes are doubled through a mirror-image effect to create a defamiliarizing sense of symmetry. This effect harkens back to the kaleidoscopic lenses that were used by Belson, Jenkins, and Heavy Water and encapsulates a New Age way of seeing that emphasizes balance, harmony, and symmetrical beauty. Here is a nice example of how visionary art adapts the surrealist impulse to "make the familiar strange" to instead "make the familiar numinous."

Several sequences in *Realms of Light* feature a female dancer who manipulates long mobile pieces of fabric. This is a variation on the "serpentine dance" form that was, like the ride film, the subject of some of the earliest motion pictures. Iasos runs these movements in slow motion and on loops, moving forward and backward, to take them out of linear time and emphasize the infinite complexity and beauty of the shapes created by the dancers.[84] The dancers are seen in surreal temple spaces that resemble paintings by Gilbert Williams and the tantric collages of the artist Penny Slinger. In fact, Iasos shot these sequences in Slinger's Blue Lotus Temple studio in Northern California, and he took part in some of her video productions from this period. Slinger's videos *Dance of the Cosmos* (2000), *Goddess Juice* (2003), and *Mother of the World* (2006)—the latter featuring music by Constance Demby—are a tantric feminist variation on New Age audiovision.

Another female artist who explored visual music with a New Age sensibility was Jeanette Stobie. Stobie created sumptuous, colorful mandala paintings that were featured in the visionary art exhibit of the Kohoutek Celebration of Consciousness in 1974 and can be seen in Dorothy Fadiman's film *Radiance*. Stobie's mandalas had a therapeutic valence, since they were made on commission to depict the holistic self of particular people, a kind of spiritual portraiture. Stobie was part of the Continuum scene that will be described in the next chapter, and through Continuum, she met New Age musician Michael Stearns. One of Stobie's mandalas can be seen on the cover of Stearns's early cassette *Morning Jewel* (1980), and Stobie used Stearns's music on her stunning video *Lightstream* (1983), which was made with two slide projectors and a dissolve unit to produce a remarkable visual journey through Stobie's mandalas.

A collection of New Age audiovision can be found on the videotape *California Images: Hi-Fi for the Eyes* (1985), which was promoted as a "video LP" with tracks organized in a two-part structure like the two sides of an LP record. *California Images* features tracks by New Agers Emerald Web, Steve Roach, and William Aura as well as San Francisco synth pioneer Doug McKechnie (who worked with Stephen Hill and Iasos on a revival of the Vortex Concerts in 1974), paired with visuals by Ken Jenkins and video artists like Denise Gallant and Ron Hays. Emerald Web released a VHS tape of their visual music titled *Photonos* (1982) and composed music for a *Radiance*-esque short film about the visionary scientist Emanuel Swedenborg, *Images of Knowing* (1982). Steve Roach released several visual albums, including a laserdisc version of *Structures from Silence* that combined his music with Marianne Dolan's motion paintings and *Earth Dreaming* (1989), with sumptuous photographs of desert landscapes and female bodies by Georgianne Cowan.[85]

This flowering of New Age audiovision reached something of a culmination with the release of *Shirley MacLaine's Inner Workout* (1989), a New Age variation on *Jane Fonda's Workout* (1982). In the video, MacLaine describes the chakra system of subtle energy within our bodies and then guides the viewer in a meditation through the seven chakra centers. For each chakra, we see a Ken Jenkins mandala that emphasizes a color that corresponds to it, and we hear a track by a notable New Age artist like Steve Roach, Suzanne Doucet, Constance Demby, and Kevin Braheny Fortune.[86]

Twelve years before the release of *Inner Workout*, Shirley MacLaine starred in another video production that will introduce us to a final manifestation of the New Age will to shine. The CBS Television special *Where Do We Go from Here* (1977), marketed as a "look at the future of entertainment," begins with MacLaine sitting in a sparkling white suit in front of a green screen.[87] "We live in the most exciting time in the history of the world," MacLaine states, but then wonders aloud, "What are we going to do with all our knowledge and know-how?" MacLaine directs the viewer's attention to a light on the screen behind her, which, she explains, is produced by a laser beam. Lasers could be a means of destruction, she says, or they could be directed to beneficial and artistic ends. As she speaks, the laser image transforms into a spinning star, and a troupe of dancers appear as laser patterns flash in the background. Later in the show, MacLaine declares that "the promise of tomorrow lies in learning to use things like lasers to make the world a happier place to live in." She proceeds to dance with four laser-created lines that move to the rhythm of a military march before transforming into spinning batons, stars, and pulsating ovals.

MacLaine's laser routine was based on a segment from the Laserium light show, which emerged as a popular form of light-based audiovisual entertainment in the mid-1970s.[88] Lasers were cutting-edge artistic tools at the time, and though MacLaine made them part of a Broadway-style musical number, their unearthly glow and abstract morphing patterns were more often accompanied by the luminous sounds of New Age music.

LASERIUM

In 1971, an article in the *Los Angeles Times* announced that "a new magic lantern" had been developed by Dr. Elsa Garmire, a research fellow in electrical engineering at Caltech. This magic lantern was a plexiglass box containing a laser that projected light through rotating bubbles of dried household cement to create lumia patterns meant to enhance the experience of listening to music. Dr. Garmire called her device a "laserium."[89] Garmire's laserium drew the attention of filmmaker Ivan Dryer, who met with her to see about filming its patterns. Dryer discovered that film could not capture the vivid color of the laser, so he began to contemplate the possibility of a live laser show. In 1973, Dryer formed the company Laser Images, with Garmire as president. She left the operation soon thereafter to pursue scientific research, and Dryer made a deal with the Griffith Planetarium in Los Angeles to debut a laser show on Monday nights, when the planetarium was normally closed. The first show took place in November 1973 and was a surprise hit. Dyer's Laserium shows were soon selling out.[90]

Laser shows brought a youth audience to planetariums around the country, and a journalist quipped in 1976 that many had arrived at

Laserium shows "having smoked something that isn't ham."[91] Laser shows presented abstract shapes like the ovals and stars in the Shirley MacLaine special as well as Wilfred-esque lumia, and critics struggled to describe these novel entertainments in words. "Huge gauzy filaments float by, their veins slowly transfusing from red to blue to yellow, the colors so bright as to be pharmaceutical," wrote a *Los Angeles Times* reviewer in 1974.[92] A London review of Laserium spoke of "ravishing mobile abstractions beautifully involved with the music." "The whole abstract school of painting can now be seen simply as groundwork for spectacles like this," the review concluded.[93]

The people who operated the laser device were known as "laserists," or laser artists, and a memoir written by one of them gives us a taste of what it was like to attend a Laserium show at this time. Glenn Thomas describes the audience arriving before the show and looking in amazement at the planetarium's imposing star projector. Once the doors were closed, a planetarium employee welcomed the audience and explained that they were about to see a live performance during which the laserist could respond to the crowd's reactions.[94] The laserist would start the music, the house lights would go down, and the appearance of the stars on the dome overhead would produce riotous applause.[95] The forty-five-minute show that followed featured a range of visual effects, including an explosion of white light from the center of the planetarium dome, lumia clouds of different colors shimmering in time to the music, rotating stars, dots transforming into lines and spinning atoms, and figures that expanded to fill the entire dome. Many of these effects were greeted by enthusiastic applause. The laser images moved in close synchronization with the music such that the images would shrink and fade as though moving off into deep space as a song faded to silence.

By the mid-1970s, laser shows with music were a new audiovisual art form that arguably fulfilled Thomas Wilfred's dreams of a popular art of light. Once again, the visionary school of New Age music was an integral part of the audiovisual mix. Tim Clark's "Second Voyage to Andromeda" was part of an early Laserium program, the same show with the dancing batons that later shared the stage with Shirley MacLaine. Laserium's

Laser Space playlist featured New Age music by Iasos, Emerald Web, Kitaro, Vangelis, Tangerine Dream and Jean-Michel Jarre. Iasos was also included in the *Laserium Starship* show, and Suzanne Ciani was part of the playlist for *Zodiacal Light*. Not only did New Age music accompany laser shows, but lasers were integrated into the toolkit of New Age audio-vision. Ken Jenkins began working with lasers in the mid-1970s, using borrowed lasers for live performances like the Transpersonal Frontiers conference in 1977. He videotaped the lumia he created with those borrowed lasers in his garage studio and used the images for the end credit sequence of Dorothy Fadiman's *Radiance* as well as his own releases, *Beauty* and *Illumination*.[96]

Lasers had a close kinship with the modular synths that were integral to the visionary school of New Age music. In fact, the operation of the laser apparatus by skilled laserists was much like the operation of a modular synth.[97] Ivan Dryer, the founder of Laserium, stated that their laser projector was a "light synthesizer." "We use the same kinds of oscillators that are used in music synthesizers," he explained. "Those oscillators control the motions of the mirrors, so if you could hear the tones that are actually creating those images, you could create music that the projector was making."[98] Likewise, Steve Roach discovered that the laserists in Los Angeles were using the same analog instruments as his electronic music compatriots.[99] Roach performed a concert as part of a Laserium show at Seattle's Pacific Science Center Planetarium in 1980 with the group Radiance, which also featured synth pioneer and laserist Danny Sofer. New Age musician Don Slepian worked for a successful laser company in Los Angeles called Laser Media in the late 1970s (more on Slepian in chapter 6). The technological kinship of laser shows and modular synths resonated with the New Age vibrational ontology discussed in the previous chapter, since the same oscillations of electrons could manifest as either patterns of sound or light.

Given their structural connection, it is not a surprise that synth groups gravitated to lasers. Tangerine Dream, the German electronic group who were a major influence on New Age music, undertook a tour in 1977 in collaboration with the Laserium light show.[100] A *Variety* reviewer described "a wide range of colors and shapes, whirling, spinning and all but boggling the mind," and concluded that "Laserium and Tangerine Dream are a natural combination in pushing technology as entertainment."[101] New Age pioneers Emerald Web were also exploring the natural combination of synth and laser show. "I think we were probably one of the only bands at that time, especially on a small scale like that, without a technician for lasers, that was doing guerilla laser effects," Kat Epple recalls. They would create spinning laser shapes as background to their shows and also shine the laser through crystals to create lumia.[102]

New Age musicians were on the cutting edge of laser technology in the 1970s, and in that regard, they were in tune with their cultural moment. In 1979, an article in the *New York Times* declared the advent of the "laser age." Lasers could be seen at rock concerts, planetarium shows, discos, and movies such as *Star Wars* (1977). There was even an emerging home market for lasers as a modern update on color organs. According to the article, lasers were poised to deliver on the promise of color organs for the home hi-fi, synchronizing music and colorful light projections.[103] We have come full circle then in our tour of New Age audiovision, from color organs to laser shows and back again. The laser show capped a remarkable decade for the New Age will to shine when the horizons of New Age audiovision seemed to be ever-expanding. In a 1979 interview, Ivan Dryer stated that the ultimate extension of Laserium would be a "media temple" with a dome twice the size of the Morrison Planetarium. "In the hubs of the space colonies of the future will be huge experience spheres," he predicted. "In these spheres will be holographic images and sound. Instead of sitting in it, the audience will float through it."[104]

Dryer's optimistic predictions didn't sound so farfetched in 1979, and that year, even pop star Michael Jackson made lasers the centerpiece of his music video "Rock with You" (1979).[105] A few years later, Jackson would help to transform the landscape of visual music as the biggest star of the new cable channel MTV, which went on the air in 1981. The Buggles song "Video Killed the Radio Star" (1980) has often been used as shorthand for this seismic shift in the music industry, but laser shows were also a victim of the rise of MTV, which suddenly made Laserium shows seem like an outdated hold-over from the 1970s. As we will see in chapter 6, New Age music eventually found a niche in the world of music video, but in 1981, New Age music was still on the periphery of the mainstream music industry.

Dryer's sci-fi prediction of audiences floating through holograms in a space colony sounds impossibly futuristic, but that was exactly the kind of experience that New Age audiovision had been providing all along. Dryer didn't need to wait to go into orbit to have this kind of experience, he only had to turn on his hi-fi or tune his radio dial to *Music from the Hearts of Space*, perhaps with an illuminated blacklight poster nearby. Dryer's reference to a "media temple" shows the continued presence of a spiritual valence to the New Age will to shine, the sense that in an important way, sound and light were not just trippy amusements but could be guides to a weary traveler on a lonesome journey in a pitch-dark night, a visionary flaming sound or sounding flame.[106]

FOUR

Cosmic Sounds

THE KOHOUTEK CELEBRATION OF CONSCIOUSNESS in 1974 was an early manifestation of a New Age fair and featured several musical performances. One of those performances was by Francesco Lupica, who played an enormous instrument he had constructed called the Cosmic Beam, which consisted of piano strings stretched across a steel girder supported by tree trunks. Lupica manipulated the Cosmic Beam's massive strings with a metal rod, playing it like a giant slide guitar to produce deep, metallic waves of sound.[1] Lupica talked about making music in a way that reveals his close alignment with the visionary school. "I surrender myself to the sun and I comprehend its infinite energy," Lupica told an interviewer. "Then, when I play, I feel the sun shine and I share it with my music."[2]

Like other New Age musicians, Lupica distributed his music on his own independent label and self-released an album featuring the Cosmic Beam in 1976.[3] Lupica's album did not find a large audience, but by the end of the decade the sound of the Cosmic Beam had been heard by millions of people—not on Lupica's independent releases but as part of the score for a blockbuster Hollywood movie: *Star Trek: The Motion Picture* (1979).[4] Lupica's Cosmic Beam had drawn the attention of prominent filmmakers as soon as he began performing in the Los Angeles area. He demonstrated it for Francis Ford Coppola during the making of *Apocalypse Now* (1979) and for Steven Spielberg, who considered using it for *Close Encounters of the Third Kind* (1977).

The Cosmic Beam's trajectory from Kohoutek Celebration to Hollywood score is indicative of how by the late 1970s and early 1980s, the circulation of New Age music was extending beyond New Age fairs, wellness centers, metaphysical bookstores, and planetarium shows as part of the soundtrack to film and television productions. New Age sounds could be heard on the soundtrack of Hollywood blockbusters like *Star Trek: The Motion Picture*, popular television programs like *Cosmos* (1980), and Ron Fricke's experimental documentary *Chronos* (1985), the latter being a New Age variation on the audiovisual aesthetic he had developed for the critically acclaimed film *Koyaanisqatsi* (1982). The emergence of a New Age soundtrack on these widely seen film and television productions was an important step in the music's gradual diffusion into the popular media landscape, allowing visionary school musicians to establish new audiovisual collaborations and reach wider audiences.

New Age music came on the scene at a time of flux and transition in film and television scoring.[5] The classical orchestral score that had dominated Hollywood since the 1930s was challenged in the late 1960s and early '70s by films such as *The Graduate* (1967), *Easy Rider* (1969), and *American Graffiti* (1973), which used popular music in an effort to reach youth audiences. The traditional orchestral score faced competition from newer musical idioms in the 1970s but didn't disappear and even had a resurgence with John Williams's popular scores for blockbuster films like *Jaws* (1975) and *Star Wars* (1977).[6] By the end of the decade, the stage was set for musical scores that could strike a balance between the orchestral tradition and newer, more popular and electronic sounds.

Two kinds of music emerged as the primary alternatives to the classical score during the 1970s and '80s. First, the minimalism of composers like Philip Glass offered a compromise to film composers who, according to musicologist Mervyn Cooke, were struggling to negotiate the demands of the traditional orchestral score and modern musical genres.[7] Second, the rise of synthesizer-based scores by Vangelis, Giorgio Moroder, and Tangerine Dream had the contemporary appeal of pop music but were better equipped to provide "sustained atmospheric underscoring."[8] The film industry's embrace of synth-based scores was signaled by

Giorgio Moroder's Academy Award for Best Score for *Midnight Express* (1978) and Vangelis's Oscar for *Chariots of Fire* (1981).[9] Tangerine Dream composed scores for a string of Hollywood productions at this time, including *Sorcerer* (1977), *Thief* (1981), and *Risky Business* (1983).

The visionary school of New Age music had a foot in each of these new idioms of film scoring; they were deeply inspired by minimalism and were fellow travelers with synth-based composers like Moroder, Vangelis, and Tangerine Dream. They were well-positioned, therefore, to offer their own numinous alternative to the Hollywood score, and in this chapter, we will see how the New Age soundtrack extends and enriches the history of minimalism in film, through New Age musician Michael Stearns's work with cinematographer-director Ron Fricke, and enhances the history of the electronic score, through the "space music" featured on Carl Sagan's television series *Cosmos* (1980).

New Age music had something to offer film and television production in the form of a timely new musical style that was more emotionally expansive than minimalism and more contemporary than an orchestral score. Conversely, film and TV production had something to offer New Age music—a new venue for the distribution and promotion of this outsider genre. Other subcultural musics of the 1970s also broke into the mainstream via soundtracks. Disco crossed over in spectacular form with *Saturday Night Fever* (1977), and punk—in the diluted form of new wave—crossed over with MTV-era films like *Purple Rain* (1984) and *Footloose* (1984). The soundtrack to *Cosmos*, released in 1981, lies at the midpoint between these two pop crossover moments, four years after *Saturday Night Fever* and three years before *Purple Rain*. Though its mainstream success was more modest, the *Cosmos* soundtrack opened the ears of many new listeners and pushed New Age music closer to the mainstream.

The films that became the vehicles for disco's and punk's crossover were updates on the Hollywood musical, but that form wouldn't work as well for New Age music's distinctive emotional and spiritual qualities. Instead, the New Age soundtrack worked best on projects that had a certain "cosmic" inclination. Note that the instrument played by Francesco

Lupica at the Kohoutek Celebration was not just any Beam; it was a *Cosmic* Beam. *Cosmic* is a word that comes up frequently with regards to New Age music and was even proposed as the name of the genre. Kat Epple of Emerald Web said that "cosmic music" was her preferred label.[10] The German word *kosmiche* has been used to describe the New Age-adjacent German progressive rock of Tangerine Dream, Klaus Schulze, Ashra, and Popol Vuh. What was "cosmic" about New Age music?

The Oxford English Dictionary defines "cosmos" as the universe understood as an ordered and harmonious system. The term suggests a complete totality. an ordered sum total that is the opposite of chaos. Similarly, the adjective "cosmic" means belonging to an ordered universal system or totality. In its all-inclusive scope, cosmic is related to holistic, but where holistic tends to concern the human-centric scale of mind-body health, cosmic points to the vast scale of the entire universe: the massive distances between stars, the eons of time in the evolution of a galaxy. the billions of chemical bases in a human DNA molecule, or the staggering velocity of subatomic particles.

If the universe is an orderly and harmonious system, how do we reconcile our everyday human scale with the very, very large and the very, very small? In the Western esoteric and alchemical tradition, this problem was addressed by dividing the cosmos into microcosm and macrocosm and asserting a fundamental interrelationship between them. This interrelationship is expressed in the famous Hermetic dictum "as above, so below."[11] Seekers in the New Age movement of the 1970s shared the alchemical faith in an orderly correspondence between macrocosm and microcosm as can be seen in their interest in practices like astrology (linking the stars and everyday life decisions) and palmistry (linking the hand and the lifetime of the individual).[12] Music has long been understood as a link between microcosm and macrocosm, as famously illustrated in the sixteenth-century alchemist Robert Fludd's image of a "divine monochord," which shows the hand of God adjusting the tuning peg on a musical instrument whose notes correspond to the elements, the planets, and the angelic orders. The visionary school of New Age music took up this occult musical orientation. Steven Halpern's second album,

Zodiac Suite (1977), links musical tones and astrological signs, and his first book, *Tuning the Human Instrument* (1979), contains a reproduction of Fludd's divine monochord.

New Age music's cosmic disposition harmonized with director-cinematographer Ron Fricke's cosmic cinema and Carl Sagan's cosmic television. Cosmic music found a niche in these film and television productions and in the process expanded the range of the film and television score. We begin by tracing the history that leads to Fricke's cosmic cinema, which will bring the New Age soundtrack into the narrative of minimalism's contribution to film music. The pivotal work in that narrative is Philip Glass's groundbreaking score for *Koyaanisqatsi.*

COSMIC CINEMA

The experimental documentary *Koyaanisqatsi*, with its pulsating minimalist score, is a landmark in the history of film music and was the result of a collaboration among three primary creatives. In the early 1970s, Ron Fricke began working with Godfrey Reggio on a media campaign funded by the ACLU that was meant to warn about the dangers of technology. That work eventually culminated in *Koyaanisqatsi*, directed by Reggio, with eye-popping cinematography by Fricke and a riveting musical score by Glass.

The visual hook of *Koyaanisqatsi* is provided by Fricke's innovative approach to time-lapse cinematography.[13] Early in the film, we see images of clouds moving over a mountainous landscape, sped up so that they resemble streams of water. Natural movements like these are abruptly interrupted by hyperkinetic shots of urban traffic, establishing the film's blunt rhetorical message that modern life is dangerously out of sync with natural rhythms and systems. This point is also made through the visual trope of moving clouds reflected on the sides of massive skyscrapers, suggesting a natural world that can only be experienced though a distorted reflection. Human experience is mostly viewed from a distance, though there are several moments when the film pauses on a cinematic portrait, lingering, for example, on a group of female workers at a Las Vegas casino.

In the context of the film, the long duration and forced stillness of these portraits produces a slightly unnerving, distancing effect. For film scholar Kathryn Kalinak, Glass's minimalist score aids in creating that effect since it avoids emotional triggers, leaving audiences adrift, forced to arrive at their own affective response.[14] *Koyaanisqatsi*'s social critique is also legible in the sequences that bookend the film: slow-motion images of the lift off and explosion of the Atlas-Centaur rocket in 1962, which underline a sense of the tragic futility of technological society. As film scholar Scott MacDonald writes, *Koyaanisqatsi*'s central message is that "the primary product of modern industrialized life is the destruction of individuality and serenity."[15]

Koyaanisqatsi became a critical and cult success, but Fricke parted ways with Reggio after the film and went on to produce his own a series of films—*Chronos*, *Baraka*, and *Samsara*—using the cinematographic approach he had developed with Reggio.[16] Fricke's inclinations were more spiritual and cosmic than Reggio's. Fricke had been inspired by Stanley Kubrick's *2001: A Space Odessey* (1968) and experimental filmmakers like Jordan Belson, who spurred his desire to make widescreen, nonverbal art films.[17] Fricke was marinating in the same cosmic sauce as the visionary school of New Age music, and so it is not surprising that when he went looking for a musical collaborator, he didn't opt for a minimalist like Glass but the visionary school composer Michael Stearns.

Michael Stearns was born in San Francisco in 1948 and grew up in Tucson, Arizona. He went to college in California where he played guitar in a psychedelic rock band. Stearns dropped out of college in 1968 and made an experimental recording that explored a new, free-form style of music. "People that took drugs and got stoned really wanted to hear this recording," he said. "That was the only context I had for it. It was a really strange piece of music that seemed to speak to the drug generation."[18]

Stearns had to put his musical evolution on hold when he received a military draft notice in 1968. He served in the Air Force for four years as a linguist, studying Haitian Creole and Haitian religious practices.

When he got out of the Air Force, he moved back to Tucson, where he studied Sufism and played guitar in a band that toured clubs in the Southwest. He also began a relationship with Susan Harper, who had just arrived in Tucson after graduating from college in Florida. Harper told Stearns about an upcoming sound-and-movement workshop that was led by a woman who had lived in Haiti. Because of his experience in the Air Force, Stearns was intrigued, and he went with Harper to the workshop.[19]

The leader of the workshop was Emilie Conrad, who had studied dance with Robert Joffrey, Katherine Dunham, and Pearl Primus. Conrad moved to Haiti during the 1950s, where she ran her own dance company. When she returned to the United States in the 1960s, Conrad descended into a spiritual crisis that culminated in the development of a system of movement meditation she called Continuum.[20] Conrad's sessions were accompanied by live music, which opened the door to an important collaboration with the musician Gary David. David's interest in music was shaped by his Arabic heritage, and he recalled how his grandfather, who was an amateur singer, took part in all-night jam sessions with instruments like the oud and the doumbek. David was intrigued by the subtly expressive musical intervals in his grandfather's singing, which he couldn't reproduce on the piano. This sparked his interest in electronic instruments, which allowed a performer to explore such microtonal nuances.[21] David crossed paths with Emilie Conrad several times during the 1960s, and in 1973 she asked him to play music for her Continuum classes. David began accompanying Conrad's classes with a Moog synthesizer, tape loops, and his voice. Conrad and David started living together in 1974 and were married in 1975.[22]

It was the team of Conrad and David that led the Tucson workshop in January 1975. For Michael Stearns and Susan Harper, the workshop was a revelation. For one thing, David's music was the closest thing Stearns had heard to the free-form music he'd been wanting to make.[23] Sensing a kindred spirit, David encouraged Stearns to join the Continuum community in Los Angeles. Stearns and Harper moved there two weeks later.[24] Stearns became a resident composer and musician for Continuum

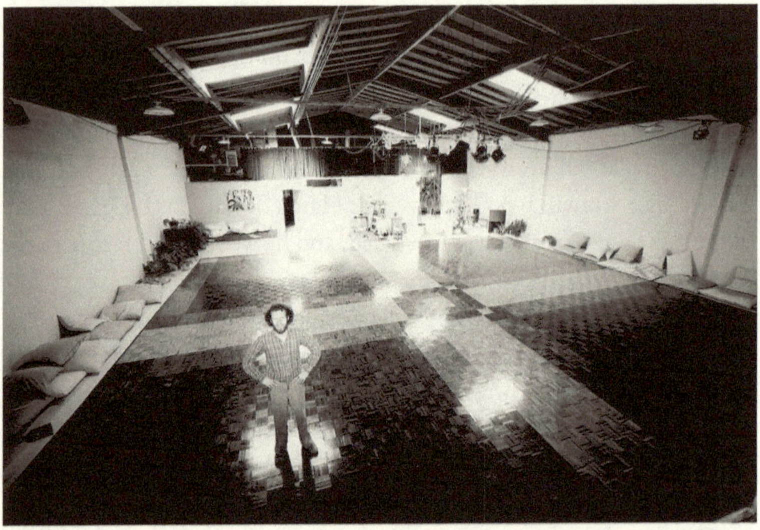

Michael Stearns at the Continuum studio, circa 1974–75. Photo courtesy of Gary David.

classes, which took place in a Los Angeles studio that had a beautiful parquet floor created by the artist George Landry, a quadrophonic speaker system, and an area for musicians with synths and unusual instruments, including a version of Francesco Lupica's Cosmic Beam.[25] Stearns and David played live for Conrad's classes and Harper became a teacher of Conrad's unique movement and meditation paradigm.

Though Conrad's background was in dance, her Continuum system was not meant to be a form of choreography or exercise. Rather, Continuum was a technique for meditation and mindfulness. Conrad wanted her students to direct their attention toward tiny, internal "particles" of movement.[26] These "micro-movements" would then become the seeds for larger, intuitive movements that she hoped would transcend the cultural habits we carry in our bodies. By developing a biological or cellular awareness of these movements, one could experience the body as an ongoing process rather than a static thing. A key concept in Conrad's approach was "fluid resonance." Starting from the premise that the body is composed primarily of water and develops encased in amniotic fluid, Conrad asserted that humans are "watery beings on land."[27] Susan Harper explained that the embodied experience of microcosm and macrocosm was at the heart of Continuum and that the name "Continuum" refers to a continuum from tiny pulsations in the body to the unfolding of the cosmos.[28] Georgianne Cowan, an artist and dancer who was active at Continuum in the 1980s, agreed that Conrad's method integrated microcosm and macrocosm. "The fluid nature of the body's systems related to the oceans and the nature of water," she said, "but also to a spiral galaxy or the way wind sweeps across a field of reeds."[29]

In a typical Continuum class, Conrad would share some of these ideas and then demonstrate a movement meditation with live musical accompaniment. The students, sometimes as many as thirty, would then join her on the floor and do their own free movements. Gary David was struck by the fluid movements of the participants, flowing across the parquet floor with their eyes closed. "It was like watching cells moving," he said.[30] David had a front-row seat on these sessions because his music was such an integral part of the experience. "We were part of the movement," David said.[31] Harper recalled that the music at Continuum, which did not have a strong rhythmic pulse or lyrics, was ideal for supporting deep, internal, and often very small movements.[32] The music provided a way to "journey and not necessarily have to take a psychedelic," she said.[33]

Music at Continuum was made with the instruments commonly found in the New Age laboratorium, both traditional and modern. The traditional sounds of the flute were provided by a musician who joined the Continuum scene around 1978. Larkin Stentz was one of the most prominent New Age flutists of the late 1970s and early 1980s. He took up the flute while he was a student at the University of California, Santa Barbara, in the 1970s and, after a life-changing visionary experience that involved being "catapulted into the loving presence of white light," he began performing at coffee shops and college campuses. In response to requests for recordings of his soothing and relaxing music, he formed his own record label, Wind Sung Sounds, and made the album *To the Essence of a Candle* (1978).[34]

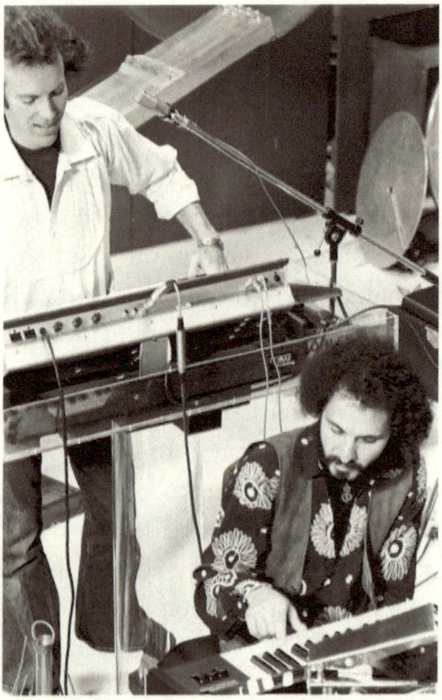

Michael Stearns and Gary David performing at Continuum, circa 1974–75. Photo courtesy of Gary David.

Larkin sold his album at bookstores and New Age fairs, and it was at a fair in Los Angeles that he met Michael Stearns and Susan Harper. They invited him to Continuum, and he began attending classes. Side two of his album *O'cean* (1980) was recorded in the Continuum studio during a session when Larkin responded on his flute to Susan Harper's movements. The back cover of the album is a black-and-white photograph that shows Harper, her head thrown back and eyes closed, next to Larkin playing his flute. Side one of *O'cean* features a low, gentle synth drone provided by Michael Stearns.

It was, in fact, the synthesizer that best characterizes the sound of Continuum music.[35] Stearns and David were using a Moog synthesizer in 1975–76, and they were joined in 1977 by the New Age musician Kevin Braheny Fortune who, as you might recall from chapter 1, developed the Mighty Serge synth. Braheny Fortune's Continuum sessions combined the Mighty Serge with tape loops and melodies played on flute or saxophone. "I had a laboratory at Continuum," he recalled. "It was a very improvisational process. I'm responding to the people in the room, and they're responding to me."[36]

The Continuum musical laboratory resulted in a distinctive subgenre of New Age music, which was given the name "cellular wave music" by Stephen Hill of "Music from the Hearts of Space."[37] Hill attended classes at Continuum, and in his *Hearts of Space* music guide he wrote that cellular wave music was "subtle movement meditation music used for deep journeys into the body."[38] Listening closely to tracks created by Stearns and Braheny Fortune reveals how their cellular wave music took part in the Continuum mission to align microcosm and macrocosm.

Stearns's "Ancient Leaves," recorded in 1976–77, features Emilie Conrad chanting over a deep drone produced on the Moog. Early in the twenty-five-minute track, we hear dissonant, overlapping voices that would not feel out of place on a horror movie soundtrack. These dark sonic clouds pass, and the track moves to shimmering harp patterns that create a mood of clarity and transcendence. "Ancient Leaves" is a good example of the complex emotional palette that can be heard on Continuum recordings, defying the common assumption that New Age music exists in a monochromatic state of blissed-out happiness. Such emotional complexity can also be heard on another early track, "Dark Journey in the Night," which was recorded at a Continuum session in 1979 and features the Mighty Serge. Long, sustained tissues of sound open the track, suggesting not stillness but a sense of urgent anticipation, as though something momentous is about to happen. The track doesn't have a steady beat, but develops a pulsating, organically evolving momentum. This driving and insistent quality is fitting accompaniment to Conrad's philosophy of perpetual movement and change, but it also reads as spiritual longing. Transcendence and inner peace are not a given here but must be achieved.

The sonic environment is fluid, watery, as though we are swimming in a vast ocean, feeling the pull of different currents as we move through sparkling streaks of light and effervescent pillars of air bubbles. Delicate synth arpeggios swirl like tiny cellular cilia while deep sub-bass notes sculpt a distant horizon. This approach to layering synthesizer tracks, with sustained drones suggesting broad vistas and rapid-fire, crystalline sequencer patterns simulating microscopic cellular processes, is a defining aesthetic of cellular wave music, manifesting a sonic representation of microcosmic/macrocosmic alignment.

Stearns's work at Continuum culminated in the album *Planetary Unfolding* (1981), which Stearns described as a cocreation with the people moving and meditating at Continuum. "They would tune in to me and take it to a different place. I would tune in with them and take it to still another place. We went back and forth that way."[39] Gary David wrote liner notes for the album that describe a dream in which the Earth was "a mass of sounds held together through resonance. Everything: atoms, cells, the Earth's core, oceans, plants, animals and humans created a complex orchestration that kept unfolding on itself. The Earth was a being of sound." David's vision of a cosmic "vibrating orchestration" is an expression of the vibrational ontology described in chapter 2 and is also an update on Fludd's divine monochord, with sound linking atoms, cells, oceans and the entire planet. The dream moves to a cosmic scale when David feels himself shot out into space to become an "Earth sensor" sent to explore the "cosmic scheme of things."[40]

Planetary Unfolding embodies the cosmic scope of Continuum, and the music is a tour de force of the expressive possibilities of the modular synthesizer. The album begins with sustained liquid tones, shimmering sequencer patterns, and a driving three-chord pattern that provides a feeling of urgent movement forward and upward, toward a distant horizon. As David's liner notes suggest, the album oscillates between cosmic space travel and a return to Earth. On the second track, "Toto, I've a Feeling We're Not in Kansas Anymore," we hear the sounds of a sci-fi spaceship launch, but a few tracks later, on "As the Earth Kissed the Moon," gorgeous synth patterns and majestic bass lines bathe earthy recordings of a mockingbird singing on a spring night in the hyper-real glow of Stanislav Grof's immanent divine.

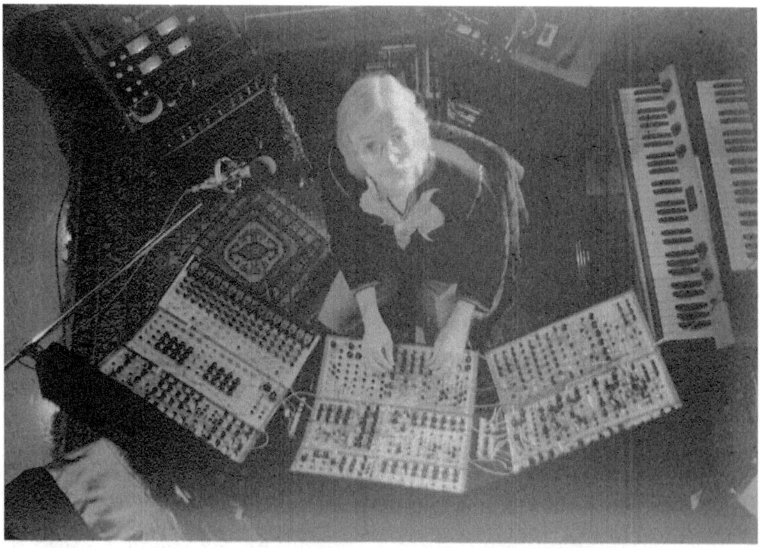

Kevin Braheny Fortune performing at Continuum, circa 1979. Photo courtesy of Kevin Braheny Fortune.

If the scene at Continuum had only produced *Planetary Unfolding* and Larkin's *O'cean*, it would have earned an important place in the history of New Age music, but Kevin Braheny Fortune also created a number of classic recordings during his time there. "After I Said Goodnight," released on cassette in 1980, captured a session at Continuum. The track begins with a host of synth-generated jungle creatures: crickets, a frog, a "space monkey," and other mysterious creatures. Ghostly sustained chords and distant rumblings create a misty ambience and an alert sense of anxious anticipation. The track gains momentum as Braheny Fortune plays a frantic saxophone solo with Terry Riley-esque tape delay. Braheny Fortune was ill with a high fever that day, and he recalled that as he finished the solo, his fever broke, and "everything cooled down, so I cooled all the music down."[41] The track cools down, but it also lifts up, as if rising out of the mist to encounter a wide, clear, starry horizon. Sparkling synth patterns in a high register are joined by a soulful mid-range chord progression. The sounds of the jungle have disappeared, creating a sense of focus, introspection, and transcendence. Deep bass notes expand the frequency range to encompass the very low and the very high, evoking a similar expansion of the listener's inner space. One has a feeling of being simultaneously grounded and floating in celestial bliss.

As with Stearns's work, Braheny Fortune's Continuum-era tracks move through a wide range of emotions, not all positive, and communicate the effort required to reach a transcendent state. "After I Said Goodnight" is a virtuosic example of synth-based composition in the Continuum style, interweaving drones and sequencer patterns that suggest cosmic landscapes and buzzing bodily and mental processes. Recordings by Braheny Fortune and Stearns show the fertility of the creative environment at Continuum, which was holistic in its mindful movement and cosmic in its dual focus on the cellular and the planetary. The subgenre of cellular wave music produced some of the most emotionally complex works in the visionary school, mobilizing the tools of the New Age laboratorium to develop a musical vocabulary for micro/macrocosmic connections.[42]

As with their fellow New Age musicians, the makers of cellular wave music faced the challenge of distributing their decidedly noncommercial recordings. "There were no record labels for this kind of music," Susan Harper recalled, "so Michael and I started one." Their label was Continuum Montage, founded in 1977. Their primary means of distribution were the New Age gatherings described in chapter 2.[43] Around this time, Stearns began working in an LA recording studio and moved into the world of film scoring through a two-year collaboration with the legendary film composer Maurice Jarre, best known for his Academy Award-winning scores for *Laurence of Arabia* (1962) and *Doctor Zhivago* (1965). Jarre became a mentor to Stearns.[44] In return, Stearns helped Jarre incorporate synthesizers into his scores for films like *Firefox* (1982), *Dreamscape* (1984), and *Witness* (1985).

Stearns was ready, then, when he was approached by Ron Fricke to compose the music for the film he was making after *Koyaanisqatsi*: *Chronos* (1985). *Chronos* has a New Age soundtrack created by Stearns, and it also has a New Age sensibility, as can be seen through a comparison of *Chronos* and *Koyaanisqatsi*. First, Fricke's film *Chronos* glows with a sense of New Age optimism not found in *Koyaanisqatsi*. "I don't agree with Godfrey's frame of reference," Fricke said in a 1986 interview. "I don't think there's anything out of control or out of balance. I think it's all in balance and that's what I wanted to show. . . . Life knows what it's doing."[45] Compare how the two films show commuters streaming up and down escalators. In *Koyaanisqatsi*, those images are juxtaposed with images of hot dogs whizzing through an industrial production line. In *Chronos*, Fricke shows a rapid escalator sequence with Stearns's dizzying musical acceleration on the soundtrack, but this sequence is later shown in slow-motion in a variation on the portrait sequences in *Koyaanisqatsi*. In the words of one reviewer, this second escalator segment is "slow, stately, almost heroic" and "shimmers with sympathy, not merely reverence, for life."[46] The individual shoppers we see on the escalator are not stiff and posed as in the *Koyaanisqatsi* portraits, nor are they backed by Glass's chilly minimalism, and so lack that film's ironic distancing.

Fricke's sense that "life knows what it's doing" was informed by his spiritual beliefs, which are more pronounced in *Chronos* than in *Koyaanisqatsi*. Scott MacDonald refers to Fricke's "Buddhist sensibility" and his fascination with "spiritual sites and activities, including natural spaces."[47] *Chronos* features many stunning shots of Egyptian temples, Gothic cathedrals, Greek monuments, and Stonehenge. Fricke saw movie-going in spiritual terms. "I've always thought of the movie theater as a sort of temple," he said, "where you can address the audience's inner being. I've been drawn to explore the sacred, the transcendent: the interconnection of life, the underlying connections beneath words."[48] In a statement that shows how Fricke's spiritual orientation is aligned with the cosmic sensibility of the New Age oratorium, he said that he thought of his films not as documentaries but as "nonverbal guided meditations."[49]

Like the visionary school of New Age musicians, Fricke's art combined the inner work of the oratorium with cutting edge technical tools, in particular, his innovative approach to time-lapse cinematography.[50] Fricke's time-lapse images create a complex tangle of multiple temporalities existing in the same shot. Fricke told an interviewer in 1985 that time-lapse photography "heightens our experience of ordinary things in an extraordinary way, helping us perceive life and ourselves in new ways."[51] Watching a time-lapse sequence where shadows play across a landscape, for example, the viewer must align a microcosmic, everyday perception of movement with a hyper-real, macrocosmic "God's-eye view" of the passing day. In some cases, Fricke's time-lapse can seem to diminish the human scale in the sublime immensity of the cosmos, hinting that all human creations will fade away in deep time. And yet a recurring trope in *Chronos* pairs macrocosmic movements of light with the resilience and stability of ancient stone constructions. In one shot, majestic celestial movements are seen in relation to Stonehenge and paired with the deep tones of Constance Demby's space bass, and in another, the sky is seen in relation to Greek temples and paired with Stearns playing the Cosmic Beam.

The fact that these human constructions tend to be ruins adds another twist in the temporal knot, prompting questions about the permanence or impermanence of human civilizations. Notably, one of the ruins we see in *Chronos* is the launch pedestal at Cape Canaveral where three astronauts died in 1967 as part of the Apollo moon missions. Compared to the use of the Atlas-Centaur rocket footage in *Koyaanisqatsi*, *Chronos* achieves a more nuanced and ambiguous critique of technology. Is the launch pedestal at Cape Canaveral, framed against the time-lapse movement of clouds, a ruin that reveals the arrogant folly of human striving, or a memorial celebrating the heroic will to journey to the stars? What is certain is that, in Fricke's hands, time-lapse is a tool of cosmic cinema, calibrating micro- and macrocosmic perspectives.

Throughout all these sequences, *Chronos* features a stunning musical score by Michael Stearns, which saturates the film with the cosmic emotional palette of Continuum's cellular wave music. Fricke stated that he wanted to work with music that fit his spiritual frame of reference, and he found it in Stearns's atmospheric style. Stearns composed the entire soundtrack as a single forty-minute piece of music, and the film was edited to his music.[52] In this regard, *Chronos* is akin to the New Age audiovision described in the previous chapter: it is a New Age musical composition given visual accompaniment. Moreover, the film was partially funded by the Reuben Fleet Space Center in San Diego, where it screened on their IMAX dome theater.[53] In other words, *Chronos* is not that far from a Vortex Concert or a trippy event at the Strasenburgh Planetarium, which is exactly how some early reviewers understood it. A review in the *Baltimore Sun* declared that it was "the closest thing to a head movie the august Maryland Science Center is likely to offer."[54]

The odd hybrid of psychedelic head movie and science museum documentary is another manifestation of the New Age blend of art and science, and *Chronos* marks the birth of one model of the New Age soundtrack.[55] Expanding the story of minimalism's place in the history of film scoring to include *Chronos* and subsequent Fricke/Stearns collaborations brings a different sensibility—a New Age sensibility—into the film music narrative. A second model of the New Age soundtrack takes us from cosmic cinema to cosmic television and adds a new case study to the history of synthesizers in film scoring. Just as Philip Glass looms large in histories of the minimalist score, so the Greek electronic musician Vangelis plays a central role in accounts of the arrival of synths on the soundtrack. Before Vangelis created celebrated scores for *Chariots of Fire* (1981) and *Blade Runner* (1982), his music was the center of gravity for a television soundtrack that greatly expanded the audience for New Age "space music."

COSMIC TELEVISION

On the evening of September 27, 1980, a special event took place at the Griffith Observatory in Los Angeles. Attendees could enjoy cocktails, a dinner of "chicken cosmos," stargazing through the observatory's telescope, and the world premiere of the planetarium show *Cosmos: The Voyage to the Stars*. This was a celebration to launch *Cosmos*, a thirteen-part science television program that was produced by PBS station KCET-Los Angeles and scientist Carl Sagan's production company.

The planetarium show was written by Sagan's cowriter and future wife, Ann Druyan, and featured a musical track that had become the theme to *Cosmos*, an excerpt from "Heaven and Hell, Pt. 1," by Evangelos Papathanassiou, popularly known as Vangelis.[56] A year after the event at Griffith Observatory, *Cosmos* was being promoted again, this time by the sale of a soundtrack LP. The *Cosmos* soundtrack featured synth-driven space music by Vangelis, Isao Tomita, Synergy, Brian Eno, Jean-Michel Jarre (son of film composer Maurice Jarre), and others. For Kat Epple of Emerald Web, the show's soundtrack was immediately legible as "our kind of music."[57] *Cosmos* helped to popularize New Age music, and the show itself vibrates at the same cosmic frequency as the visionary school. The show's innovative soundtrack was paired with Emmy Award–winning visual effects made by a team of artists who worked in a style of space art that overlapped with visionary art and had an unmistakably New Age sensibility. *Cosmos* was one of the most consequential pairings of New Age music and visuals and was perhaps the era's most popular manifestation of the genre's ambition to blend visionary art and cosmic science.

The story of *Cosmos* begins, of course, with Carl Sagan, who was born in Brooklyn in 1934. After earning a master's degree in physics and a PhD in astronomy and astrophysics from the University of Chicago, he taught genetics and exobiology at Stanford and later astronomy at Harvard and Cornell University. Sagan worked closely with NASA on the Apollo moon missions and the Pioneer and Voyager space probes. One of his primary research interests was the possibility of extraterrestrial life, and he oversaw the design of plaques for the Pioneer and Voyager spacecrafts that were meant to communicate with any alien species they might encounter. Sagan was passionate about presenting science to a broad audience, and he wrote several popular books, including *The Cosmic Connection* (1973) and the Pulitzer Prize–winning *The Dragons of Eden* (1977). Sagan's public visibility was greatly increased in the early 1970s with his appearances on Johnny Carson's *Tonight Show*. Sagan first appeared on the show in November 1973 and returned in January 1974 to talk about Comet Kohoutek.[58]

Sagan defies easy categorization. He worked across the scientific disciplines of astronomy and biology, was simultaneously a scientist, a best-selling author, and a media celebrity, and he struck a balance between the 1960s counterculture and the scientific and academic establishment.[59] A close collaborator stated that Sagan was "very much a child of the sixties, much more so than a typical physics professor at the time."[60] It is now well known that Sagan was the author of an anonymous essay on the benefits of marijuana in which he made a statement that Ken Jenkins would appreciate: "Looking at fires when high," Sagan wrote, "especially through one of those prism kaleidoscopes . . . is an extraordinarily moving and beautiful experience."[61] Sagan also corresponded with countercultural icon Timothy Leary about the feasibility of building a ship to travel to nearby stars.[62]

Sagan was already open to poetic and countercultural approaches to communicating scientific ideas when he received a fan letter in 1971 from the artist Jon Lomberg.[63] Along with the letter, Lomberg sent artworks he had created that were inspired by ideas in Sagan's coauthored book *Intelligent Life in the Universe* (1966). Lomberg wrote that he was interested in depicting "the joint realizations of minuteness and vastness," from the humbling scope of our galaxy to the beauty and proportion of a seashell.[64] One of the images Lomberg sent to Sagan was a design for a starship organized into five flower-like petals, linking interstellar technology with organic forms and the chakra system of energy centers in the body.[65]

Sagan responded to Lomberg's letter to say that he liked the art and that he felt there was "far too little effort to express artistically and musically what is clearly the expanding cosmic consciousness of mankind."[66] The two continued to correspond, and Sagan asked Lomberg to illustrate his book *The Cosmic Connection* (1973).[67] "We liked working with each other," Lomberg said, "and I guess we both felt that we could do something together that neither of us could do on our own."[68] Lomberg was as much a child of the sixties as Sagan, and had experimented with psychedelic drugs and been inspired by the renaissance in music and graphic arts during the 1960s.[69] He also had a long-standing interest in astronomy and felt an affinity with the genre of "space art," which depicts as-yet-unseen aspects of outer space. Space art was popularized by Chesley Bonestell's illustrations in *Life* magazine during the 1940s, but Lomberg distinguished his approach from the dominant tradition, which was based in realistic landscape painting. "The art I was interested in was much more ecstatic and graphic," he said, "less concerned with realism and more concerned with expressing ideas."[70]

One of the primary ideas that Lomberg expressed in his art was the connection between microcosm and macrocosm.[71] Lomberg's painting *The Great Chain of Being* (1975) moves from atoms and diatoms at the bottom of the image, up through plants and insects, past a person playing the guitar, to a sunrise seen from Earth, and a galaxy seen from outer space. "You're seeing the whole gamut of creation in one image, atoms and galaxies as part of the same continuum," Lomberg explained. "Humans sit between the micro and the macro, unifying it with music, art, and science."[72] Sagan shared Lomberg's inclination to see the universe as one piece, and included this image in the book version of *Cosmos*. Sagan liked to point out that the elements in our bodies were forged inside the heart of stars. "Not many scientists would make that leap," Lomberg stated. "Not many scientists who were interested in what was forged in the heart of stars were also interested in what atoms are in the human body."[73]

Given their shared cosmic perspective and established working relationship, it is not surprising that Sagan asked Lomberg to be head of the art department for his new television series. Sagan had started a film and television production company in 1976 and was contacted that year by a producer at PBS station KCET in Los Angeles about hosting a show to be called *The Heavens*. Production on the series, now called *Cosmos*, began in 1978, with Lomberg leading a team of artists to create astronomical images and visual effects.[74] The visual sequences created by this team, when paired with the soundtrack, reveal *Cosmos* to have a New Age sensibility not that far removed from works by artists like Ken Jenkins, Jordan Belson, and Ron Fricke.

If you've ever seen *Cosmos*, you can likely bring to mind the striking opening credit sequence. As we hear the soaring theme from Vangelis's

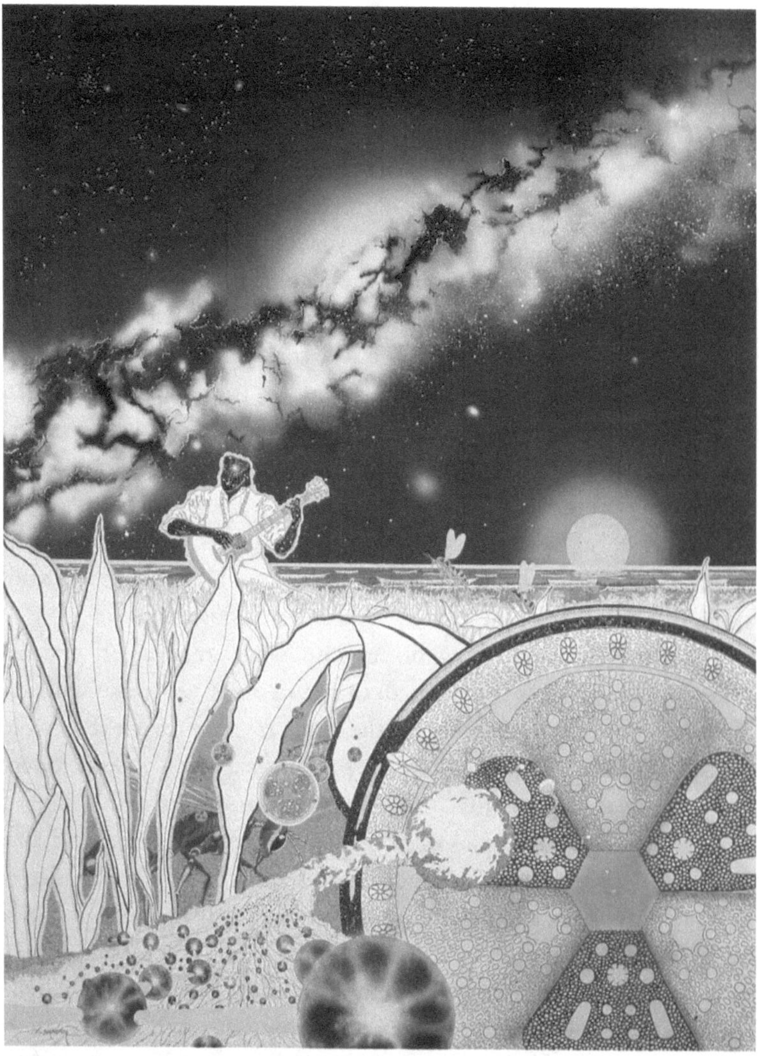

Jon Lomberg's painting *The Great Chain of Being*. Image courtesy of Jon Lomberg.

"Heaven and Hell," orange galaxies and stars move toward us as a powder-blue title appears: "Cosmos." Vangelis's music begins with a gentle piano that is joined by high, gleaming synth notes. The chord progression on the piano resolves, seeming to pause on a precipice overlooking a sublime landscape. Then a repeating pattern of stately piano chords evoke inexorable, powerful processes, as organ arpeggios swirl in the high register like whirling galaxies, and a choir of voices add the emotional yearning of a church service. As we hear these uplifting sounds, the stars on the screen move outward toward the viewer, giving an effect of moving through outer space. The intensity of the contrast between orange and blue has a distinctly psychedelic flavor; in fact, the show was criticized by some scientists for using such a bright color palette. "We definitely pumped up the color," Lomberg admitted, explaining that one of the reasons for that stylistic decision was that the team of artists on *Cosmos* had been deeply influenced by the psychedelic posters, album covers, and blacklight posters of the era. "That was a look we liked," Lomberg said, and it was also a look that had taken on cosmic associations.[75]

The first episode of *Cosmos* begins with Sagan standing on a beach, where he says that "the cosmos is all that is, or ever was, or ever will be." The beach becomes a metaphor for the Earth as the shore of the "cosmic ocean." The vehicle for this micro/macro transformation is the introduction of a visual trope that recurs throughout the series: Sagan's "ship of the imagination." Sagan picks a dandelion and removes one of its fuzzy seeds. We see him release the dandelion seed into the wind, and the next shot presents a dandelion-seed-shaped spacecraft drifting through interstellar space. As Vangelis's "Heaven and Hell" plays on the soundtrack, we move inside this ship, where Sagan sits at a control desk while watching the stars through a large view screen. The ship of the imagination features prominently throughout the rest of the series as a method to present astronomical phenomena.

Sagan's ship of the imagination is reminiscent of Thomas Wilfred's "imaginary space liner" described in the previous chapter, but Wilfred was not the source of the design.[76] Instead, Sagan was inspired by a painting by Jon Lomberg. "Carl did not want a realistic spaceship," Lomberg remembered. "He wanted something more abstract." When he saw Lomberg's painting *Starseeds*, which shows a sparkling cluster of dandelion-like objects against a starry backdrop, he found the concept he was after.[77] In the first episode of the series, the ship of the imagination takes viewers on a stunning "cosmic zoom" from the edge of the known universe to the Earth, with a good portion of the journey accompanied by Vangelis's celestial track "Creation du Monde."

Another visual trope established in the first episode of *Cosmos* is the "cosmic calendar." First developed in Sagan's book *The Dragons of Eden* (1977), this was a technique for compressing the fifteen-billion-year lifetime of the universe into a single year, with approximately every billion years of history corresponding to one month.[78] "The cosmic calendar was a way of putting that story in a scale that ordinary people could grasp," Lomberg said. "It takes the macro time of the history of the universe and puts it into the micro time of a single year."[79] The cosmic calendar is an interactive visual prop for Sagan, who enters it with the help of video effects. The cosmic zoom and the cosmic calendar sequences of *Cosmos* are techniques that align micro- and macrocosmic realities and can be placed alongside the drones and sequencers of cellular wave music and Ron Fricke's time-lapse experiments in *Chronos*.

Sagan's cosmic calendar was first described in *The Dragons of Eden*, a book whose cover image was created by Don Davis. An integral part of the *Cosmos* creative team, Davis worked on paintings and models of planetary surfaces for the show. Davis developed an interest in space art as a boy, and in 1971, he got a job at the US Geological Survey branch of astro-geologic studies, where he made maps of the moon and Mars. It was there that he learned how to use what Lomberg called the "defining tool" of space art: the airbrush.[80] The airbrush, like space art more generally, is a link between scientific illustration (astro-geologic surveys) and the "deviant" science of New Age visionary art. Held like a pen, an airbrush uses controlled streams of air to project ink. Airbrush art was first widely seen as part of commercial advertisements of the 1930s and the photorealistic pin-up girls of the 1940s but proliferated in the 1960s and '70s when it became associated with countercultural posters and album art, as well as a host of popular forms like motorcycle helmets, T-shirts, and van murals. Its capacity for fine detail and hyperreal images, when combined with a surrealist aesthetic, could produce dreamy visionary works by artists like H. R. Giger and Gilbert Williams.

The airbrush was also useful for space art's realistic depictions of planetary surfaces and astronomical phenomena. Don Davis noted the airbrush's ability to create cloudy textures and layers of light.[81] In the 1970s and '80s, airbrush art could be found on science fiction book covers and as illustrations in science magazines like *Omni* and *Discover*. In addition to Davis, another airbrush artist on the *Cosmos* creative team was Adolph Schaller.[82] Schaller's masterpiece in the series can be seen in episode 2, when Sagan describes the life forms that might inhabit a giant gas planet like Jupiter. We see huge panels created with an airbrush by Schaller of the "hunters, floaters, and sinkers" that might exist on such a planet, as Vangelis's track "Alpha" plays on the soundtrack. "Alpha," which can be heard in multiple episodes in the series, develops from a simple synth pattern to an epic rock anthem: a musical manifestation of micro- and macrocosm.

Looking at Schaller's sci-fi airbrush art while listening to Vangelis's synth-driven track is an audiovisual blend akin to gazing at visionary cover art, like Roger Dean's covers for albums by the band Yes, while listening to New Age or progressive rock music.[83] In fact, Don Davis created the cover art for Francesco Lupica's album *Cosmic Beam Experience*, which depicts a microcosmic/macrocosmic alignment that encapsulates the cosmic concerns of New Age music. We see a human figure whose brain is connected to a glowing network of energy from the Earth, and whose outstretched hand makes an energetic connection to the center of a distant spiral galaxy.[84] Davis's New Age album cover did not appear in a vacuum, and he was associated with the New Age music scene through his interactions with Ken Jenkins and Iasos (who included Davis's work in his online gallery of visionary artists).

Another person who bridged these worlds was the musician and visual artist Geoffrey Chandler, whom we met briefly in the previous chapter. Chandler began painting "spacescapes" in 1973 and became connected to

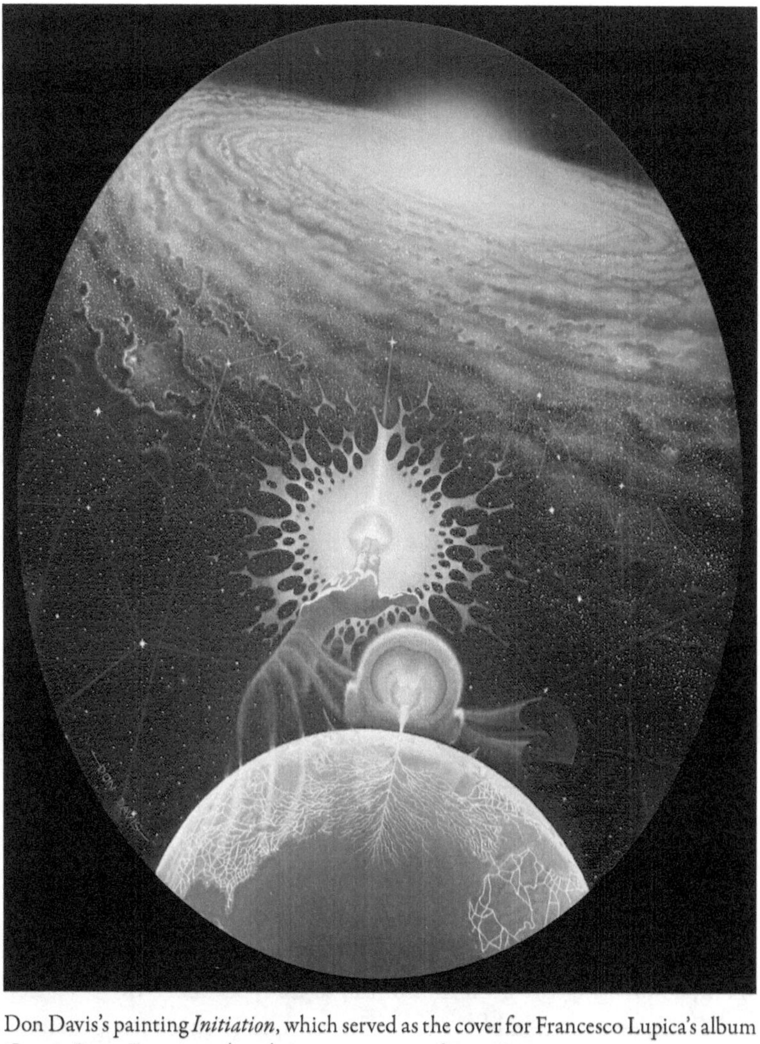

Don Davis's painting *Initiation*, which served as the cover for Francesco Lupica's album *Cosmic Beam Experience* (1976). Image courtesy of Don Davis.

the New Age music scene through an association with Iasos and Stephen Hill.[85] He made one New Age album, *Starscapes* (1980), which features synth-driven tracks with astronomical titles like "Polaris," "Starmaker (Sirius)," and "Stellar Solitude," and his own space art painting on the cover.[86] Chandler curated a festival of "Space Music and Art" in 1987 that included paintings by space artists like himself and Don Davis, as well as a stellar musical line-up of New Age artists like Michael Stearns, Emerald Web, Constance Demby, and Steve Roach.

Don Davis and Geoffrey Chandler embody the permeable boundaries between astronomical science, space music, and space art and indicate how the airbrush style seen on *Cosmos* could register at the time as both science illustration and trippy visionary art. The airbrush, like the modular synth, is a decidedly predigital tool, but the *Cosmos* team of artists was working on the cusp of the technological sea change to digital production. In fact, *Cosmos* was both the last major science TV show to rely on techniques like airbrush, models, and cell animation, and a showcase for some of the earliest digital animation seen on television.[87] For some animated sequences on the show, Jon Lomberg had initially considered hiring the psychedelic light show Heavy Water, who worked with Tim Clark at the Strasenburgh Planetarium.[88] That idea didn't pan out, so instead, they worked with Jim Blinn and Charlie Kohlhase from NASA's Jet Propulsion Laboratory (JPL).[89]

In episode two of *Cosmos*, an animated sequence depicts the evolution of life from the first cell to humans.[90] The sequence presents beautiful line drawings created by artist Susan Brown, which morph from one creature to the next in a graceful, Continuum-esque watery movement, condensing the evolution of life to forty seconds. The evolution of life sequence is notable as an early example of computer-generated morphing and is paired with music on the soundtrack.[91] The first time the sequence is shown, it is accompanied by a Bach violin partita, but when it is shown again in episode eight, Brown's line drawings are given a starry, cosmic background and are accompanied by Vangelis's "Alpha." Indeed, as you will have noticed throughout my description of the show's visual techniques, music by Vangelis or a similar New Age/space music artist is called upon to depict the most cosmic moments of the show: when we zoom through the galaxies, contemplate the deep time of the universe, or travel inside a cell to see the workings of a DNA molecule. Just as Michael Stearns's music was the right fit with Ron Fricke's cosmic cinema, so Vangelis struck the right chord for Sagan's cosmic television.

It was the artist Susan Brown who brought Vangelis to the team's attention. Brown was a Vangelis fan and introduced Lomberg to the album *Heaven and Hell* (1975). One evening during the production, Sagan and producer Adrian Malone came to Lomberg's apartment to hear his ideas about music for the show. Lomberg played them a selection of music that he and other artists on the team thought could work well, including the Vangelis track that became the title theme.[92] Vangelis is not the only electronic artist on the *Cosmos* soundtrack, which also includes music by Edgar Froese from Tangerine Dream, Jean Michel Jarre, Isao Tomita, Synergy, Brian Eno, Fuhrs & Frohling, and Teddy Lasry. Documents in the Carl Sagan Papers reveal that a host of other New Age-adjacent musicians were considered, including German *kosmiche* artists like Klaus Schulze, Roedelius, Cluster, and Neu, French synth-pop group Space Art, and American synth pioneers Wendy Carlos and Tonto's Expanding Headband.[93] All these musicians are the more industry-established, major label-backed cousins of visionary school musicians like Iasos, Deuter, Emerald Web, Steve Roach, and Michael Stearns.

This kind of music resonated with Sagan and the *Cosmos* artists, and when *Cosmos* was broadcast in 1980, the soundtrack provoked a surprising response from the television audience. PBS reported that it had received between twenty and thirty thousand telephone calls asking where they could find the music from the show. There had been no plans to release a soundtrack album, but due to this outpouring of interest, the producers worked with RCA Records to put out an LP.[94] The album was promoted on local PBS station fund drives, in bookstores nationwide alongside Sagan's publications, at planetariums, and on radio advertisements.[95] The *Cosmos* soundtrack is thus a supercharged update on New Age music's alternative distribution network, now with major label support.[96] That said, the *Cosmos* soundtrack circulated through the New

Age alternative distribution network of metaphysical bookstores and head shops: Ethan Edgecombe of Fortuna Records remembered stocking it on his Bay area circuit.[97]

Kat Epple of Emerald Web was one of the viewers who was excited about the music of *Cosmos*. "It was groundbreaking," she said, and she felt that it made her kind of cosmic electronic music more acceptable. She remembered overhearing someone say, "I thought I hated electronic music and then I heard *Cosmos*."[98] Epple had been aware of Carl Sagan as a celebrity scientist and had seen his appearances on *The Tonight Show*. "I was always such a science nerd," she said, "and to have this really likable and attractive professor hosting a science show was really thrilling at the time." When *Cosmos* was broadcast, she found it to be even better than she had hoped it might be, and she felt very connected to it.[99] That connection grew even stronger when Emerald Web began to work with Sagan on subsequent iterations of the show.

For the original broadcast of *Cosmos* on PBS, the production team did not need to negotiate and pay for each individual musical cue. The copyright procedure changed when the show was released on video, and Sagan was unable to afford Vangelis, who had become a major star with his soundtracks for *Chariots of Fire* (1981) and *Blade Runner* (1982). Vangelis's rise to fame is a familiar tale in histories of film music, but another, lesser known narrative concerns the way in which the success of the *Cosmos* soundtrack opened the door for other manifestations of the New Age soundtrack.[100]

No longer able to afford Vangelis, Sagan asked his associates to seek out other artists who sounded like him, and several suggested Emerald Web. Epple got a phone call out of the blue from a producer but was soon fielding calls from Sagan himself. "When Carl Sagan would call, sometimes I would go into my schoolgirl crush mode," she recalled. "I would get all giddy. 'Come on, Kat. You gotta be professional here!' But it was just so cool to talk to this person who I admired for all these years."[101]

Emerald Web were included on a video rerelease of *Cosmos*, and after that, worked with Sagan on a number of television projects, including KCET's *Together to Mars* (1987).[102] Emerald Web also provided music for two space-related episodes of *Nova*, "Is Anybody Out There?" (1986) and "Can the Next President Win the Space Race?" (1988), as well as a series of science programs on the brain. Emerald Web were not the only musicians of the visionary school to move into television soundtracks. Peter Davison began composing for film and TV in the mid-1970s and became one of the main composers for Churchill films, a producer of classroom films. Davison later composed the score for a twenty-six-episode PBS series on geography, *Earth Revealed* (1992).[103]

Emerald Web's presence on the *Cosmos* rerelease and Michael Stearns's presence on Ron Fricke's films of the 1980s and 1990s are milestones in the widening circle of the visionary school's cosmic sound. *Cosmos*, after all, was a major media event, billed as the most ambitious American-made PBS series to date, with an $8 million budget and an estimated viewership of half a billion people in sixty nations.[104] That huge international viewership was also a huge international listenership, and an unintended outcome of the show's success was to promote New Age music, aiding its move from the cultural periphery towards more mainstream audiences.

In retrospect, *Cosmos* might have been less successful in its primary mission to promote science. Sagan was worried about anti-science sentiment and the erosion of scientific knowledge, and that became an explicit theme in *Cosmos*.[105] Looking back from the present moment, Jon Lomberg feels bittersweet about the show's legacy. On the one hand, it was "a high watermark in the appreciation of science by the American people." On the other hand, the current political climate in which science is in disfavor makes him feel that in some ways they failed. "Carl's ultimate goal was to increase the literacy of not only the American public, but the global public, and to show them what a wonderful thing science is, and how reliant we are on science to navigate our modern world," he said. "We've slid so far from that. The whole venture of science is at risk. That's profoundly disturbing to me."[106]

As a lesson in how we might regain that high watermark, we could do worse than revisit Sagan's method of building bridges and forging dialogue.[107] *Cosmos* stitched together art, science, and spirituality using tools like airbrushes and synthesizers, genres like space art, and, perhaps most effective of all, a visionary soundtrack. One set of issues that *Cosmos* called to our attention were environmental, and the show contains dire warnings about the threat of greenhouse warming as well as the need to protect whales from extinction. These environmental concerns were shared by the visionary school, as we will see in the next chapter.

FIVE

Environmental Sounds

"TODAY WE ARE CONSCIOUS of the ecological necessity of being in harmonious balance with the earth" declared the program for the Kohoutek Celebration of Consciousness in 1974. A room at the event was dedicated to displaying the latest developments in alternative energy, including solar power. Other exhibits concerned natural foods, communication between plants and people, and a talk on the subject of "planet management."[1] The New Age movement, it is clear, overlapped with the environmental movement of the 1970s, and New Age music flowed with those ecological currents.

The 1970s have been called the Green Decade, when the baby-boom generation, who had wept watching *Bambi* (1942) as kids and absorbed the public controversy over Rachel Carson's *Silent Spring* (1962) as they grew up, saw, as young adults, the troubling evidence of America's polluted rivers and coastlines.[2] The first Earth Day took place in 1970, as did the formation of the Environmental Protection Agency, as concerns about the environment became widespread. Environmentalism moved into popular culture at this time as well, in films like *Silent Running* (1972) and *Soylent Green* (1973).[3]

Environmental sentiments can be found in the music of the period, scattered across folk, rock, R & B, and jazz recordings, but it is New Age music that, as a genre, had the most sustained and meaningful connection to environmental ideas and activism.[4] That's the way it seemed to Lee Underwood, a musician and music writer, who wrote an unpublished book manuscript on New Age music.[5] A keen observer of the New

Age music scene, Underwood defined this emerging genre through reference to the then recent Gaia theory of scientists James Lovelock and Lynn Margulis, which asserts that the total ecosystem of the Earth is a self-regulating system.[6] Underwood wrote that many of the musicians in the New Age scene "consciously or unconsciously recognize at a profound level their bio-spiritual relationship to the organic ecosystem of Gaia."[7] Underwood perceived correctly that, in addition to being visionary, holistic, luminous, and cosmic, New Age music was *environmental*.[8]

We saw in chapter 2 that New Age music's investment in the therapeutic function of music resulted in a blend of art and science, music and medicine. The music's investment in environmentalism provided another avenue for hybrids of art and science. Gaia theory demonstrates that an important touchstone for both environmentalism and the New Age movement was the "systems view" of reality, associated with cybernetic anthropologist Gregory Bateson and popularized by author and physicist Fritjof Capra.[9] Bateson, along with his wife, the eminent anthropologist Margaret Mead, helped establish a "second-order" cybernetics that is less detached from the systems it observes and widens the analysis to include the observer.[10] Bateson in particular showed how a cybernetic perspective could be applied, not only to thermostats and weapons systems but to human societies, family relationships, biological processes, and "ecologies of mind." Such an approach was in harmony with the New Age movement's holistic urge to overcome reductionism and mechanism, as well as its interest in micro- and macrocosmic resonances and integrated multisensory experiences.[11] Bateson and Mead were influential thinkers in the environmental movement, with Mead giving the keynote speech at the first Earth Day in 1970.[12]

Music offered a way to synthesize and embody the ecological systems thinking of the 1970s, and the historian Daniel Belgrad describes how composers like Pauline Oliveros, La Monte Young, Terry Riley, Steve Reich, and Philip Glass explored music as "a natural, open system, organized by feedback relations rather than having been put in order by the composer's dictatorial authority."[13] Belgrad doesn't mention them, but the visionary school of New Age music was doing something similar, especially those working with analog synthesizers. The New Age musician Steve McLinn, who recorded under the name Ojas, told an interviewer that when he looked with his "mind's eye" inside his synthesizers, he could see "all the energy currents running around. These instruments have life too. They are alive." McLinn saw his creative process as a cybernetic system that integrated self, synth, and spirit and that produced music from complex electronic feedback circuits in a way that blurred the lines between human and nonhuman intelligence. The result was a musical vision that was "running as much through those circuits as it is through me. Sometimes I see myself as just one module sitting within the synthesizer, and the Spirit is running the whole operation."[14] In a similar way, Steve Roach compares his home recording operation to tending a houseplant or home aquarium. "I'll set up a modular synth patch, and it just lives," he said. "It's breathing and living as it's evolving over time. It's like the growth of a beautiful exotic, surrealist plant, a living sonic life form that is in your space." He referred to this as tending an "analog modular garden."[15]

New Age musicians, then, were early adopters of systems thinking and hands-on practitioners of cybernetic creative processes, which fostered a distinctive set of audio alloys of art and ecological science. In the first section of the chapter, we consider the overlaps between New Age music and acoustic ecology (the study of the relationships between living organisms and their sonic environment). The combination of field recordings and studio-based music is a distinctive characteristic of New Age music and was an expression of both environmental politics and the visionary impulse to merge inner and outer realities, the numinous and the everyday. The integration of environmental sounds was one manifestation of the genre's interest in the creation of sonic environments through space-creating techniques like echo and reverb, with alternative names for the genre like "space music" and "ambient music" indicating its spatial preoccupations.

In the second section of the chapter, we move to New Age music's intersections with bioacoustics (the study of the ways in which animals transmit and receive sound) and biosemiotics (the study of processes of sign relations and their function in the biological processes of life). The central case study here is whale vocalization, which was featured on multiple New Age records, most notably those by Larkin, Paul Horn, and Paul Winter. New Age music's whale tracks shimmered with the visionary luminosity of the lab-oratorium, but they resulted in real world activism as well as inner trips, and initiatives to protect whales and other endangered species brought members of the visionary school into contact with the environmental movement of the 1970s. Modular synthesizers, fixtures in the New Age home studio, could also be found on board ships bound for missions to protect and study whales and were potent emblems of the ecological thinking of the 1970s.[16]

The third and final section focuses on Paul Winter, who embodies many of the themes of the chapter. He is the New Age musician most associated with environmentalism, and he released three classic albums on his own independent label, Living Music, that combined his unique style of cosmopolitan jazz with the sounds of whales, wolves, eagles, and seals. Winter's term for these difficult-to-categorize records was "Earth music." Winter's Living Music releases were richly multimedia affairs, with LP packaging that included booklets brimming with poetry, myth, insights from biological science, and wildlife photography. Winter's multimedia releases are another manifestation of New Age audiovision, and we will also revisit the New Age soundtrack in this chapter, in the form of several documentaries about human-animal encounters that feature a New Age score. We begin with an influential album that established a model for the New Age approach to combining music and field recordings.

AN AMALGAM OF THE NATURAL AND THE SYNTHETIC

Wendy Carlos is best known for her landmark album *Switched-On Bach* (1968), which presented her multitracked performances of Bach compositions on the Moog synthesizer. *Switched-On Bach* opened many people's ears to the expressive possibilities of electronic instruments, but it was Carlos's third release that had the biggest influence on New Age music. *Sonic Seasonings* (1972) mixed realistic recordings of birds, rain showers, ocean waves, and frog choruses with analog synths to create four atmospheric tracks that evoke the mood of each season. Carlos's collaborator, Rachel Elkind, described the album as "an amalgam of the natural and the synthetic."

Elkind wrote that *Sonic Seasonings* was designed to be "a part of the decor," a "sonic ambience that enhances the listener's total environment." *Sonic Seasonings* is clearly a precursor to Brian Eno's "ambient music," which was first heard three years later on the album *Discrete Music* (1975). As with ambient music, there was a functional element to *Sonic Seasonings*, and Elkind wrote that by listening to the album, "the weary urbanite can eavesdrop on the conversation of chattering birds; the mountain dweller can lave his soul with the sound of the surf." *Sonic Seasonings* was not explicitly connected to environmental politics, but as ecocritic Lawrence Buell points out, artworks that use natural cycles like the seasons as an organizing principle offer a first step toward encouraging an ecological consciousness.[17]

Several musicians of the visionary school list *Sonic Seasonings* as a major influence, and a similar amalgam of natural and synthetic sounds became a hallmark of New Age music in the decade after the release of Carlos's album.[18] Several New Age pioneers were working with field recordings well before the release of *Sonic Seasonings*. Suzanne Doucet had been a pop star and television host in Germany in the 1960s but made a break with her previous career by releasing the triple album *Trip—Flip Out—Meditation* (1970). Doucet worked with her sister Diane on the project, and the two spent six months making location recordings with a portable cassette recorder. As the album title suggests, they were tripping on LSD during some of the sessions.[19] The sisters edited these recordings into sound collages, which were released under the name Zweistein.[20] After this first exploration of the psychedelic uses of environmental recordings, Doucet developed a variation on the *Sonic Seasonings* amalgam.

During the early 1980s, Doucet released a series of New Age albums on her own label, Isis Music. *Transformation* (1982) contains the track "Drop Out," a trippy, drippy collage of water drops akin to Iasos's "Bubble Massage," which immerses the listener in an elemental experience of watery rhythms. On the same album, "Love" combines gentle guitar arpeggios with crashing waves. The title track on *Transmission* (1983) concludes with recordings of birdsong, and *Reflecting Light, Vol. 1* (1984) features "Seacliff," which is a blend of real and synthesized wind and waves. Field recording remained a significant part of Doucet's career with the "Sounds of Nature" and "Tranquility" series of releases. Albums like *Thunder over Shasta* (1994), *Cosmic Night* (1997), *Moonlight in the Canyon* (1998), and *Desert Dreams* (1999) combine New Age music and natural sounds. Doucet said that her process on such recordings was to listen to the sounds of nature and play along just as one would play with another musician.[21] "I feel that music is everywhere, in every environmental sound," she said. The fusion of environmental sounds and instrumental music "*is* the music," she explained.[22]

Another German New Age pioneer, Deuter, developed a similar approach to working with field recordings. Deuter recalled saving money as a boy to purchase a tape recorder and using it to record birds, water, and wind in the trees. "That, for me, was a type of music," he said.[23] As with Doucet, Deuter talked about creating duets with field recordings: "You record birds when they're singing, and there is an incredible music there," he said. "You take a flute and you want to answer it or play with it. There's a rhythm in water, and you take a drum and play with it."[24] On Deuter's album *Celebration* (1976), we hear this approach on tracks like "Solitary Bird," which combines footsteps and waves with echoing guitars, and "Easy Is Right," where gorgeous double-tracked guitar chords and harmonica melodies emerge from birdsong. The founder of the Celestial Harmonies label, Eckart Rahn, who signed Deuter, said that "you can't take the nature out of Deuter's music."[25]

The New Age amalgam of the natural and the synthetic can be heard on many other New Age recordings by visionary school artists like Iasos, Michael Stearns, Steve Roach, and Kitaro, among others.[26] Their tracks show how field recordings were put to the visionary purposes of the New Age genre, merging the tangible, natural world of field recording with the numinous glow of electronic sounds and studio effects, thereby manifesting the hyper-real quality of Stanislav Grof's immanent divine.[27] As a form of visionary art, the New Age audio amalgam creates sonic landscapes akin to paintings by California visionary artists like Bill Martin and Gage Taylor, whose Edenic natural spaces could function as metaphors for states of consciousness in which inner and outer realities were united in "a spiritual symbiosis."[28]

New Age tracks using field recording could be dismissed as an example of what ecocritic Leo Marx calls a "simple pastoral," a presentation of the natural world that is sentimental and escapist. Marx preferred a more stylized "complex pastoral" that used irony and juxtaposition to offer an explicit critique of industrialization.[29] I'm suspicious of aesthetic judgements based upon a stark dichotomy between works that are deemed either complex-unsettling-avant garde or simple-harmonious-popular, as though a musician need only insert the sound of a bulldozer and suddenly a track is transformed from a neoliberal tranquilizer to a radical call to arms. New Age field recordings created their own sonic dialectic, not between nature and industrialization but between inner and outer environments, which could result in navel-gazing introversion but could also bring a new sense of intimacy and urgency to environmental politics.

Moreover, at least some visionary school musicians were cognizant of the fact that the use of natural sounds could become an empty cliché. Steve Roach and Robert Rich talked about wanting to avoid the generic "classical piano meets soothing waterfall" style of ambient music, and they preferred to trouble the boundary between natural and electronic sounds or find organic textures in traditional instruments as well as field recordings. Other New Age musicians did not so much place natural sounds alongside synths as create representations of natural sounds *with* synths. On Peter Davison's early albums, one can hear tracks like "Leaves Shimmering," "Grass Waving in the Wind," and "Songs in the Wind" that use the Serge synthesizer to represent natural scenes. Davison was inspired by composers like Olivier Messiaen, Maurice Ravel, and Claude Debussy, as well as by impressionist painting. "I love impressionistic painting," he said, "and they do all these beautiful landscapes. I try to make music like that."[30]

Whatever particular approach they took to cooking up amalgams of the natural and synthetic, New Age musicians as a cohort listened to the natural world with the same intensity that they brought to music. It makes sense, then, that a person close to their milieu would help develop a branch of ecological science that uses field recordings as scientific data. The sound recordist Bernie Krause was a pioneer of electronic music who also experimented with his own amalgam of synthesizers and field recordings on the album *In a Wild Sanctuary* (1970) by Beaver & Krause, an early electronic duo that got airplay on *Music from the Hearts of Space*.[31] Beginning in the late 1970s, Krause reoriented his career from electronic music to wildlife field recording and developed pathbreaking ideas about how audio recordings could measure the health of ecosystems. These ideas became foundational for the fields of acoustic ecology and ecoacoustics.[32]

New Age musicians of the visionary school were not scientists, but their careful attention to field recordings as music, their exploration of the sonic poetics of natural spaces, and their manipulation of soundscapes helped to prepare the ground for scientific work at the intersection of audio and ecology. The visionary school's environmental disposition also fostered intersections with the science of bioacoustics, a subset of the study of animal behavior concerned with animal communication in sound. The key ingredient in the alloy of bioacoustics and New Age music was a type of wildlife recording that had strong cosmic overtones for spiritual seekers: the vocalization of whales.

WHALE TRIP

An advertisement for a new release on Capitol Records appeared in the November 26, 1970, issue of *Rolling Stone Magazine*. Directly above an ad for the new Pink Floyd album *Atom Heart Mother* (1970), we see a drawing of a man in a rowboat. The man occupies only the uppermost righthand corner of the image, however, and he looks down into the water where the head of a huge humpback whale dominates the frame. This was an ad for biologist Roger Payne's *Songs of the Humpback Whale* (1970), and accompanying the image was a blurb from a *Rolling Stone* review by Jon Carroll, who describes the album as more than an oddity. It was, he insists, a *good record*, one that belonged in any up-to-date record collection alongside current favorites like The Band's *Music from Big Pink* and Van Morrison's *Moondance*. "It's especially good for late at night and peaceful, together moments," Carroll wrote. "It stretches your mind to encompass alien art forms. The kids can't dance to it, but they can't dance to Satie either." In his review, Carroll compared the sounds on the album to electronic music, Tibetan chanting, and Jimi Hendrix's psychedelic track "1983 . . . (A Merman I Should Turn to Be)."[33]

Payne began his work studying humpbacks in the late 1960s and *Songs of the Humpback Whale* was initially released by a small, independent publishing company called Communications Research Machines before it was picked up by Capitol.[34] Payne's recordings are still arresting today, fifty years after their novelty has worn off. On tracks like "Solo Whale," one hears a range of tones moving from deep seismic rumbles to high plaintive calls and from clear bell-like chimes to raspy growls. These kaleidoscopic tones move at a slow pace that, according to Payne, requires a special kind of listening, one attuned to "long, slow rhythms, where things occur very lingeringly. In order to observe whales, you must be willing to set your metronome on adagio."[35]

In other words, listening to Payne's album is a lot like listening to New Age music, which could also be glossed as a synthesis of electronic music, Tibetan chanting, and progressive, psychedelic rock. In terms of their long, slow rhythms, humpback recordings resemble New Age tracks like Steve Roach's "Structures from Silence" or Iasos's "Cloud Prayer." Payne's album also resembles New Age music in its sonic representation of space. Payne wrote that the first time he heard recordings of the songs of humpback whales was also the first time he heard "the abyss": "Normally, you don't hear the size of the ocean when you are listening, but I heard it that night." Whale song gave the ocean "its voice," he continues, a voice that "is ethereal and unearthly. You put on headphones, and after a while a whale starts to sing, and the echoes from the abyss come tumbling and roaring back, and suddenly you are aware of the vastness of the mystery that underlies your boat."[36] Humpbacks vocalizing in the vast reverberant space of the ocean was a biophonic variation on New Age music's space-creating application of echo and reverb.

Payne's account of putting on headphones and experiencing vast and mysterious spaces can easily be mapped onto the psychedelic experience of recorded music. The final track on *Songs of the Humpback Whale* is titled "Three Whale Trip," and the liner notes suggest listening with stereo headphones to best approximate the "beautiful, mystical mood" of the original recording session, when Payne listened to three humpback whales from a sailboat near Bermuda. The track's title is an intentional reference to the meaning of "trip" as "a mental voyage," an acknowledgement that humpback songs produce "an extraordinary inner experience" for listeners.

People were taking that mental voyage, as indicated by another review of the album published in 1970. After putting on the record and a pair of earphones, this reviewer encountered a sound that was "unlike anything I had ever heard. My experience contained no precedent."[37] This review was published in the *Los Angeles Free Press* and written by Gary David, whom we met in the previous chapter as one of the founders of the Continuum studio in Los Angeles. David describes "the absolutely mystical way" the humpback's voice echoes and moves through the water, a sound that suggested "the soul of all the living organisms that have ever populated this planet" or even "the sound of the universe itself." As he listened, David felt compelled to vocalize in kinship with the whale:

> I could roar like no other beast on earth, fling my sound toward the surface, feel it bounce back like echoes in a gigantic cavern, and ripple through my massive body. I was an underwater artist who took delight in the endless ways I could create sound upon sound; I could sound like a massive horn ringing through the water galaxies. . . . I could sound like

> a gentle, mysterious, heavenly flute unlike any flute known to the ears of man. . . . I could sound like a giant motor creating pulse waves that traveled the entire ocean floor.[38]

David's exuberant reaction to the album shows how whale recordings, which presented a radically different kind of embodied sonic expression, could scratch the same itch as the New Age aspiration for an expanded musical vocabulary through microtonal systems and modular synths. Payne's recordings seemed to be moving through the same watery galaxy as Continuum and exploring a similar kind of fluid resonance. David's review is a wonderful illustration of how *Songs of the Humpback Whale* resonated with, and would become an influence on, New Age musicians. David, for example, used whale recordings as part of his musical performances at Continuum and side one of the album *O'cean* (1980), by fellow Continuum musician Larkin, is built around whale recordings he was given by Roger Payne.[39]

Songs of the Humpback Whale would eventually sell over a hundred thousand copies and become a much-discussed example of environmental communication with real-world impact.[40] Humpback recordings were not the only bridge between bioacoustics and New Age music, however. Equally significant was the work being done on the acoustic communication of orcas, or killer whales. The key researcher in that area was Paul Spong, who took a job at the University of British Columbia in 1967, where he worked with the Vancouver Aquarium. Concerned that captive whales were suffering from sensory deprivation, Spong began playing music for them.[41] He ran into trouble with his employers after he gave a speech in June 1969 in which he stated that the captive orcas at the Vancouver Aquarium should be released into the wild as quickly as possible.[42] A week later, he made headlines when he talked about taking mescalin as a means of getting in tune with the orcas. Soon thereafter he was prevented from his plan to swim nude in the tank with the orcas while playing them electronic music. He retaliated with a sonic protest, hooking his zither to an amplifier and playing it outside the Aquarium.[43]

Spong continued his research on orcas after leaving the academy, and in June 1971, he invited the New Age musician Paul Horn to play his flute for the orcas at Sealand of the Pacific, a commercial enterprise in Victoria, Canada.[44] The next year, Horn's interactions with the Sealand orcas were captured in the short documentary *We Call Them Killers* (1972), sponsored by the Canadian National Film Board.[45] The fifteen-minute film has two distinct sections, the first showing the orca Haida performing at Sealand, where he is cued by a trainer to jump out of the water and splash the audience. In the second half of the film, we are taken backstage to witness a more intimate interaction between Spong, Horn, and the orcas, with narration by Spong. The effect of this two-part structure is to expose the shallowness of the Sealand performance and the potential for deeper and more authentic interactions between humans and orcas. Over the course of the film, the orcas transform from performing circus animals to something much more complex and mysterious.

Spong's voiceover describes the orca's highly developed senses. When discussing their sense of touch, we see images of the orcas Haida and Chimo seeming to delight in the caress of a feather. Tactile interaction is taken a step further when Spong swims with them in the tank, an act that would have inspired terror a few years earlier, given their reputation as vicious predators. Spong explains that the sense of hearing is primary for whales, and that in fact, they have "the most marvelous hearing systems on the planet." Spong delicately clinks two wine glasses together as the two whales raise their heads in what appears to be rapt attention. Spong asserts that since music transcends language barriers in our own species, there is "no reason why we shouldn't explore the possibility that it may transcend interspecies barriers." Spong's words are paired with images of Paul Horn playing his flute for Haida. With the entrance of Horn's New Age music, *We Call Them Killers* becomes an early example of the New Age soundtrack.

In addition to Paul Horn's New Age sounds, the film advances ideas that would resonate with New Age musicians. Recall the New Age emphasis on intention described in chapter 2, which links the musician's inner state and the positive effects intended for the listener.[46] That approach is translated here to human-animal interaction. "I achieve the greatest rapport with whales when I'm least afraid of them," Spong says as we see him swimming in the tank.[47] Spong compares the intention of the orca trainer to the musician. "The more a musician can project himself into his music, the more responsive a whale is," Spong states. "Paul Horn, of course, is a fantastic musician, and *a fantastic person*. . . . The whales, I'm sure, appreciate him in both areas." The suggestion is that Horn's status as a fantastic person, perhaps implying his spiritual practice (he was a well-known meditator), helps him connect with the orcas. The film presents the event at Sealand as a duet, with Haida vocalizing in response to Horn's flute and images that alternate between close-ups of Horn's lips on the flute and the whale's blowhole.

If Horn is an ideal musician, the orcas are, in a sense, ideal listeners. Recall from the discussion of guided meditation cassettes in chapter 2 that the New Age audile technique involved listening with one's entire body. The orcas in *We Call Them Killers* do exactly that. In fact, whales and dolphins have sound receivers in both the forehead and lower jaw, and Spong explains that whale's bodies "pick up the sound directly, without ears. In essence, cetaceans literally hear with their whole bodies, sound traveling through the surface of their skin directly from the water until it hits the jawbone or forehead." For the orcas, sound is delivered to the brain as "a tactile message from the whole body."[48] In *We Call Them Killers*, we see the two orcas immersed in the water as well as in Horn's music: the quintessential New Age listeners.

In addition to New Age theories of intention and listening, Horn's interactions with Haida were also colored by a New Age belief in the healing power of music. The orca Chimo died in the autumn of 1972, and Horn returned to Sealand to see Haida, who had not been eating and had developed cracks around his blowhole.[49] To some, these were signs of an infection. To others, they were signs of grief as he mourned the loss of Chimo. Haida's condition improved after Horn's flute sessions, and Horn wrote that this was a "dramatic example" of music's ability to "bring a nonhuman, intelligent life-form out of a state of depression."[50] Horn's claims are debatable, and Haida's changes in behavior could just as easily be attributed to the massive doses of antibiotics he was given. The veterinarian at Sealand echoed Georgia Kelly's distinction between "healing music" and "therapeutic music" when he stated that "playing music has exactly the same benefit as putting a television set in a kids' ward. . . . It keeps them involved. But I'd never trade ten million units of penicillin for a television set or a flute."[51] Whatever the efficacy of Horn's healing intervention, his interactions with Haida, as captured in *We Call Them Killers*, were an embodiment of a New Age amalgam of art and science that understood music as something more than entertainment.

Horn's encounters with orcas were documented on several commercial recordings. Sealand released the record *Haida and Paul Horn* (1972), which includes a spoken commentary by Horn about the mythology of whales, their evolution, physiology, and behavior.[52] Horn also released a track entitled "Haida" on the album *Inside II* (1972), which was released the same year as Wendy Carlos's *Sonic Seasonings* and, like that album, presents a model for New Age applications of field recording. In the album's liner notes, Horn writes that he had initially wanted to continue the location recording approach he had pioneered on his *Inside the Taj Mahal* album. His plan was to play his flute in natural spaces with a portable tape machine, but concerns about sound quality made him reconsider. Instead, he decided to work in the studio with recorded sounds of nature to create his own amalgam of the natural and the synthetic. The first track on the album, "The Mahabhutas," is a twenty-minute epic that takes the five-element framework—earth, air, fire, water, and space—as an alchemical organizing principle. Horn applies a remarkable range of flute techniques to recordings of roaring winds, crackling fires, intimate whispers, and rainstorms. The last section of "The Mahabhutas" depicts inner space through a spacey haze of gossamer tones created by setting the strings of the studio piano to vibrate in sympathetic resonance with his flute. This sonic effect had "mystical meaning" for Horn, depicting the resonating spiritual centers as they awaken within the individual, from the base of the spine to the "thousand-petalled lotus" in the brain.[53]

"The Mahabhutas," along with Carlos's *Sonic Seasonings*, is a blueprint for the New Age blend of cosmic music and field recordings. The second

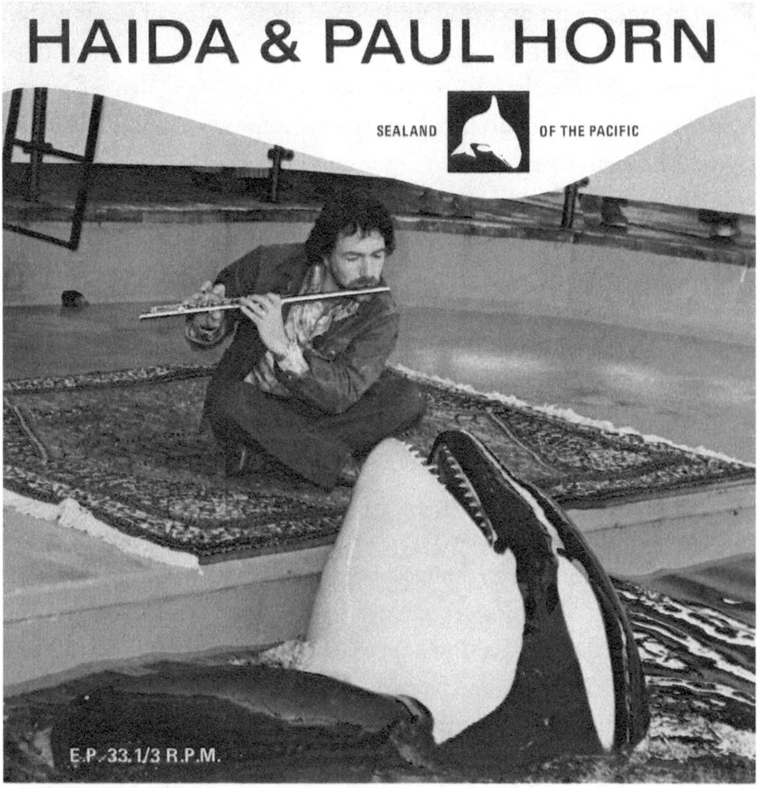

Cover art for *Haida and Paul Horn* (1972). Image courtesy of Robert Williston, Museum of Canadian Music, citizenfreak.com.

track on *Inside II*, "Haida," is a New Age variation on whale vocalization records. "Haida" is not a documentary recording of Horn and Haida interacting but a studio creation with Horn overlaying his flute onto five minutes of orca sounds made by Haida and Chimo at Sealand, as well as orcas recorded in the wild. Horn's track begins with a slow, two-note descending pattern that mimics the sound of someone calling the name "Hai-da." From the start, we are not in the zone of music but semiosis; this is not a musical duet, but a greeting, an exchange of calls. The field that is most relevant here is biosemiotics, the study of the ways in which living organisms produce and understand signs.[54] One of the founders of biosemiotics, Thomas Sebeok, argued that "the phenomenon that distinguishes life forms from inanimate objects is semiosis," defined as "the instinctive capacity of all living organisms to produce and understand signs."[55] Biosemiotics is interested in the wide variety of biological semiosis, and Sebeok pointed out that some animals have individual names. "In well-organized vertebrate societies—such as are found among birds and especially mammals—individual members tend to bear a singular proper name," Sebeok wrote, "marking each carrier animal as unique." These semiotic marks were used to assess social rank, mark territory, and maintain family bonds, and they could be communicated as visual, sonic, tactile, or chemical signs.[56] Sebeok also pointed out that animals in captivity tend to be given proper names by humans, as with the orcas at Sealand.[57] Horn's recording is given the name "Haida," and uses naming as a semiotic bridge between species.

After Paul Horn's initial musical mimicry of the name "Haida," the track develops a studio-based collage that represents a playful interaction between flute player and captive orca, with a simulated call and response of similar tones and pitches. There is a biosemiotic link between naming and play. Sebeok writes that singular proper names in animals are established in social activities like play, and he draws upon Gregory Bateson's influential model of play as metacommunication. Play involves the classification of signals, since a given action could be either an act of serious aggression or part of a game. In Bateson's famous example, play is a negative message. Play behavior involves signaling that a bite is a *play* bite; not a real act of aggression.[58] Horn's "Haida," then, is less a session of interspecies communication than a recreation of interspecies *meta*communication.

The track ends as Horn's flute fades out and an orca's synth-like calls are treated with reverb and echo, leaving the listener with a sense of mystery as the unknowable whale sounds recede into the depths. "Haida" documents the kind of intimate play session that could only occur with a whale in captivity. Paul Spong wrote that the responsiveness of captive orcas like Haida was in part due to the monotonous conditions of captivity and the "acoustic deprivation" of concrete enclosures.[59] Spong and his wife Linda continued their work at a station off Vancouver Island, where they played music for wild orcas, with varying degrees of interest from the animals.[60] The Spongs made recordings of orcas in the wild beginning in 1969 and released an LP and cassette of their recordings, *Songs and Sounds of Orcinus Orca*, in 1987.[61] The title of the album indicates a biosemiotic, rather than a purely musical framework; it is "Songs and Sounds," not just "Songs," as was the case with Roger Payne's humpback album.

The Spongs' *Songs and Sounds* album presents all manner of orca sound-making, including echolocation, the coordination of group behavior, and the dialects of specific family pods. The unifying theme of the album is relationship.[62] The tracks on *Songs and Sounds of Orcinus Orca* provide glimpses into the ways in which sounds establish social relationship for orcas. On the track "Last Words," we hear an underwater recording of a young orca being lifted out of the water in a sling to be taken to captivity in California. The captured orca calls to his family, and we hear their anxious cries of alarm in response. "There is a poignancy in their voices which cannot be dismissed as mere anthropomorphism," Spong writes. "We hear it. We can share the pain of the capture." As with names and play sessions, alarm calls are an important area of biosemiotic research and a bridge between human and nonhuman communication.

"Last Words" also shows that the whale recordings in circulation were not limited to slow, graceful, trippy songs, but also included edgier sonic experiences. In fact, Spong's work with orcas was a critical link between scientific study, the "whale trip" as heard on commercial recordings, and political activism to protect whales. Bob Hunter, who founded the environmental organization Greenpeace in 1971, was turned on to whale activism by an encounter with a captive orca facilitated by Paul Spong in 1974.[63] Paul Horn's 1972 musical encounter with Haida helped shape Greenpeace's activism as well. When Greenpeace made their historic voyage to intercept Russian whalers in 1975, the crew included the electronic musician Will Jackson, who brought his Serge modular synthesizer onboard as a way to communicate with the whales.[64] Spong had played a zither and Horn a flute during their musical sessions with orcas, but modular synths were thought to have a unique capability to make sounds that resembled whale vocalization.

Two years before the Greenpeace mission with Jackson's Serge, another expedition had mobilized a modular synth to communicate with whales. The synth operator on this mission was Erich Hoyt, who had been part of the back-to-the-land movement in British Columbia for two years, living as a subsistence farmer while experimenting with an early ARP synthesizer. Through community connections, Hoyt got involved with an initiative called Project Apex, whose aim was to make a film of orcas in the wild. The plan was to attract the orcas with sounds from Hoyt's synthesizer and then film them. They were aware of Paul Horn's interactions with Haida, but, as Hoyt put it, "that was a captive audience, and a very bored whale, and an ill whale at one point. . . . We were going to try to engage orcas in the wild."[65]

The expedition set out in the summer of 1973 and is documented in a twelve-minute film titled *Orca* (1973).[66] The film begins with an opening speech by Hoyt, who explains that the ARP synthesizer is capable of simulating the vocabulary of the killer whale and that their goal was to "communicate with them in their own language or in musical variations of it." The title of the film appears on the screen, followed by images of the sailboat riding the waves and crewmembers working on deck, accompanied by a New Age soundtrack consisting of Hoyt's dreamy and droney organ-like music, reminiscent of Terry Riley or Randall McClellan.

After two weeks on the water, they met a group of whales and heard some of their calls with underwater microphones. The film depicts this first encounter with distant shots of dorsal fins in the water and the sounds of spouting orcas. When they encountered this group of whales a second time, Hoyt tried to mimic their call on his ARP synth, which was connected to an underwater speaker. "We didn't know what their call meant," he said, "but it was something they repeated a few times." Hoyt played his version of the call on the synth, and the orcas responded

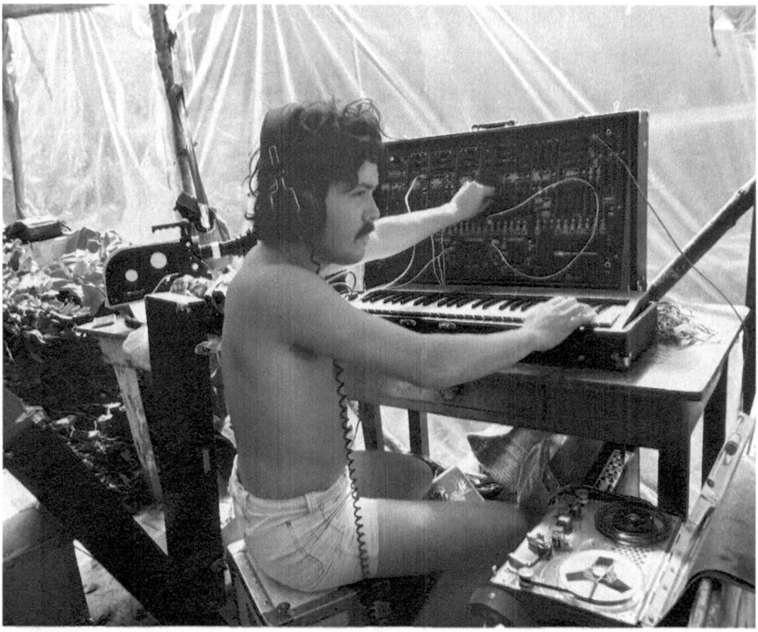

Erich Hoyt working with an ARP synthesizer connected to underwater speakers in Robson Bight on northern Vancouver Island. Photo by Stan Waterman, courtesy of Erich Hoyt.

with what Hoyt described as an "extraordinary rendition of what I'd put in the water."[67] *Orca* captures this moment with recordings of the interaction on the soundtrack paired with shots that cut between Hoyt's fingers on the keyboard and long shots of orca dorsal fins disappearing under the water.

The film manifests a tension between sound and image in whale encounters: the intimate communication occurring on the soundtrack is juxtaposed with distant glimpses of a disappearing fin. Hoyt said that in this regard, the expedition's premise was flawed. They thought that sound would attract the whales to come closer for filming, but orcas can communicate with sound from distances up to sixteen kilometers away. "We learned a lot about what closeness actually means in an audio sense," Hoyt said.[68] The film's reliance on distant shots of orca pods ends up being a strength of the film, not a weakness, as it emphasizes the stunning surrounding landscape, and situates the whales in their wider ecosystem. Like the echoey ending of Paul Horn's "Haida," *Orca* maintains a respectful distance from the pod, in contrast to the "false intimacy" of the interactions with captive whales we see in *We Call Them Killers.*[69]

Hoyt's ethereal synth music returns to the soundtrack as the expedition shifts to a new location near the shore. The filmmakers ride out in a canoe, and the film cuts between Hoyt playing the keyboard and the orca pod moving around the canoe. The soundtrack lets us hear the call and response between Hoyt's synth and the orcas, while we see whales breaching the surface of the water and shots of their underwater environment. The film ends, like Horn's "Haida," with a sense of mystery and an emphasis on what has *not* been seen and heard. Noisy, distorted underwater audio of distant orcas and partial views of orcas seen through clouds of bubbles seem to underscore the limits of human perception and understanding.[70]

Despite the film's ambiguous results with regard to the expedition's initial goals, Paul Spong declared that it was "a wonderful statement, the closest glimpse we have yet gained of these creatures," and that *Orca* documented "the first ever unquestioned communicative exchange between free orcas and humans."[71] The film premiered to a sold-out crowd of over two thousand people at the Queen Elizabeth theatre in Vancouver as the climax of Paul Spong's Christmas Whale Show in 1973 and was praised for its first-ever underwater footage of killer whales in the wild.[72] *Orca* was part of the "whale trip" of the 1970s, which among other things fostered early manifestations of the New Age soundtrack.[73] Paul Horn's flute, and the synths used by Erich Hoyt and Will Jackson, were links between bioacoustics, biosemiotics, environmental activism of the 1970s, and New Age music.[74] We turn now, in the final section of the chapter, to a New Age musician who worked at a similar crossroads and developed his own unique variety of bio-spiritual music.

In some ways, Paul Winter does not fit with the visionary cohort of New Age musicians. Like Paul Horn and James Newton, Winter was an established jazz instrumentalist before making records that were categorized as New Age, whereas most of the visionary school had either classical training or a background in progressive rock or electronic music. Winter plays the saxophone, and though he was aware of developments in electronic music and was friends with the synth pioneer Don Buchla, he never made synthesizers part of his music. He built a home studio akin to the New Age lab-oratorium in the 1970s, but he was more of an ensemble player than a self-sufficient jack-of-all-trades like Iasos. Winter wasn't part of the LSD culture of the 1960s and was generally wary of drugs, having seen their devastating effects on jazz icons of the bebop era. "I never wanted to work with anyone who took anything stronger than aspirin," he said.[75] Nevertheless, Winter aligns with the visionary school through his status as a spiritual seeker, his gently cosmic music—which has often been categorized as New Age—and his creation of an ecological variant of *musica sancta*.[76]

Born in 1939, in Altoona, Pennsylvania, Winter began playing the saxophone as a teenager in the 1950s. He put together his first ensemble, a jazz sextet, while attending Northwestern University. In 1961, Winter's group won the Georgetown University Intercollegiate Jazz Festival, which resulted in a recording contract with Columbia Records.[77] The group recorded their first LP in 1961 and embarked on a tour of Latin America, sponsored by the US State Department.[78] The tour was a pivotal experience for Winter, exposing him to new sounds and cultures and showing him that music was a powerful way to bring together people from diverse backgrounds.[79] When the Winter Sextet returned to the United States, they became the first jazz group to perform at the White House, playing at the invitation of First Lady Jacqueline Kennedy.

Winter spent the following year in Brazil, where he collaborated with musicians in the Bossa Nova scene. With his musical horizons expanding, Winter was inspired to create a new kind of musical ensemble. In 1968, he formed the Winter Consort, which featured the novel combination of saxophone, cello, guitar, English horn, flute, and percussion.[80] The designation "consort" was carefully chosen, referring both to a small group of musicians and to the act of collective music making, as in the verb "to consort," meaning to associate, accord, or harmonize.[81] The Winter Consort took various forms over the next several years, and for a time, Winter played with the harpist Joel Andrews, who released New Age albums in the 1970s and '80s. Winter recalled that Andrews would do past-life sessions for people, playing the harp and guiding them through their previous incarnations.[82]

Winter had learned from his international travels that music could bridge cultures, and in 1968, he became interested in how music might also be a bridge between humans and other species.[83] That year, he attended a lecture in New York City on the topic of whale songs. "I couldn't imagine what that meant," he remembered, "but I was curious about all things relating to sound." He was also intrigued when a friend told him that if you listened to whale songs on earphones, it was better than an LSD trip. The lecture, by Roger Payne, was a life-changing experience for Winter. The whale's voices amazed him. They covered a startling range of frequencies, had the emotional power of a great blues singer, and their songs had the structural complexity of a Beethoven symphony.[84] "It was sort of like hearing Charlie Parker for the first time," he said, which for a jazz musician is a potent way of expressing the paradigm-exploding force of the experience. On top of the musical epiphany was a moral and political one. Payne made clear in his talk that the cetaceans who created these sublime and mysterious sounds were being exterminated to make products like dog food and lipstick. "I was so astounded by that," Winter said. "I became an activist that night."[85]

Payne's lecture introduced Winter to "the greater symphony of the Earth" and inspired him to make music that celebrated whales.[86] Winter contacted Payne soon after the lecture and asked if he could work with some of the biologist's recordings. Payne appreciated Winter's music—he was a cellist himself—and the two became friends. Winter began to

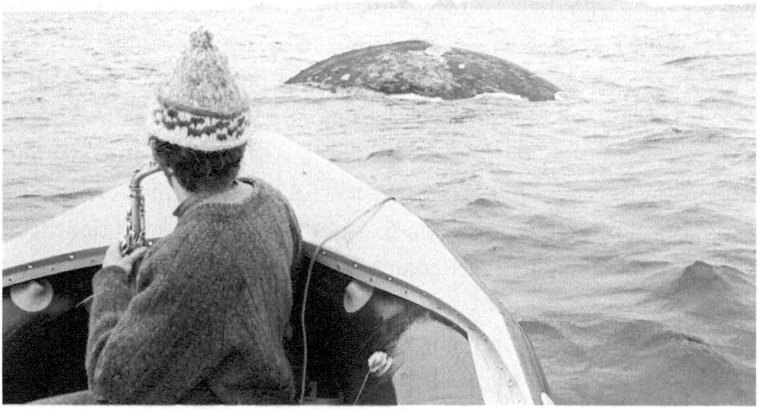

Paul Winter consorting with a gray whale. Photo courtesy of Rex Weyler.

weave recordings of whales into his live performances, which drew the attention of Greenpeace, which invited him to take part in a benefit concert in 1973.[87] Greenpeace was training on the Pacific coast of Vancouver Island for their historic confrontation with Russian whalers. After the benefit concert, Winter was invited to go out on the Greenpeace boat.[88] At one point, he sat in a small boat, playing his saxophone for gray whales. "They're huge and beautiful," Winter remembered. "When a creature as big as a locomotive emerges from the sea right next to your raft and looks at you with this giant eye before it dives again, it was just so moving."[89]

The 1975 mission produced iconic images of Greenpeace members positioning themselves between Russian harpoons and escaping whales, which created a media sensation and galvanized the Save the Whales movement.[90] California governor Jerry Brown announced California Celebrates the Whale Day in November 1976 and appeared at a keynote event that resembled a New Age fair.[91] There were exhibits from thirty environmental groups, the screening of a documentary with live narration by Roger Payne, and a concert featuring the Paul Winter Consort, Country Joe McDonald, John Sebastian, and Joni Mitchell.[92] The Winter Consort accompanied a reading by the environmental poet Gary Snyder and began their own set in total darkness, asking the audience to imagine themselves as whales swimming in the deep ocean.[93]

Winter's whale collaborations continued in 1977, when he, cellist David Darling, and harpist Joel Andrews took part in the making of a film, still unreleased, shot in Magdalena Bay in Baja California Sur, Mexico. Winter recalls a bizarre scene with dancers, inflatable whales, and musical performances meant to capture the whales' attention.[94] An unexpected outcome of that eccentric venture was Winter's discovery of the creative spark that occurred when a group of people spent time together outdoors. "Each night, after supper, we had nothing to do but sit around the fire and talk," he said. "People would take turns telling their stories, and this seemed to draw everyone out."[95]

Winter decided to make an album in a similar way, assembling a group of creative people living in an outdoor environment. He had moved to a farm in Litchfield, Connecticut, in 1974, and this proved to be the perfect setting. This album project, undertaken in the summer of 1977, was produced by Winter in his version of the New Age home studio. Winter transformed a horse barn with a cathedral-esque loft into a recording studio. A remarkable group of international musicians pitched their tents on his property and collaborated on the album: drummer Kwaku Dadey from Ghana, percussionist Laudir de Oliveira and guitarist Oscar Castro-Neves, both from Brazil, Sufi Choir director William Allaudin Mathieu, singers Susan Osborn and Janet Johnson, and Consort regulars cellist David Darling and oboist Paul McCandless.[96]

Together, they produced *Common Ground* (1978), which creates an amalgam of music and recordings of whales, wolves, and eagles, all animals that were threatened with extinction as well as sonically compelling.[97] Side one of *Common Ground* ends with a track called "Trio," featuring Winter, Darling, and McCandless in a trio of sax, cello, and oboe, the Consort's counterparts to wolf, whale, and eagle. Side two ends with "Trilogy," which blends recordings of a humpback whale, timber wolf, and African fish-eagle, over a deep drone note on the organ to produce a sonic harmonization of water, land, and air. Each animal gets its own track on the album: "Eagle Song" features a solo oboe improvisation in response to the cry of an African fish-eagle, "Ocean Dream" has a theme taken from a recording of a humpback whale and casts a dreamy, trance-like spell, with Winter singing the lyrics "Ocean child / Come now home," and the track "Wolf Eyes" opens with a recording of a timber wolf, moves to Winter's sax variations over somber piano chords, and closes with a recorded duet between Winter's sax and a captive wolf.

Common Ground was the first of a trilogy of albums that established Winter's "Earth music" genre, music that had the aspiration "to celebrate the creatures and cultures of the whole earth."[98] Winter didn't label his work as interspecies communication, which he saw as a buzzword of the 1970s. "I was not drawn to that. I think you'd really have to be a devoted scholar even to approach that subject," he said. "To me, it's just consorting."[99] He also made a distinction by saying he was involved in "communing; not communication. Communication immediately gets the cerebral cortex involved. Communing is the whole being. You could call it a spirit thing, maybe."[100] As is the case with other New Age uses of wildlife recordings described in this chapter, the goal was to celebrate, consort, and commune, not to directly communicate with animals. Winter's "spirit thing" was informed by science, but he didn't claim to be doing science. Winter's was a holistic amalgam not unlike Carl Sagan's blend of cosmic awe and science education.

On Winter's Earth Music, the New Age blend of art and science took the form of innovative album packaging. Winter had wanted *Common Ground* to include extensive liner notes. There are descriptions of each track on the back cover, but he wanted to include even more information about the natural history of the species featured on the record.[101] Winter convinced Jerry Moss (the "M" in A&M Records, his major label distributor) to include a text-heavy insert with the album.[102] Moss agreed but after a period of time, Winter discovered that A&M had stopped including the insert. When he inquired about this, Moss replied, "Well, those cost us a penny a piece."[103] Winter was discouraged by this penny-pinching, and he doubted whether A&M, or any other major label, would support his concept for the follow-up to *Common Ground*. "I knew that no record company would entertain the idea of producing an album about sea mammals," he said. "I didn't even ask anybody about it."[104]

Winter wanted his album about sea mammals to have extensive accompanying text and images, and that would require creating his own company. "The idea of having my own label in the sixties would have been unthinkable," he said, given that the tools of recording, manufacturing, marketing, and distribution were so firmly in the hands of the major labels. "Through the seventies things began to change," he recalled, "and artists began to take charge of different aspects of it."[105] Winter created a label called "Living Music" and rented office space next to the *Whole Earth Catalog* offices in Sausalito, California.[106] He could record in his Connecticut home studio, but the real challenge was distribution, especially since his music didn't fit neatly into existing genres. New Age was still not a recognized industry category, and the Winter Consort puzzled retailers. "They never knew where to place us," Winter said. "In record stores we'd find ourselves in the bins of folk music, or jazz, classical, and more often, nowhere." Like other visionary school musicians, Winter sought out alternative retail outlets like metaphysical bookstores and holistic health centers like Esalen and the Kripalu Yoga Center, where he gave music-making workshops.[107]

The first release on Living Music was the album *Callings* (1980).[108] A double LP with a twenty-page booklet, *Callings* is a nexus of many of the themes of this chapter: an amalgam of field recordings and New Age music, a showcase for whale recordings by Roger Payne and Paul Spong, and a multimedia blend of art and ecological science. The *Callings* booklet contains drawings of sea mammals, seashells, and Native American totem poles; quotes from poets, scientists, and environmentalists; a collection of color photos of "seal kin"; and a section of "Lifenotes" with information on the natural history and evolution of sea mammals.[109] The album thus has a similar multimedia collage aesthetic as the *Whole Earth Catalog* or Joan McIntyre's *Mind in the Waters* (1974), the latter being an influential text in the whale protection movement that aims at a holistic truth about cetaceans through overlapping accounts from science, myth, religion, and historical accounts of human-cetacean encounters.[110]

Spiritual art merges with ecological science in the form of field recordings, wildlife photography, and scientific information. The music has a similar collage aesthetic. The track "Lullaby from the Great Mother Whale" uses a humpback recording from Roger Payne, and "Sea Wolf" features the sounds of an orca pod recorded at Paul Spong's research station. "Blue's Cathedral" speeds up the sound of a blue whale to twice its normal frequency to make it audible to humans. Drenched in cosmic reverb and accompanied by a pipe organ, the song evokes the cathedral ambience that Roger Payne described from his initial encounter with humpback songs. In fact, Payne compared that experience of hearing the space of the ocean to hearing Paul Winter's saxophone in New York's Cathedral of Saint John the Divine. "Paul played his first note and the nave roared back at him, half-burying him in a deluge of echoes," Payne wrote. "It is the same with the abyss."[111] This parallelism of ocean and cathedral, the sacred and the ecological, is at the heart of Winter's next album, *Missa Gaia / Earth Mass* (1982), which was recorded in the Church of St. John the Divine in New York City, where Winter was an artist-in residence.[112]

Missa Gaia / Earth Mass was commissioned by the dean of the cathedral and written and performed by the Winter Consort, along with the cathedral organist, Paul Halley. "I wanted to create a mass that was both ecumenical and ecological, one which would embrace all the voices of the earth," Winter said.[113] The New Age approach to reverberant sonic spaces is given an environmental valence here, with the liner notes explaining that the mass celebrated a vision of "the entire Earth as a cathedral." The album continues Winter's multimedia approach, with a sixteen-page booklet containing collage-style combinations of drawing and photography, poetry by Gary Snyder, quotes from scientists James Lovelock and Lynne Margulis, and spiritual wisdom from St. Francis of Assisi, the Book of Job, and Winnebago wise sayings.

Missa Gaia / Earth Mass captures cathedral acoustics, and it also highlights the fact that the rise of the New Age movement coincided with, and was in part fueled by, a dramatic decline in attendance at traditional churches during the postwar decades. The baby boomers were perhaps the last generation to have grown up going to church en masse, and the New Age movement offered them personalized spirituality rather than traditional religion. "The 1960s moral authority for most Americans was increasingly located in the self rather than in family, church, or nation," writes scholar of religion Sarah Pike. "Secularization and personal religious seeking displaced denominational affiliation and institutional commitment."[114] As their peers were leaving churches during the 1970s, New Age musicians were heading back into them to capture a cosmic acoustic, like hermit crabs creeping into semi-abandoned stone shells. Paul Winter's long association with St. John the Divine in New York City is a case in point. Winter told an interviewer that "organized religion no longer seems to be the dominant re-linking force of our time." He thought that music could help fill the gap, especially if it could capture "nature's spirit." Music can "re-link us to nature very quickly, even when we don't get a chance to go directly to nature itself," he said. "That to me is music's value: it reconnects us to the larger world."[115]

Winter's words illustrate how New Age music's ecological concerns harmonized with its visionary, holistic, and cosmic qualities. One of the most striking tracks on *Missa Gaia / Earth Mass* links the cosmic and the ecological. "Return to Gaia" is a musical fantasy depicting a view of Earth from space that was inspired by Winter's conversations with the astronaut Rusty Schweickart, who was part of the Apollo 9 mission in 1969. The track is a sonic narrative that starts with the perspective of an astronaut looking at a tiny blue-green planet. The astronaut comes closer to the Earth, given musical embodiment by the cathedral's organ, reenters the atmosphere, and returns home with a salutation by the voice of a loon.[116] "Return to Gaia" braids science fiction, spirituality, ecological thinking, music and field recording in a distinctly New Age amalgam.

Four years later, a similar amalgam of ecological sci-fi hit movie screens worldwide. *Star Trek IV: The Voyage Home* (1986) was directed by

Leonard Nimoy from a story he had written about the crew of the *Enterprise* traveling back in time to find humpback whales, which had been driven to extinction and whose wisdom was needed to save humanity from a mysterious intergalactic probe.[117] In the film's climactic moment, the crew uncloak their starship to block the harpoons of whalers in hot pursuit of two humpbacks. This crowd-pleasing moment is a dream-logic cinematic restaging of Greenpeace's historic 1975 mission.[118]

Star Trek IV is one indication that, as we will see in the next chapter, New Age ideas were entering the mainstream by the mid-1980s. The film also shows the subterranean influence of New Age music's ecological sounds. Roger Payne had provided humpback sounds to the film's production team, and when it was released, Nimoy allowed him to premiere the film as a fundraiser for his organization, Ocean Alliance. Paul Winter participated in the event and was delighted that the film would bring whale activism to a wider public. Payne and Winter stayed up all night after the premiere, talking about ideas for new initiatives. One idea was to work together on an album that would combine whale recordings, music, and Nimoy's narration of prose and poetry about whales.

Payne and Winter flew to California to meet Nimoy and record his narration for what would become the album *Whales Alive* (1987).[119] When they arrived on the Paramount lot, Nimoy was in the far end of a bungalow where he had his office. "He came walking toward us, holding an LP cover," Winter recalled. "The first thing he did was to hand me the LP and say, 'Would you please autograph this for me?'" It was the *Common Ground* album. "That's the first place I heard the whales," Nimoy said.[120]

SIX

Now Age

IN 1987, a record store opened on Melrose Avenue in Los Angeles called Only New Age Music. True to its name, the store stocked only New Age recordings and was designed to resemble an art gallery, with lots of empty space, and LPs and cassettes hung on white walls, illuminated by tasteful track lighting. The store also carried New Age videocassettes, samples of which could be seen on an in-store television.[1] Only New Age Music was owned by the visionary school musician Suzanne Doucet, who had moved to the United States from Germany in the early 1980s and discovered that music like hers could not be found in record stores or heard on mainstream radio. She and her husband traveled by car across the country to meet with New Age musicians and distributors and then decided to open a store where people could learn about the music as well as buy it.

Only New Age Music was the site of seminars, workshops, and in-store appearances by artists. "The seminars are to educate people," Doucet told *Billboard*. "We'll do seminars for professionals, like people who do massage."[2] "All the New Age musicians came to us," she recalled. "We put the New Age music community together."[3] In addition to fostering community in her store, Doucet organized three conferences on New Age music and established the Crystal Awards to celebrate accomplishment in the field. Doucet told *Billboard* that she envisioned opening a chain of Only New Age Music stores as the market for New Age music expanded. "First there was yoga, then there were health food stores, then it was metaphysical bookstores," she said. "I think the next step is 'Only New Age Music' stores."[4]

The opening of Doucet's store, the conferences that followed, and her optimistic outlook on the future are all indications that by the mid-1980s, the wave of New Age music that had been rising for a decade was beginning to crest. 1986–87 was a period of transition for the genre when it grew beyond its initial scene to become an established category in the broader entertainment industry. New Age music's trajectory follows a pattern described by the sociologist Jennifer C. Lena, who explains that genres of popular music tend to move from a scene-based phase of development to an industry-based phase.[5] Scene-based genres are characterized by the intense activity of a cohort of artists, audience members, and small-scale supporting organizations. From 1974 to 1987, New Age music was a scene-based genre, supported by independent distributors and regional radio shows like *Music from the Hearts of Space.*[6] Scene-based genres sometimes draw the attention of large media companies that orchestrate a shift to an industry-based genre, which has the organizational structure of the multinational corporation and a set of conventions for presenting artists to a mass market.[7]

In this final chapter, we ride the crest of the wave that brought the New Age genre into the mainstream of the music industry during the mid-1980s. We will then let that wave break and roll on without us as we remain in its wake with the original cohort of visionary school musicians. How did the visionary school respond to the transition to an industry-based genre? How have they coped with subsequent shifts in the music industry? How does the music they made forty or fifty years ago speak to listeners today? Have they retained the optimistic worldview that characterized the New Age movement of the 1970s and '80s? To answer these questions, this chapter will move from the New Age to the *Now Age*, a term I borrow from several of my interviewees.[8]

Since the mid-2010s, New Age music has moved into a third phase in Lena's life cycle of musical genres. After the industry-based phase, Lena describes a traditionalist phase, when efforts are made to preserve the heritage of the original scene and communicate its history and aesthetics to a new generation.[9] If New Age music transformed to an industry-based genre around 1987, it entered its traditionalist phase around 2012, with reissues of classic recordings, a new community of collectors, fans, and writers, the formation of a canon of essential tracks on streaming service playlists, and a new appreciation by academics like myself. As we will see, a number of factors in the 2010s and '20s set the stage for a resurgence of the visionary school: music streaming platforms made previously obscure recordings more accessible; a growing interest in wellness, mindfulness, and mental health gave new life to sound therapy; and the legalization of cannabis and a rising interest in psychedelic therapy generated new demand for soundtracks to non-ordinary states of consciousness.

Musica sancta, originally created in the 1970s–80s for numinous, holistic, cosmic, and environmental purposes, could sound different when transposed to the cultural key of the Trump era. The fact that New Age music lacked lyrics and moved into hard-to-define emotional terrain has always made it politically ambiguous. Understanding New Age music as a school of visionary art, as we have done throughout this book, draws attention to its relationship to an imagined future, which provides a fresh perspective on its potential political valence. In this final chapter, I will argue that there are still treasures to be discovered in New Age sounds that are relevant to both our troubled now and our possible tomorrows. To build a bridge to those possible futures, we first return to the past, with one more visit to the Kohoutek Celebration of Consciousness in 1974. It is there that we will meet someone who, thirteen years later, would become the catalyst for an event that propelled New Age ideas into the media spotlight.

THE CREST OF THE WAVE

One of the events at the Kohoutek Celebration was a slide presentation by José Argüelles titled "Mandala." An artist and art historian, Argüelles had a PhD in art history from the University of Chicago, and during the 1970s and '80s, he taught at a number of universities, including Princeton, the University of California, Evergreen State College, and the

University of Colorado. In 1987, Argüelles published a book, *The Mayan Factor*, in which he laid out an impressionistic, sci-fi-flavored interpretation of the Mayan calendar.[10] Ideas in *The Mayan Factor* became the blueprint for the Harmonic Convergence celebration, which was held around the world on August 16–17, 1987.

According to Argüelles, those dates were the time of a galactic synchronization that was possible for the first time since the detonation of atomic weapons in the 1940s.[11] Nuclear explosions had sent a negative signal from the Earth to higher galactic intelligences, and Argüelles urged humanity to counter it with a positive signal. That would prompt the galactic intelligences to transmit a planetary vision to the "rainbow humans" who took part in events on August 16–17.[12] The Earth, Argüelles claimed, had been thrown out of its natural resonant frequency by toxic chemicals, radioactivity, and the electromagnetic frequencies of radio and television broadcasting. The Harmonic Convergence was an opportunity to get back in tune.

Argüelles's ideas about resonant frequencies are a good example of the New Age vibrational ontology described in chapter 2, and his method for fixing the imbalance resembles a planetary session of cymatic sound therapy. If the rainbow humans were successful, he predicted, extraterrestrials would come to our assistance in 2012 to dismantle governments, the military, and corporations that were polluting the environment. "The Earth will have been cleansed and purified," Argüelles said, and "we'll take our rightful place in the galactic community."[13] The purification process was to begin at planetary acupuncture points—a micro-macrocosmic alignment of planet and body—where people gathered to generate an intergalactic signal by chanting, praying, dancing, holding hands, and blowing conch shells.[14] Over the two days, five thousand people gathered at Mount Shasta, California, three thousand attended an event at Serpent Mound in Ohio, and one thousand convened at Chaco Canyon, New Mexico. There were also events held at the Great Pyramid in Egypt, Niagara Falls, Central Park in New York City, Mount Fuji in Japan, Machu Pichu in Peru, Glastonbury in England, Ayers Rock in Australia, and many other locations.[15]

The rainbow humans may or may not have communicated with higher galactic intelligences, but they certainly sent a signal to the American public via the mass media. The Harmonic Convergence received extensive press coverage and brought the fringe ideas of the New Age movement onto the front pages of major newspapers and into American living rooms on primetime television news segments. It was not José Argüelles who became the figurehead for the New Age movement however, but the Hollywood actress Shirley MacLaine. MacLaine was on the cover of *Time* magazine's December 1987 issue, which contained a feature story called "New Age Harmonies." By that time, MacLaine oversaw a New Age media empire, with books discussing reincarnation, extraterrestrials, and out-of-body experiences, a five-hour primetime ABC miniseries, *Out on a Limb* (1987), and a fifteen-city tour of a seminar called Connecting with the Higher Self.[16]

The Harmonic Convergence and MacLaine's multimedia celebrity brought the New Age movement a new level of visibility in the mainstream of American cultural life. New Age music was experiencing its own crossover moment around this same time. *Time* magazine published a story on New Age music in September 1986, and a month later, the trade journal *Billboard* announced that New Age music had "arrived as a viable commercial category."[17] Independent record labels that specialized in New Age music were seeing a surge in sales, and major record companies were jumping on the bandwagon. The most dramatic New Age success story was Windham Hill Records. Founded in 1976 by Will Ackerman, the company was named after the building company where Ackerman was a carpenter. Ackerman played solo acoustic guitar, and when friends asked him for a recording of his music, he collected five dollars each from sixty people to fund his first record, *In Search of the Turtle's Navel* (1976). Ackerman pressed a few hundred records and received some radio airplay. He then used the proceeds from sales to fund a recording by his cousin, the guitarist Alex De Grassi, who was also a worker on the construction crew.[18]

As the operation grew, Anne Robinson, then married to Ackerman, oversaw the label's distinctive visual style, with album covers featuring tasteful landscape photographs on a minimal white background.[19] The effect was to foster listener loyalty to the Windham Hill brand rather than to individual artists, a loyalty further engendered by the label's release of an annual sampler album. The Windham Hill sampler of 1981 was a surprise hit, selling a hundred thousand copies. The label's big breakthrough release, however, was the pianist George Winston's *Autumn* (1980), which was produced for under $2,000 and eventually sold more than a million copies. In industry jargon, it went platinum. Two subsequent Winston albums, *December* (1982) and *Winter into Spring* (1982), also went platinum.[20] By 1983, Windham Hill's sales had reached $8 million. That figure jumped to $30 million in 1986.[21]

Due to this success, the Windham Hill aesthetic came to epitomize New Age music for many people, but the company's approach is significantly different from the visionary school I've been describing throughout this book. For one thing, Windham Hill's sound was distinct from the *musica sancta* of the visionary school. Winston's *Autumn* features simple, gently melodic solo piano pieces, recorded with pristine audio quality. Ackerman's early albums are similar, with solo acoustic guitar performances that create the relaxed atmosphere of a front porch on a quiet evening. As a music critic for the *New Age Journal* put it in 1982, the Windham Hill sound is "contemplative . . . coloristic, slightly spiritual, and plenty sophisticated," with an emotional palette centered on "melancholy" and "good old-fashioned adult loss."[22]

The "slightly spiritual" comment is significant in comparison with the visionary school. Windham Hill's music is decidedly not numinous; it is neither drawing on nor aiming to support ecstatic, visionary experiences. A 1983 profile of George Winston reveals that he "never touches drugs" and has a certain skepticism about "woo-woo" New Age types.[23] The tracks on George Winston's *Autumn* have titles like "Moon," "Sea," "Stars," and "Woods," suggesting a nonspecific realistic setting. This is not the visionary school's terrain, where instead of a generic "Sea," we are more likely to visit a "Sea of Bliss," "Crystal Waves," or "Siren Shallows." Windham Hill also lacks the trademark studio techniques of the New Age lab-oratorium, like spacey reverb and the "contemporary ancient" blend of modular synth and traditional instruments. The Windham Hill approach to recording was not the homebrew, multitrack studio experimentation that characterizes the visionary school. Instead, the aim was to capture what Winston described as "a musician at home playing on an instrument . . . without the clutter of overdubs."[24] Ackerman described his formula as "good music, played well, recorded well without piling on overdubs; nothing fancy, just good, simple music."[25]

Windham Hill music was not using alchemy to cook up unusual sounds, nor was it harmonizing pulsating sequencers and celestial drones to align the cellular and the galactic. It was New Age music with the cosmic aperture reduced to the melancholy of here and now. We might say that Windham Hill was part of the New Age genre, but not part of the visionary school movement.[26]

The Windham Hill aesthetic of "nothing fancy" kept recording costs low, and that helped make the company highly profitable.[27] It's not a surprise that major labels took an interest, and in 1983, Windham Hill signed a distribution deal with A&M Records.[28] Over the next few years, other New Age labels followed suit, with Narada signing with MCA, Global Pacific with CBS, and Private Music with RCA.[29] The New Age genre was appealing to major labels in part because of its association with high quality audio. New Age music emphasizes the nuances of timbre and was often intended for a focused listening experience, so it makes sense that its fans were often audiophiles. A genre that attracted audiophiles was a good vehicle for pushing the new compact disc format introduced by Philips and Sony in 1982. CD players were quite expensive at first, but prices dropped throughout the decade, and CDs were outselling cassettes by 1994.[30] New Age labels were early adopters of CDs, and the genre's rising popularity aligned with the major labels' desire to get consumers to switch to the new format.[31]

Major label distribution deals were only one indication that New Age music had arrived in the mainstream music industry. There was also a Grammy Award category for Best New Age Recording created in 1987 and a *Billboard* chart introduced for tracking sales of the genre in 1988. One beneficiary of this new industry infrastructure was Paul Winter, an artist who, as we saw in the previous chapter, didn't fit easily into jazz, classical, or pop categories. Winter found a niche in New Age and was nominated for his first New Age Grammy in 1987. He ended up with six Grammy wins over the course of his career, the most of any artist in the New Age category.

Another beneficiary of this new major label interest was Kitaro, who signed a contract with Geffen Records in 1985. Kitaro played in the Japanese progressive rock band Far East Family Band and then launched a synthesizer-based solo career after working with German synth pioneer Klaus Schulze. He rose to international prominence thanks to his work on the soundtrack for the television series *The Silk Road* (1980). A coproduction by Japan Broadcasting (NHK) and China Central Television (CCTV), *The Silk Road* is a documentary that follows a Japanese film crew as they retrace the titular trade route connecting China and the West. Every episode of *The Silk Road* begins with a credit sequence backed by Kitaro's soulful and memorable synth-driven theme song. Kitaro's atmospheric music is heard throughout the series, often paired with panoramic landscapes, aerial views of ruined cities, and artifacts from archeological digs. *The Silk Road* aired the same year as *Cosmos* and was extremely successful internationally, inspiring two sequels. It established Kitaro as an international star the likes of which had not been seen before in the realm of New Age music. Eckart Rahn, founder of the New Age record company Celestial Harmonies, recalled that when German television broadcast *The Silk Road* in prime time, his company sold forty-five thousand Kitaro albums, a spectacular number for a small label with no promotion.[32] In 1987, Kitaro went on a world tour playing in huge arenas, the first time a New Age artist had accomplished such a feat. That year, *New Age Journal* called Kitaro one of New Age music's only "bona fide superstars," who was doing for New Age music "what the Beatles did for rock n' roll."[33]

New vistas opened up on radio as well.[34] Stephen Hill and Anna Turner's *Music from the Hearts of Space* moved from serving a regional scene to a national audience after the show was syndicated on National Public Radio (NPR) in 1983. On commercial radio, the watershed event for New Age music came in 1987, when the rock station KMET in Los Angeles announced that it would inaugurate a New Age music format. The station changed its name to KTWV—"the Wave"—and program director Frank Cody boasted that it was the first station to present the music in a "mass appeal fashion."[35] KTWV's New Age format was a hot topic at the National Association of Broadcasters convention in 1987, and by the end of the year, KTWV was broadcast via satellite to nine stations in major markets and had been joined by *The Breeze*, a New Age and jazz fusion syndicated show heard on twelve affiliate stations around the country.[36]

The Wave promoted a cohort of musicians like Yanni, Enya, John Tesh, and Andreas Vollenweider, who, like the Windham Hill artists, differed in sound and attitude from the visionary school. Suzanne Ciani was an exceptional case, a break-out star featured on KTWV who also had ties to the visionary school via her pioneering work on the early modular synth scene. Ciani's second album, *The Velocity of Love* (1986), was supported by KTWV, and the title track became a radio hit. "KTWV rolled with 'The Velocity of Love,'" Ciani remembered. "They sponsored my first concert in LA, and they were very instrumental in solidifying this concept of New Age."[37] As it was for Paul Winter, the New Age category was a boon for Ciani, who felt that it served a legitimate purpose, especially when it came to retail. "In those days," she recalled, record stores "didn't know where to put my stuff. They didn't know if it was vocal because I was a woman—they assumed that all women sang. They thought it might be jazz. They thought it might be classical. There was no category for it. The category of 'New Age' gave a place for new instrumental music."[38] Ciani's third album, *Neverland* (1989), was nominated for the New Age Grammy Award.

Ciani's position between the visionary scene and the industry-based model of New Age music is evident in her music videos. On the one hand, Ciani worked with visionary school denizen Ken Jenkins on the video for "The Velocity of Love," which features some of Jenkins's most ecstatic kaleidoscopic creations. On the other hand, Ciani also made videos that adhered to the standard MTV formula: glamorous shots of the artist interwoven with a narrative thread featuring actors and eye-grabbing visual effects.[39] In "Neverland" (1989), we see Ciani playing the piano, intercut with shots of a young girl building a sandcastle on the beach. The girl is transformed into a young woman and rides an animated horse to a castle in the sky where she meets a handsome prince. "Neverland" looks less like a Jordan Belson film or a Heavy Water light show than a major label, MTV-friendly music video from the mid-1980s—think A-ha's "Take On Me" (1985), which has a similar animated aesthetic. Ciani's videos were not in heavy rotation on MTV, but they did get played on VH1 (Video Hits One), a twenty-four-hour music video cable channel that launched in 1985. VH1 targeted an older demographic than MTV, and New Age music was part of its programming mandate.[40] With more than twenty million subscribers, VH1 represented a massive expansion of the potential audience for New Age audiovision since the days of planetarium shows and experiments with video synthesizers.

Cable television created new outlets for New Age audiovision, as did the market for home videocassettes, which exploded in the 1980s. Ken Jenkins's *Beauty* (1978) and the collection *California Images: Hi-Fi for the Eyes* (1985) were early forays into this market. Yoga and massage videos provided new professional opportunities for Peter Davison, who was hired by a company called Healing Arts to compose the music for their first video, *Massage for Health, Featuring Sherry Belafonte* (1987). The founder of the company, Steven Adams, was on a mission to bring yoga to the masses, and under the new name Living Arts, they pioneered the field of yoga videos, with Davison's music on the soundtrack. Living Arts helped to popularize the once-fringe practice of yoga, and its VHS tapes and DVDs were eventually sold in chain stores like Wal-Mart. Living Arts also released ten CDs of Davison's New Age music.[41]

The landscape and time-lapse cinematography of Ron Fricke, as seen in *Koyaanisqatsi* (1982) and *Chronos* (1985), was a common point of reference for New Age visual music in the era of home video.[42] Miramar Productions released a series of VHS tapes that combined nature imagery with New Age music: *Natural States* (1985) showcases the forests and mountains of the Pacific Northwest; *Desert Vision* (1987) explores the landscape of the American Southwest; and *Canyon Dreams* (1987) combines images of the Grand Canyon with music by Tangerine Dream. The photographer David Fortney produced a number of similar videos, including *Natural Light: Windance* (1987), which features New Age music by Steven Halpern, William Aura, and Richard Burmer. Windham Hill released VHS tapes and laserdiscs, like *Western Light* (1984), *Water's Path* (1984), *Autumn Portrait* (1984), and *Winter* (1985). In line with their brand, the Windham Hill videos eschew time-lapse, preferring a "nothing fancy" visual aesthetic characterized by slow motion, helicopter shots of Western landscapes and sepia-toned Americana like antique cars, prairie windmills, and cozy fireplaces. As with the label's approach to music, their audiovisual aesthetic jettisons the cosmic concerns of the visionary school.[43]

By the end of the 1980s, a radically different industry landscape could be found outside the door of the New Age lab-oratorium. The music was now supported by major record companies, distributed in chain stores across the country, acknowledged on charts and awards, and promoted on national radio, cable television, and home video. For the musicians of the visionary school, this newfound status in the industry came at a price. One result of the new level of major label backing was that it became harder for independent New Age musicians working in home studios to compete in terms of sound quality. Kat Epple of Emerald Web remembered that they felt an unmistakable shift in the New Age music scene around 1986. "That's when corporations started putting money into it," she said. The album that showed them that the bar had been risen was Enya's quadruple platinum album *Watermark* (1988), which was released in America on Geffen Records. "We just loved that album," she said, but they thought "there's *no way* we can ever afford to do that level of production." What stood out to Epple was the album's high quality reverb. "It had the best reverb," she said. "We thought, with our little home four-track, there's no way we can do that."[44] The New Age alternative production and distribution network was starting to feel outdated and amateurish by comparison.

Ideological as well as technological divides were developing. Sociologist Jennifer Lena describes how the transition from a scene-based to an industry-based genre can create a rift in the community between "old heads" and newly arrived "tourists."[45] That rift is often fueled by a dispute over the shared goals and assumptions that brought the scene together in the first place.[46] We see such a dispute over genre ideals as the discourse around New Age music moved from spiritual growth and mind-body health to marketing and demographics. Program director Frank Cody said that KTWV/the Wave had identified "an untapped market of the best educated and most affluent baby boomers."[47] A music distributor told the *Chicago Tribune* that New Age music was bringing people in their mid-30s, who didn't relate to current pop music, back to record stores.[48] The *New York Times* rock critic Jon Pareles cited marketing reports on the genre's popularity with "UltraConsumers," who were said to seek "self-validation by buying products and services that telegraph who they are and what they want to be."[49] The association with aging baby boomers was cemented with popular press articles about New Age music bearing titles like "New Age Music Wins Wider Following as Many People Grow Too Old for Rock" and "Mellowing Out with New Age Music."[50] The *Time* magazine article on New Age music stated that it was "the perfect music for washing one's BMW."[51]

Press coverage like this, which associated the music with rich yuppies and narcissistic consumption did much to sour New Age music in the minds of critics. Decades later, critics still made sweeping generalizations about the genre based on this brief period in its history. In the book *The Ambient Century* (2000), the music writer Mark Pendergast asserts that New Age music emerged in the mid-1980s and became known as "hot tub music" because it was "so bland that it was only good for playing as background Muzak in the bath." He connects New Age music to the "greedy '80s" and claims that it was aimed primarily at "overheated executives who needed to unwind after a Wall Street–style day at the office. Most of it was emotionally shallow," he writes. "Pitching through cover design and title at a quasi-mysticism that was ephemeral at best."[52] As we've seen, New Age music is a product of the spiritual '70s, not the greedy '80s, and the best of it was not emotionally shallow; quite the opposite. In fact, it had an expansive emotional palette that included numinous emotions rarely explored in genres of popular music. Like many other critics, Pendergast mistakes the discourse surrounding New Age music's crossover moment for the genre as a whole.[53]

Some of the harshest critics of the industry-based version of New Age music were the visionary school cohort themselves, who were concerned that the genre they had created was drifting out of their control. Suzanne Doucet wrote a commentary for *Billboard* in 1988 in which she argued that the newfound popularity of New Age music had created a paradox. The music's original purpose was "to slow down the listener, to relax, balance, and heal." New Age music was meant to evoke "intuition, imagination, and altered states of consciousness" and so was opposed to the rigidly analytical mindset of success-oriented businesses like the music industry. When New Age music became part of that industry, Doucet wrote, it became subject to "the disease it was trying to heal."[54] Doucet distinguished between the genre's originators, who thought in terms of the music's healing and visionary qualities, and the industry newcomers who were mostly concerned with making it accessible to the greatest number of people. Doucet ends her commentary by doubling down on the genre's visionary ideals, making a reference to the archetypal visionary artist, William Blake. The full appreciation of New Age music, she writes, requires "opening up one's inner doors of perception."[55]

The growing rift between visionary originators and industry newcomers became clear over the course of the three conferences on New Age music organized by Doucet. At the first conference, in 1989, John Sebastian, the program director of KTWV/the Wave, gave a keynote address and claimed to be a true believer, saying he viewed the music as more of a cause or a mission than "simply a radio format." His aim, he said, was to strike a balance between the music as a "pragmatic business concept" and as "something that can change the world."[56] By the third conference, that balance was faltering and a rift was becoming apparent. An executive at Narada Records said the company was working diligently to make New Age a mainstream music and wanted to get "as far away from the culture surrounding it" as possible. "We've worked hard at dismissing the crystal factor," he said.[57] Even Stephen Hill from *Music from the Hearts of Space* was stepping back from the New Age moniker. "We never billboarded the program as a New Age program but a space music program," he said. "I'm not comfortable being identified with many of the attributes of the New Age lifestyle. It's just music. It doesn't need to be burdened with those complex associations."[58]

Such were the tensions as New Age music moved from a scene-based to an industry-based genre in the late 1980s. For the "old heads," it was not so easy to strip the music away from the lifestyle; to take the *musica sancta* out of the lab-oratorium. Despite these inevitable growing pains, New Age music from 1973 to 1987 presents a dramatic music industry success story. From the Kohoutek Celebration of Consciousness to the Harmonic Convergence, the horizons of the music's circulation expanded while it maintained a set of ideals that resonated with a generational cohort of listeners and seekers. That association with a generation—the much maligned baby boomers—made the genre impossibly unhip in the Gen-X 1990s, but in hindsight, the rejection of the music industry's modus operandi of targeting a youth market was perhaps the most radical aspect of its crossover success. Where most pop music has a Freudian orientation to childhood and adolescence, New Age music has a Jungian orientation to ongoing spiritual growth at midlife and beyond. It is visionary art for mature listeners. A genre of music that succeeds in the youth-oriented industry landscape by addressing the spiritual concerns of middle-age, mind-body health, and cosmic wonder is a rare thing indeed.

The stars had aligned for New Age music in 1987, as José Argüelles was spreading the word about the Harmonic Convergence. In Argüelles's thinking, 1987 was just an overture, and the cosmic curtain would rise in 2012, when the rainbow humans would make direct contact with intergalactic higher intelligences and usher in the New Age. Argüelles's timeframe is surprisingly useful when it comes to New Age music. Higher galactic intelligences did not arrive in America in 2012, but a "celestial jukebox" did: Spotify was launched in the United States in 2011. That same year the media producer Douglas Mcgowan—who became a driving force in rebooting the genre—gave his first public talk about New Age music. In 2012, Colorado and Washington become the first two states to legalize cannabis for recreational use. A new era was dawning for New Age music, and one visionary school musician who felt the warmth of that new dawn was Don Slepian.

NEW DAWN

Don Slepian's recording of "Sea of Bliss" nicely encapsulates some of the changes I've been describing between the 1980s and the 2010s. Slepian was born in 1953 and grew up in Summit, New Jersey. His father was a mathematician at Bell Laboratories, and as a child, Slepian developed an interest in electronics, delighting in disassembling old radios and television sets. His passion for electronics expanded to include music after his father brought home an LP called *Music for Mathematics*, which contained early computer music made by his colleagues at Bell Labs. "I wore that record flat," Slepian remembered. Soon thereafter he built a homebrew synthesizer out of slot-car motors for a third-grade science project. By the time he was fifteen years old, his path toward electronic music was solidifying, and he found inspiration in Wendy Carlos's album *Switched on Bach*.[59]

Slepian got his first modular synthesizer, an ARP 2500, in 1971. After graduating from college, he spent a year in Los Angeles, where he worked as a laser projectionist, and then returned to the East Coast, where he landed a position as an artist in residence at Bell Labs. His job at Bell Labs was to explore the musical possibilities of an early digital synthesizer created by Hal Alles known as the "Alles machine."[60] While a few other musicians, like Larry Fast and Laurie Spiegel, spent an hour or two with the Alles synth, Slepian worked with it every day for two years. "I'm the only musician who really got to know it," he said.[61]

Slepian composed and recorded six pieces of music with the Alles machine. One of them, "Sea of Bliss," is now a landmark of New Age

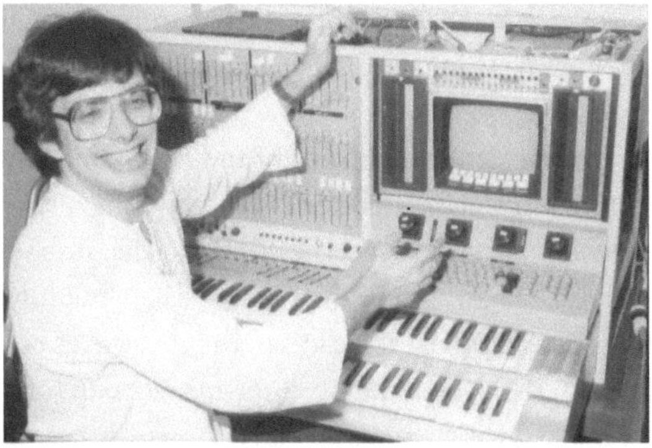

Don Slepian and the early digital synthesizer known as the "Alles machine." Photo by Chris Kluge.

music. This twenty-nine-minute track rises and falls like a slow-motion seascape, with spiraling, misty arpeggios, crystalline sustained tones, and intermittent melodic patterns that gently move the listener from one tonal center to another. All these elements are bathed in the Alles machine's unique digital reverb. "If you buy a modern digital reverb," Slepian explains, "it's silky smooth and perfect." By contrast, the reverb on the Alles machine was "crunchy and zingy and had all sorts of flaws. It made a unique ambient environment." The machine's software enabled Slepian to create ever-changing arpeggio patterns triggered by multiple clocks running at close to, but not exactly, the same rate. The effect of musical patterns coming in and out of sync with each other, he explained, is what gives the music a "feeling of timelessness."[62]

Created in March 1980, "Sea of Bliss" was on the cusp of a new digital era in the production of music. The *distribution* of music, however, was still in the analog era, and "Sea of Bliss" was released as a cassette tape with a hand painted cover. "Sea of Bliss" did not make waves when it was first released. "I didn't get any money," Slepian recalled. "No feedback. Nothing. Zero." The track got some attention a few years later when it was used on *Music from the Hearts of Space* as the background to Hill and Turner's spoken announcements.[63] It was forty years after its release, Slepian said, that he really started to get some feedback on "Sea of Bliss." For one thing, Slepian began to see a rise in his streaming activity on Spotify.

Online streaming services like Spotify and Apple Music have played a significant role in resurfacing recordings of the visionary school. Though streaming provides very little income to musicians, it makes available cassette-only releases like "Sea of Bliss" that were previously difficult to find. Streaming sites have the capacity to stock New Age tracks that are longer in duration than the standard three-minute pop song and would have caused problems for previous formats. Moreover, the calming sense of timelessness created by "Sea of Bliss"—and advertised by the track's title—fits nicely with Spotify's decision, around 2013, to organize music into playlists based on mood.[64]

The fact that much of New Age music was released only on cassette once made it seem outdated and amateurish, but there was a revival of interest in cassettes in the 2010s, spurred by the rise of independent, cassette-only labels and the prominent role of a mixtape in promoting the film *Guardians of the Galaxy* (2014).[65] The materiality of cassettes is now part of the appeal of the New Age genre for some collectors, as indicated by the YouTube channel Sounds of the Dawn, where audio of New Age recordings is paired with their original cassette art.[66] Predigital modular synthesizers have also enjoyed a resurgence of interest since the early 2000s, fueled in part by the popularity of Dieter Doepfer's Eurorack hardware. Modular synth enthusiasts have rediscovered visionary school records as some of the earliest explorations of that predigital audio technology.[67]

YouTube channels like Sounds of the Dawn and streaming service playlists like Apple Music's New Age Essentials have established a canon of classic New Age music, a good indication that we have entered the traditionalist phase of a genre, when a scene's musical heritage is codified and preserved. The most prominent curator of New Age music in the 2010s was Douglas Mcgowan, who oversaw the seminal compilations *I Am the Center* (2013) and *The Microcosm* (2016). Mcgowan's label, Yoga Records, has reissued albums by New Age artists like Joel Andrews,

Alice Damon, and Smith & Erickson. Mcgowan also worked closely with the Numero Group label, which released a beautiful reissue of Don Slepian's *Sea of Bliss* in 2019, as well as reissues by Laraaji, Joanna Brouk, and Master Wilburn Burchette. Recordings by Emerald Web have been reissued by the label Finders Keepers, which also released early work by Suzanne Ciani.

Developments in the music industry during the 2000s and 2010s aided in the rediscovery and appreciation of visionary school recordings, and a number of developments in the broader cultural landscape made them timely and appealing. Browsing the playlists on Apple Music, one finds many playlists under the category of "well-being"; there are playlists for sound therapy, guided meditations, natural sounds, sound baths, healing voices, and sleep meditations. These curated playlists reflect the rise in the mindfulness industry during the past several decades, spurred in part by the COVID lockdown and a mental health crisis. According to one national survey, the percentage of American adults who practiced meditation more than doubled between 2002 and 2022, greatly increasing the number of people who might use audio as a mindfulness tool.[68]

The exploding market for guided meditation apps is a clear indication that meditation has gone mainstream. The leading company in this category is Headspace, founded in 2010. Another app, Calm, won the 2017 iPhone App of the Year Award from Apple's App Store. In 2018, an article in the *Wall Street Journal* explained that the rise in meditation apps was driven by business owners who were "eager to help employees tap into their higher consciousness in the hopes that it will improve productivity and reduce stress-related health-care costs." The resulting boom in corporate mindfulness trainings was said to be fueling a "digital bonanza."[69] The founder of Calm, Michael Acton Smith, perhaps hoping to woo the corporate market, distanced his company from associations with the spiritual seekers of the 1970s. Acton Smith said that the "light bulb" moment for the company was the realization that meditation "wasn't about incense or counterculture or religion. It was neuroscience, a way to rewire the human brain."[70] In a pattern similar to the marketing of New Age music in the late 1980s, the goal was to strip away the countercultural lifestyle—remove the "crystal factor"—and sell the commodity that remained. Despite this streamlining, meditation apps created an opening in the digital marketplace for New Age musicians. The visionary school artist Aeoliah has close to eight thousand followers on the meditation app Insight Timer, and the app has become an important part of his current career.[71]

Options for healing meditations can be found on apps like Calm and Headspace, and sound healing has had a resurgence in recent years. Laraaji has been very active in the 2010s and '20s, not only releasing and performing music but offering a variation on the sound healing theme in the form of workshops on laughter meditation. Laraaji's laughter sessions work much like a body-scan chakra meditation, with participants visualizing their laughter moving into the head, throat, chest, and abdomen.[72] Laraaji's laughter therapy recalls the New Age audile technique, although rather than listening with the whole body, one is laughing with the whole body.

Many of the options on well-being playlists and meditation apps have to do with sleep, an area of growing concern in the era of overwork, mobile phone distraction, caffeine addiction, and political insecurity. One of the first declarations of a sleep crisis and its health implications was Arianna Huffington's bestselling book *The Sleep Revolution* (2016).[73] New Age music works well as a soothing backdrop to sleep, which has opened another niche in the digital landscape. New Age musicians were always interested in sleep, not in terms of a health crisis, but in the context of the study of states of consciousness. Visionary artists have long been drawn to dreaming as well as the twilight states between wakefulness and sleep.[74] The visionary school musician most associated with sleep research is Robert Rich, who was born in 1963 in the San Francisco Bay area. Like Don Slepian, Rich developed an early interest in electronics, and around 1978, he built his first synthesizer kit. Drawn to drone music, he began recording his own compositions and selling cassettes at a local New Age bookstore.[75]

In high school, he became interested in the research being done on sleep and dreaming by Stephen LaBerge at Stanford University.[76] Rich went to Stanford and got a degree in psychology, studying with LaBerge. He combined his interests in sleep science and electronic music when he put on his first "sleep concert" in a dormitory at Stanford in 1982.[77] Rich's sleep concerts were eight-hour events during which the audience was encouraged to fall asleep. Rich had been trying to figure out a way to perform his long-form, atmospheric music for an audience. "How do you get people to experience something for seven or ten hours, while encouraging them to journey inside themselves?" he wondered. Rich realized that encouraging the audience to fall asleep would be just the way to gently usher them into altered states of consciousness.[78] His sleep concerts, performed throughout the 1980s and '90s, enact the New Age aspiration to combine art and sleep science in a manner that is still relevant today.

In the 1980s, Rich's sleep concerts offered a legal alternative to other means of achieving altered states of consciousness. By the 2000s, psychedelic states of mind were becoming more legally available. Medical marijuana was first legalized in California in 1996, and recreational legalization began in 2012. The use of hallucinogenic drugs in therapeutic contexts gained new momentum at this time as well. Michael Pollan's popular book *How to Change Your Mind*, which describes the history and resurgence of psychedelic therapy, was published in 2018 and turned into a Netflix documentary series in 2022. Pollan's book was one of the *New York Times Book Review*'s best of 2018, and the Netflix series describes the use of psychedelics like LSD, MDMA, and psilocybin in therapeutic contexts.

Steven Halpern, still releasing music two decades into the twenty-first century, has always been quick to identify emerging trends and incorporate them into the marketing of his music. His most recent releases are a barometer of cultural changes with regards to psychoactive drugs. His album *Cannabis Dreams* (2021) was the result of his work as a brand ambassador for the Natural Cannabis Company. "I smoked the sample they gave me every time I recorded tracks for the album, and had a marvelous time," he said.[79] In 2023, Halpern released *Psychedelic Therapy Music* (2023), which he hoped to promote at the

Multidisciplinary Association for Psychedelic Studies (MAPS) conference, a nice bookend to his presence at the Kohoutek Celebration of Consciousness fifty years earlier.[80] His most recent album is *Music for Microdosing* (2025), which features a blurb by James Fadiman, one of the founders of transpersonal psychology who had been a speaker at the Kohoutek Celebration of Consciousness and held the Transpersonal Frontiers conference in 1977. Fadiman is one of the main proponents of microdosing, which involves taking very small doses of psychedelic substances like LSD or psilocybin to obtain health and wellness benefits such as improved creativity, greater physical energy, emotional balance, increased problem-solving ability, and the treatment of depression, anxiety, and addiction.[81]

Fadiman begins his book on microdosing by distancing himself from a more ecstatic and visionary psychedelic experience. Recounting his own introduction to psychedelics in 1961, which he described as "a belief-shattering awakening," Fadiman makes clear that his book is not about such "astounding, amazing, fantastic trips. It is, instead," he writes, about how people have improved their health and their capacities "without the razzle-dazzle, heaven-opening, reality-expanding experiences that made the sixties such an optimistic, culture-changing decade."[82] Fadiman likely realized that, as with the corporate uses of meditation apps, some his most avid readers were likely to be Silicon Valley professionals; an early article on microdosing in *Rolling Stone* had the headline "Hot Business Trip."[83]

We can see, then, that when Don Slepian saw an uptick on his Spotify streaming numbers in the 2010s, it was the sign of a broader resurgence of interest in the visionary school. New Age music like Slepian's had become available on music streaming services and reissue LPs, but it had also gained historical cachet in relation to cassette culture and analog synths and was newly relevant in its conjunction with sound therapy, mindfulness, sleep aids, and psychedelics. It was a new dawn for New Age sounds, though they were often stripped of their original esoteric context. A question could arise then, about New Age music's politics, but that had always been a question.

To the extent that it became part of corporate mindfulness trainings and attempts to maximize productivity, New Age music in its twenty-first-century manifestation could be critiqued as a Band-Aid on a capitalist nightmare. The musicologist Victor Szabo has written eloquently about how holistic living and relaxed awareness don't challenge the underlying tenets of "exploitative capitalism and neocolonial globalism" and arguably divert attention away from the political and interpersonal dimension of social problems.[84] A pithier expression of the same critique can be found in a first-person account of the Kohoutek Celebration of Consciousness in 1974. The author recounted a moment when a Black man interrupted a panel discussion to assert that the speakers were "full of cosmic crap" and asked what any of this high-flying talk had to do with the plight of Black people.[85] This is obviously a valid complaint, and we might say that while New Age thinking is adept at the cosmic alignment of micro and macro, it has the regretful tendency to neglect or evade the meso or middle level of the social world where political action takes place. Moreover, since the 1980s there has been a growing awareness of and sensibility to dynamics of cultural appropriation and "orientalism," and the New Age movement has been the target of valid critique in that regard.[86]

The political valence of the New Age movement has always been ambiguous. The *Time* magazine cover story from 1987 noted the uncertain politics of the movement. "Is it some kind of neoleftist response to the Age of Reagan, or is it an ultrarightist extension of Reaganism?" the author wondered. "While some see in the New Agers' chants and nebulous slogans a revival of the shaggy '60s, others see the devotion of many New Agers to moneymaking as simply a new variant of yuppieism."[87] Then and now, health and wellness are politically slippery, and in recent years a concern about healthy food and environmental pollutants has shifted from the political left to the right as part of the Make America Healthy Again movement, which takes aim at pesticides and chemical additives in the food system and questions established medical advice about treating disease.

The sociologist Colin Campbell, writing about the emerging New Age movement in 1972, observed that it had rejected organized religion in favor of a more individualistic and experiential pursuit of the divine. On the one hand, this made the movement quite tolerant, as there was no central organization to dictate a set of beliefs or practices. At New Age fairs, wildly different paradigms and worldviews could be placed side by side. On the other hand, with spiritual orientation left up to the individual seeker, and lacking a shared set of agreed-upon facts, the door was open to "post-truth" conspiratorial thinking.[88] Iasos certainly fell prey to such thinking, and talked in interviews about secret space programs, hollow Earth theories, and super-advanced alien technologies that he was confident would soon be made available.[89]

It's easy to see how New Agers of this generation could fall prey to the culture of conspiracy theories, resulting in a phenomenon that has been called "conspirituality," a merging of New Age holism and conspiracy theory.[90] Ken Jenkins's study of JFK assassination conspiracy theories was the means by which he became politically active in the 2000s. Jenkins grew up in an apolitical household in Palo Alto but felt a shift in his politics during the Vietnam war. He went to a few protests in college, though his main focus was on his artwork.[91] "What could I do?" he wondered. "Where could I make any kind of a difference?" His anti-war political outlook and artistic aspirations converged in a peace-oriented science fiction film he hoped to produce.[92]

After the film project failed to materialize, he began to study the JFK assassination. "Obviously it was a huge conspiracy," he asserted, and "the fact that it was covered up bothered me."[93] His studies expanded to the RFK and MLK assassinations, but it was the 9/11 attacks that tipped the scale. When he first saw TV coverage of the World Trade Center, his reaction was, "I hated it. I just hated it. It felt like a monumental setback for the New Age vision. This is going to put us back decades."[94] Jenkins came to believe that 9/11 was allowed to happen as an excuse to start the Iraq War, and he became involved with a group of like-minded people in the Northern California 9/11 Truth Alliance. As part of this community, he felt that he could apply his media skills to the issue, and he worked for twenty years on their annual film festival.[95]

The tragedy of 9/11 clearly poses a challenge to the optimistic anticipation of a dawning New Age of peace and enlightenment. It was not the only source of cognitive dissonance for the visionary school generation. Perhaps the first glitch in the New Age narrative came on January 28, 1986, when the space shuttle *Challenger* exploded, killing a crew that included the first "teacher in space," Christa McAuliffe. Don Davis, the space artist who was part of the *Cosmos* team, wrote that the dream of "widespread access to space ended that day for a generation."[96] The *Challenger* explosion forever dented the chrome-tinted, airbrushed futurism of space art and space music; 9/11, the Iraq Wars, and COVID have continued the turbulence.

The harpist Georgia Kelly also became more politically oriented in the first decade of the twenty-first century. In 1988, just as the New Age music scene she helped to create was having its crossover moment, she discovered that she had relatives in the former Yugoslavia and went to visit them. She returned to Yugoslavia several times, but her visits were interrupted in 1991 with the outbreak of civil war. "I was leaving the US from the first Gulf War," she said, "and I thought, 'Oh, I'm so glad to be getting away from all the war talk.' Then I get there, and there's war again, and I thought, 'There's just no escaping this.'" She began to wonder, "Why do we do this over and over and over again?"[97] To address that question, Kelly applied the same do-it-yourself initiative that had fueled her independent distribution of albums in the 1970s, and she put together a seven-day conference in Dubrovnik, Croatia. The conference went so well that she decided to continue the initiative and created a nonprofit organization, Praxis Peace Institute in 2000, which continues, twenty-five years later, with the mission to manifest peace, social and economic justice, environmental sustainability, and civic participation.[98]

Comparing herself to many of her New Age music cohorts, Kelly noted that she had been active in the peace movement since the Vietnam war. "I was always political," she said.

I started learning about politics very early and got involved very early. A lot of the people I met in the New Age movement weren't politically sophisticated at all. They had ideas and opinions, but they didn't know history, they didn't know politics. They weren't studying it. They weren't interested in it. There are certainly exceptions, but I've seen a lot of the New Age movement go to this anti-vaxxer place. . . . That's wacky, in my mind."[99]

"There's a lot of optimism in the New Age movement," she observed, and "some of it is purely wishful thinking. It's not, 'How do we get from here to there?' It's, 'Oh, it's gonna be fine!' To me, that's BS. It doesn't just happen. We're on a default mode that doesn't get us to a better place. . . . . To get out of that isn't going to take just believing and hoping and meditating. It's going to take action."[100]

I'm extremely sympathetic to Kelly's comments, but they make me wonder: What counts as taking action? Can making relaxing instrumental music count? In his study of Japanese ambient music, the media scholar Paul Roquet argues that critiques of ambient media tend to imply that "an ethical choice must be made between a strong, active, socially and historically aware subjectivity and a passive, therapeutic, mood-regulating one." Roquet asserts that there is a danger here of "reducing complex social and emotional contexts to a simple divide between 'active' and 'passive' social positions, denouncing comfort and presenting discomfort as a corrective in and of itself." Critiques of comforting, healing music can discount the real needs of listeners in maintaining health and resilience in a chaotic world, and risks "falling into a vapid nostalgia for a less 'emotionally sensitive' time," as in the more explicit political commitments of 1960s radicalism.[101]

Consider the case of Peter Davison, whose father was a card-carrying communist and the chief administrator of the People's Educational Center in Hollywood in the 1930s, a gathering place for progressive Hollywood radicals. When Peter was four years old, his parents were called before the House Un-American Activities Committee (HUAC) and as a result lost their livelihood. His father opened a laundromat, and the family moved to the Jewish Bush Belt of Los Angeles, where they were under FBI surveillance. Davison remembers being with his mother when he was eight years old and running into the actor Edward G. Robinson on an elevator. Robinson had cooperated with HUAC, and when he smiled and said, "Oh, what a nice boy," his mother slapped the actor in the face.[102] With this upbringing, Davison grew up oscillating between an optimistic and pessimistic outlook and often found his family's beliefs out of step with peers and teachers.

Davison said that he was "attempting optimism" when he looked at the world in 2025 but that it was "the worst I've ever seen it. I had no idea that the United States would become a fascist nation." When Donald Trump ran for president in 2016, Davison wrote a long rant to a friend in which he declared that from now on, all his music was going to be "really smooth New Age music that's beautiful and uplifting and enlightening," but "what I am saying while I'm working on it is, 'FUCK YOU TRUMP!'"[103] Davison's quote adds a new wrinkle to New Age ideas about intention, and it complicates overly simple dichotomies between quiet, comforting, seemingly apolitical artworks and loud, explicit, political engagement.[104]

Regardless of their intentions, in the streaming era, the visionary school's music is not curated and contextualized by the managers at wellness centers and metaphysical bookstores but by online platforms that tend to organize music by mood. The music writer Liz Pelly argues that functional music, which has become the "defining phenomenon of the streaming era," sells listeners on the empty promise that they can control their moods. Moreover, the range of emotions curated by streaming services like Spotify tends to be reduced to "the maximization of positively charged emotions."[105] As we have seen, it is a misconception that New Age music presents only a monochromatic emotional palette of happy and peaceful emotions, and even when the focus was on positive emotions, they were framed in a way that was very different from "lo-fi beats to study to." Consider that Iasos talked about how his music aimed to depict new, *emergent* emotions. Emotions, he said, "repeat at higher octaves," and positive emotions extend to infinity: "Gladness an octave higher is happiness, an octave higher joy, then ecstasy, then rapture. It just keeps going," he said, though we have no words for these "higher octave emotions, since they are realms where humans seldom tread."[106]

Iasos's higher octave emotions elude easy classification in the "chill" music categories of the streaming era and show instead the visionary school's unflagging optimism. Don Slepian sees "great potential in all manner of awakenings, both political, sociological, technological, and cultural." Though the world is more dangerous, he sees positive signs in a political resistance movement that utilizes theater, dance, and poetry. "I'm seeing ordinary people step up because the present day demands it," he said. "I think it's really important for us to stay sane as a society. We must find truth within each of us, and for me truth is an enduring optimism."[107] When I asked Suzanne Doucet if she was still optimistic, she replied, "Why should I not have optimism? There are always things happening that you don't expect, sometimes positive, sometimes negative. I'm just open to every possibility, and I think that's the most important thing, that you stay open. Don't close yourself off to any possibility of change or what *can* happen."[108]

This, perhaps, is how New Age music, when understood as visionary art, offers its surest contribution to the meso- level of social and political life. Visionary art is strongly orientated toward the future, to what *can* happen. Recall that the title of this book is taken from an essay on visionary art by Carl Jung, who described it as a bridge to an unseen shore. It is also a bridge to an unknown future, a "vision of other worlds."[109] For visionary artist Ernst Fuchs, the function of art in society is "giving, by means of utopianism and visionary perspective, those impulses and ideas which are not typical of the world we live in but which may be typical in the future."[110] Visionary art taps into numinous experiences and nonordinary states, and in the process, it represents how the world *could be otherwise*, blurring tangible and imaginary worlds to suggest that we might have the best of both.

Whatever else it was, the New Age movement was a vehicle for hope. New Age music, like other embodiments of visionary art, explores the art and politics of the future. It is an incubator or alchemical retort for vital new mixtures and energies, rarely the end of the story in terms of social and political life but often the fertile start, the spark of a new life. It is important to assess New Age music in terms of politics, but too much of a critical emphasis on the meso-level seems a little unfair. New Age, after all, was primarily a spiritual movement, not a political one. As we saw in the last chapter, the rise of the New Age movement coincided with a decline in church attendance, but that trend has recently reversed, and there has been much discussion of a revival of interest in organized religion in the past few years.[111] New Age music has maintained a special relationship to sacred spaces and church architecture, with musicians performing in cathedrals and churches or simulating their acoustics with cosmic reverb.

In August 2024, I saw Steve Roach perform at the Epiphany Center for the Arts in Chicago. Roach was celebrating the fortieth anniversary of his landmark *Structures from Silence* album, and he sold out the venue, a refurbished church built in 1885, with tall arched ceilings and rows of stained-glass windows. Roach has been performing in churches and cathedrals since the 2000s, working with the immersive event series Age of Reflections since 2023.[112] Roach explained that sacred spaces are the perfect container for the kind of music he has been creating for forty years and that his recent church concerts allow for a sense of spiritual integration with a community and space.[113] Other visionary school artists like Laraaji, Suzanne Ciani, and Robert Rich have also been on the church concert circuit.[114]

At his Age of Reflections show in the Chicago Epiphany Center, Roach carefully crafted his music to fit the acoustics of the space, and the accompanying visual projections, by the artist Eric Epstein, brought the space to life by tracing wall panels, illuminating stained glass windows with ghostly radiance and making the walls and ceiling shimmer and pulse with prismatic and ever-evolving lighting effects. The show was a sublime continuation of the tradition of using sound, light, and sacred architecture as a vehicle of numinous and enveloping experience. The climax of the concert was when Roach moved from behind his rack of synths and sequencers to take a seat at the front of the stage. It was there that he played the iconic title track to *Structures from Silence* on his Oberheim synth. The airy chords of the piece rose up from silence and gently fell back into it, moving at the pace of slow, deep, relaxed breathing. Roach talks about the sublime sensation of playing "Structures" live, feeling everyone in the church venue breathing together. "That's the beautiful part of playing 'Structures' live," he said. "We're on the same breath wave."[115] Less like linear melodies and more like three dimensional living entities, the Oberheim chords expanded to fill the church and surrounded us all, Roach included. I felt a profound sense of embodied communion, with the space, the sound, the light, and the listening community immersed in it all.

In the still point on the crest of that breath wave, the various points on the timeline of this chapter—and of this book—collapse into each other: an album of the visionary school released in 1984, reissued and celebrated during the revival of the 2010s, alive and relevant in the present moment and offering tantalizing whispers of a possible future. This is not just *Now Age*, it is—to borrow a term Roach uses to describe the feeling of creating music—*Front Side of Now Age*, a focused awareness of the present moment so intense that it leans forward into a blossoming future.[116] Like his visionary school cohorts, Roach has created visionary artworks that are bridges thrown out towards an unseen shore, an unknown future, and perhaps—most difficult of all to imagine—toward a less fractured, fragmented, and divided world.

CODA: THE BRIDGE

"Would you like to have your own Spirit Guides communicate to you personally through sound and music?" This is how Kevin Braheny Fortune advertises a "music channeling" service on his website.[117] For a fee, Braheny Fortune will channel your spirit guides and under their guidance produce a personalized musical track that conveys their message. I was intrigued by this possibility, but I was hesitant to take the step. Over the course of writing this book, I had been walking a razor's edge between what Gregory Bateson called the Scylla of scientific materialism and the Charybdis of romantic supernaturalism. Would exploring music channeling be crossing a line? Had I completely lost my scientific objectivity and fallen under the sway of the supernatural?

After much back and forth, I decided to hire Kevin to undertake a session of music channeling. I have to admit that I was motivated as a fanboy as well as a scholar, excited to get a personalized synth composition by an artist I admired. There was a conceptual component to my motivation as well, since I was inspired by Carl Jung's introduction to the Chinese divination book the *I Ching*. Jung applied the *I Ching*'s system of divination to consult the book about its own situation of being presented to Western readers and then included its divinatory response in his essay.[118] I decided to take part in that most characteristic of New Age practices—channeling—and ask New Age music about my intention to present it to new listeners.[119]

Kevin Braheny Fortune, the Continuum composer and creator of the Mighty Serge, is perhaps the world's only practitioner of music channeling.[120] Here's how the process worked. I sent Kevin a brief written statement about the topic I wanted to address in the session. Kevin is a multi-instrumentalist, so I also had to specify the instruments I wanted to be used. As a modular synth buff, I asked that he use only the Mighty Serge in his channeled composition. Kevin told me that he would tune in to me and open himself to whatever my spirit guides wanted to share. That information would be communicated through a musical composition that was created in a way that epitomizes New Age ideas about the author as medium. "I don't know how long the piece will be or what musical form it will take," Kevin said. "I will not know what it means, but I trust that the message your guides have for you will be encoded in the sounds. As I'm just dropping off into trance, I hit record, and then I go someplace. I wake up and I hit save."[121]

In my written statement, I wrote that I wanted to gain insight into the creative energies that fostered the visionary school of New Age music in the 1970s and '80 and how those visionary impulses related to the present. Kevin suggested that the best way to receive the spiritual message was through the New Age listening technique we've encountered throughout this book. The spirit guides would be interacting with me "on a cellular level," he explained. "When you experience the sounds by deep listening—being present without analyzing, and by noticing how you feel—you will receive the most benefit."[122] This experiment would clearly test my ability to listen with my whole body.

I waited eagerly for the audio message to arrive, and when it did, I listened to it wearing headphones in the dark. Fourteen minutes later the track was over and I was wiping the tears from my eyes. The track begins with a repeating musical tone with an abrupt attack and long fade, suggesting a gentle but abrupt reawakening, or return to life. Long synth tones enter, expanding the sonic horizon, and then slow cascading melody lines float past, like clouds reflected in a still lake. I felt myself enter the full body listening attitude as my breathing fell into sync with the slow, meditative pulse of the track. From this calm, misty atmosphere, an extremely high and plaintive melody enters with a delicate beauty, its warm tone suggesting a morning sun and a dawning of optimism and new possibility. A sonic constellation begins to take shape around this solar melody, with richer, heavier tones orbiting around the listener.

Now the sense of forward movement heard on other Continuum recordings kicks into gear, as I feel the track gaining momentum and moving me into a larger-than-human space and perspective. Five and a half minutes into the piece, a sparkling cloud of sound moves from right to left with the bristling energy of a comet passing across the viewscreen of a space liner. Something has changed through the encounter with this sonic entity, as though we have now moved out of Earth's atmosphere into a broader cosmic ocean. There is now a sense of distance from the track's initial warm glow, as colder ambiences surround us. A feeling of doubt and hesitation arises. Have we frozen in place? Has the journey come to an end?

At the eight-minute mark, the crystalline cloud returns, moving from left to right this time and signaling another transition, perhaps a return to Gaia or a continuation of movement that takes us to an entirely different planet or reality. There is another plateau here, another period of uncertainty, as we linger in clouds of reverb. Is our momentum dissipating? Uncertainty vaporizes at the ten-minute mark, when a sublime deep bass tone enters with a visceral sense of mass that shifts our perceived movement from the horizontal to the vertical plane. There is no denying now that I am listening with my whole body, not just my ear, and that this is a physical and emotional, as well as a mental experience. The visceral power of the bass frequencies is almost overwhelming: listening with your entire body can be frightening.

The emotional valence shifts as the bass tone begins to climb slowly upward, a movement that brings an exhilarating sense of gradual but persistent growth. I feel a wave of gratitude for being shown something sublime, like an encounter with a locomotive-sized whale in a small boat. The high solar melody returns, now given new meaning since it is paired with the bass line, which rises, falls, and rises again, suggesting a resilient determination. The track ends as the high and low frequencies of this widescreen conclusion fade away, leaving only the looping tone that began our sonic journey.

The fanboy in me was overjoyed. Here was a brand-new work in the Continuum style, which Kevin named "The Bridge" and can be heard on his Bandcamp page.[123] The historian in me was pleased as well, with a fascinating sonic document from a key creator in my historical narrative that functioned as a kind of nonverbal oral history interview. "The Bridge" is a New Age musician telling me about New Age music in the music's own idiom. I was conscious of the fact that my prompt, which asked about the music scene of the 1970s and '80s, would have personal resonance for Kevin, and on one level, I heard the track as a wistful reverie on the passing of time, a bittersweet recollection of a life now fifty years in the past. "It reminded me of time traveling," Kevin told me about working on "The Bridge." "It reminded me of the Continuum days, because it was sort of a Continuum-style piece."[124] Though I couldn't share Kevin's lived connection to that time and place, his track certainly had an emotional effect on me, eliciting tears every time I've listened to it.

"The Bridge" spoke to me in an emotional language about the passing of time, and in its structure I heard the rise and fall and rise again of the New Age movement, as well as its aspiration to a timeless, perennial, visionary experience. Kevin's track seemed to balance a horizontal movement in space and time with another kind of travel, as manifest in that ecstatic concluding expansion of high and low frequencies. Those two movements, horizontal and vertical, coexisted in the track, and that dynamic provided an answer to my question about how the visionary impulses of the past relate to the present. The vertical potential remains ever present, the track suggests, like the unseen sun at dawn, illuminating the sky while remaining invisible. At any time, a comet could pass your viewscreen and the picture could change, or you could tumble into the gravitational pull of a massive black hole and find the constellation of your life realigned.

"The thing about the spirit world," Kevin told me, "is that there's no time there. It wasn't thirty years ago for spirit. It's always now. When you're listening to it, that presence is still there, the energy is still present."[125] I had asked about the historical relationship between the past and the present, and "The Bridge" seemed to be gently reminding me that visionary music aspired to transcend linear models of time, at least momentarily, by making contact with an expanded now that blurred the distinction between past and future.

"The Bridge" gave me a lot to think about, but in the end, what Kevin's track means is a mystery. Moreover, I worried that maybe I was deviating from Kevin's suggestion to experience the sounds and be present with them without analyzing. Even Carl Jung confessed that "the less one thinks about the theory of the *I Ching*, the more soundly one sleeps." Jung concluded that the *I Ching* "offers neither facts nor power, but for lovers of self-knowledge, of wisdom—if there be such—it seems to be the right book." New Age music offers neither facts nor power, nor a strong beat you can dance to, but it too is right for lovers of self-knowledge and wisdom. "Let it go forth into the world for the benefit of those who can discern its meaning."[126]

ACKNOWLEDGMENTS

This book crystallized quickly, in large part due to the interest, support, and guidance of Raina Polivka, whose suggestions profoundly shaped its final form and tone. I am extremely grateful for her encouragement and insight. I have been very lucky to work with everyone at the University of California Press, in particular Sam Warren, who has been exceedingly kind, patient, and diligent. Thanks also go to Jeff Anderson and Richard Feit.

I also want to thank everyone who helped me with my research while writing the book: Chelsea Vasquez, Elizabeth Alecki, and Joe Ricci at the Strasenburgh Planetarium in Rochester; the staff at the University of Iowa Library; Bruce Kirby at the Library of Congress; and David Stiver, the Special Collections Librarian at the Graduate Theological Union, for all his help with the William "Will" Noffke Papers.

Thanks to Jason Whittaker and Sibylle Erle at the Blake Society and Beate Oschsner and Christine von Nell at the University of Konstanz for the opportunity to present some of the early ideas that grew into this book. Izzy Fradin was an important source of knowledge and valued interlocutor from the start of the project.

My colleagues at Northwestern University continue to offer me support and inspiration, and I want to thank in particular Thomas Bradshaw, Catherine Carrigan, Zayd Dohrn, Alex "The Synth Doctor" Inglizian, Dean E. Patrick Johnson, Michael Metzger, Chris Mercer, Stephan Moore, Christina Nguyen, and Neil Verma. My thoughtful and brilliant students at Northwestern were also an important inspiration and imagined readership for this project, and I hope the book will speak to them.

My sons, Jonah and Henry, are my favorite readers and listeners, and contributed much to my thinking both through their excellent suggestions and gentle critiques. Freda continues to be my best editor, a fellow seeker, and the love of my life. Thanks so much to my family for all your time listening, watching, reading, and talking with me.

Finally, I want to thank all my interviewees. I was deeply moved by your kindness, generosity, thoughtfulness, and abiding optimism. I learned much more from our conversations than can be contained in these pages.

NOTES

INTRODUCTION

1. Timothy Leary, *Starseed: A Psi Phy Comet Tale* (Level Press, 1973), 7, 11.

2. Kohoutek Celebration of Consciousness program, annotated, Paul Mariah Papers, Yale University Library, GEN MSS 2096, box 7, folder 134. See Theodore Roszak, *Unfinished Animal: The Aquarian Frontier and the Evolution of Consciousness* (Harper & Row, 1974), 31–33; Robin Roberts, "Sorry, No Comet," *Foothill Sentinel* 16, no. 12 (January 25, 1974): 1, 3.

3. On definitions of the New Age movement, see Wouter Hanegraaff, *New Age Religion and Western Culture: Esotericism in the Mirror of Secular Thought* (State University of New York Press, 1998); Sarah M. Pike, *New Age and Neopagan Religions in America* (Columbia University Press, 2004), 22–23; Christopher Partridge, *The Re-enchantment of the West: Alternative Spiritualities, Sacralization, Popular Culture, and Occulture*, vol. 1 (Continuum, 2004), 32–33; Paul Heelas, *The New Age Movement: Religion Culture, and Society in the Age of Postmodernity* (Blackwell, 1996); J. Gordon Melton, *New Age Encyclopedia* (Gale Research, 1990); James R. Lewis and J. Gordon Melton, eds., *Perspectives on the New Age* (State University of New York Press, 1992); David J. Hess, *Science in the New Age: The Paranormal, Its Defenders and Debunkers, and American Culture* (University of Wisconsin Press, 1993); Michael Hill, "The New Age: A Sociological Assessment," in *The Encyclopedic Sourcebook of New Age Religions*, ed. James R. Lewis (Prometheus Books, 2004).

4. For the sake of clarity and consistency, I will capitalize "New Age," whether referring to the movement or the music.

5. Victor Szabo, *Turn On, Tune In, Drift Off: Ambient Music's Psychedelic Past* (Oxford University Press, 2023), 40.

6. Gene Youngblood, *Expanded Cinema* (Fordham University Press, 1970), 54.

7. I take the term "non-ordinary states of consciousness" from Stanislav Grof; see *The Cosmic Game: Explorations of the Frontiers of Human Consciousness* (State University of New York, 1998), 4–5. Erik Davis defines visionary art as "art that resonates with visionary experiences, those undeniably powerful eruptions of numinous and multidimensional perception that suggest other orders of reality." Erik Davis, "Visionary Art: The Vanguard of Tradition," in *True Visions*, ed. Massimiliano Geraci and Federica Timeto (Betty Books, 2006), 5.

8. C. G. Jung, *Modern Man in Search of a Soul* (Mariner Books, 1933), 155–56.

9. Jung, *Modern Man in Search of a Soul*, 155–56, 158.

10. Jung, *Modern Man in Search of a Soul*, 158.

11. C. G. Jung, *The Spirit in Man, Art, and Literature* (Princeton University Press, 1966), 75–76.

12. Suzanne Doucet, interview by author, April 18, 2024.

13. Georgia Kelly, interview by author, August 8, 2024.

14. Christopher Partridge's insightful studies of the film, literature, and music associated with "occulture" is an important exception to this claim. See Partridge, *The Re-enchantment of the West*.

15. See Szabo, *Turn On, Tune In, Drift Off*, 28.

16. Dick Hebdige, *Subculture: The Meaning of Style* (Routledge, 1979), 113–14.

17. Colin Campbell, "The Cult, the Cultic Milieu and Secularization," in *The Cultic Milieu: Oppositional Subcultures in an Age of Globalization*, ed. Jeffrey Kaplan and Helene Loow (Altamira Press, 2002), 14. On the New Age as alternative culture, see April D. DeConnick, *The Gnostic New Age: How a Countercultural Spirituality Revolutionized Religion from Antiquity to Today* (Columbia University Press, 2016), 17; Hanegraaff, *New Age Religion and Western Culture*, 1, 517.

18. Campbell, "The Cult, the Cultic Milieu and Secularization," 14. On Christopher Partridge's related concept of "occulture," see *The Re-enchantment of the West*, vol. 1, 68.

19. José Argüelles, "Open Letter to 144,000 Rainbow Humans," in *The Encyclopedic Sourcebook of New Age Religions*, ed. James R. Leis (Prometheus Books, 2004), 588–89.

20. Ryan Hibbett, "The New Age Taboo," *Journal of Popular Music Studies* 22, no. 3 (2010): 288. Chris McGowan, "Instrumental Inroads: Outburst of Quiet Fusion Signals That New Age Has Arrived," *Billboard*, October 25, 1986, N3.

21. See Geeta Dayal, "New Age of New Age Music: 'It Used to Be Just Hippies and Unassuming Types,'" *The Guardian*, October 12, 2016; Harley Brown, "The State of New Age Music in the Always-On 'Wellness' Era," NPR, October 2, 2019; Nathan Taylor Pemberton, "The Case for New Age Music as American Folk Art," *The New Yorker*.

22. Stephen Hill, "New Age Made Simple" (1988), Hearts of Space (website), www.hos.com/about/new-age-music-made-simple, reprinted in *On Minimalism*, ed. Kerry O'Brien and William Robin (University of California Press, 2023), 220–21.

23. See Annette Kuhn and Guy Westwell, *A Dictionary of Film Studies* (Oxford University Press, 2020), 269, 305. Kristin Thompson and David Bordwell, *Film History: An Introduction* (McGraw-Hill, 2010).

24. Michael Stearns, interview by author, April 9, 2024.

25. From Blake's *Jerusalem*; see *Blake's Poetry and Designs*, ed. Mary Lyn Johnson and John Ernest Grant (Norton Critical Edition, 2008), 310.

26. See Mack Hagood, *Hush: Media and Sonic Self-Control* (Duke University Press, 2019); Paul Roquet, *Ambient Media: Japanese Atmospheres of Self* (University of Minnesota Press, 2016); Szabo, *Turn On, Tune In, Drift Off*; Tara Rogers, *Pink Noises: Women on Electronic Music and Sound* (Duke University Press, 2010).

27. Music historian Douglas Mcgowan refers to a "golden era" for New Age music between 1978 to 1984. Douglas Mcgowan, "New Age Music," in *The Acid Archives*, ed. Patrick Lundborg (Lysergia, 2010), 381.

28. Sarah M. Pike, *New Age and Neopagan Religions in America* (Columbia University Press, 2004), 22. Note that there was a display at the Kohoutek Celebration of Consciousness titled "Cosmically Attuned Meditational Sounds." Kohoutek Celebration of Consciousness program, annotated, Paul Mariah Papers, Yale University Library, GEN MSS 2096, box 7, folder 134.

29. Kohoutek Celebration of Consciousness program, annotated.

30. Erik Davis, "Visionary Art: The Vanguard of Tradition," in *True Visions*, ed. Massimiliano Geraci and Federica Timeto (Betty Books, 2006), 7. Davis writes, "Today's visionary artist draws from, and feeds, the 'lowbrow' legacy of psychedelic poster art, comic books, skateboard stickers, concert fliers, SciFi paperback covers, and fantasy illustration."

31. Visionary art has a complex relationship to time: pointing towards an expanded sense of the present moment through heightened mindfulness, while simultaneously referencing a primordial past and a possible future. Erik Davis argues that visionary art has long served as "evidence of a world that does not

yet fully exist; a world that we are calling into being through the very act of creating and participating in the Work." Davis, "Visionary Art," 8.

32. Ernst Fuchs interview, in *True Visions*, ed. Massimiliano Geraci and Federica Timeto (Betty Books, 2006), 16.

CHAPTER 1: VISIONARY SOUNDS

1. Peter J. Forshaw, "Oratorium—Auditorium—Laboratorium: Early Modern Improvisations on Cabala, Music, and Alchemy," *Aries* 10, no. 2 (2010): 170.

2. Elizabeth Kent, "The Magical Music of Iasos," *Yoga Journal*, January 1977, 16. See also Iaso's self-produced 1979 documentary on his music, available on YouTube, www.youtube.com/watch?v=4OSn_RJcwlo.

3. Lee Underwood, *World Music and Inner Transformation* (unpublished manuscript, 1984), 1-4. "Athol Cassidy Interviews Iasos," Iasos.com, accessed July 12, 2024, https://iasos.com/media/mp3/AtholCassidy-interviews-Iasos-8-13-2020.mp3.

4. Alexander Roob, *Alchemy & Mysticism* (Taschen, 2014), 331; Andrea De Pascalis, *Alchemy: The Golden Art* (Gremese International, 1995), 105.

5. The artist and writer Laurence Caruana asserts that visionary art is a mode of creation that is guided by a desire to bear witness to realities made evident in alternative states of consciousness. Laurence Caruana, *The First Manifesto of Visionary Art* (Recluse, 2010), 3. See also Erik Davis, "Visionary Art: The Vanguard of Tradition," in *True Visions*, ed. Massimiliano Geraci and Federica Timeto (Betty Books, 2006), 5. For artist Alex Grey, visionary art is based on "personal experience of the divine" and an attempt to make "inner truths" sensible via "an external material-world manifestation." Alex Grey, *The Mission of Art* (Shambala, 1998), 25. See also Northrop Frye, *Fearful Symmetry: A Study of William Blake* (Princeton University Press, 1947), 8. Frye's prime example is William Blake, a paradigmatic visionary artist, who asserted the ultimate reality of "vision or imagination." William Blake, *Blake's Poetry and Designs* (W. W. Norton, 2008), 433–34. Blake begins *Milton: A Poem in Two Books* with the call to "Rouze up, O Young Men of the New Age!" Blake's line is sometimes given as the source of the name "New Age," and he has long been recognized as an important influence on the poets and visual artists of the counterculture. See, for example, Stephen F. Eisenman, *William Blake and the Age of Aquarius* (Princeton University Press, 2017); Christoph Bochinger, "Esoterism and the New Age," in *The Encyclopedic Sourcebook of New Age Religions*, ed. James R. Lewis (Prometheus Books, 2004), 21.

6. Stanislav Grof, *The Cosmic Game: Explorations of the Front Line of Human Consciousness* (State University of New York Press, 1998), 50.

7. The term "auditives" comes from André Breton, one of the founders of surrealism, who asserted that "great poets have been 'auditives' not visionaries. At least, with them, vision, 'illumination,' is the effect and not the cause." André Breton, "Silence Is Golden," *Modern Music*, 1944, 153–54. In a manifesto on visionary art, Laurence Caruana writes that artists of this type attempt to "see the unseen." Laurence Caruana, *The First Manifesto of Visionary Art* (Recluse, 2001), 1.

8. "Christopher Toussant Interviews Iasos," https://vimeo.com/38694958, Accessed, July 12, 2024. As I mentioned in the introduction, there was a consequential meeting in 1980 to settle on a label for promoting this new music, and while the consensus was to call it "New Age," several attendees, including harpist Georgia Kelly, had preferred "visionary music." Georgia Kelly, interview by author, August 8, 2024.

9. Elizabeth Kent, "The Magical Music of Iasos," *Yoga Journal*, January 1977, 17.

10. Kent, "The Magical Music of Iasos," 17.

11. Manuel Montes, "Iasos: Interview to a Theoretician/Practitioner of the New Age," Amazings.com, www.amazings.com/articles/article0014.html; Kent, "The Magical Music of Iasos," 17. Iasos's experience with Vista is characteristic of a culture of "channeling" that permeated 1970s New Age culture. "The term channeling refers to the conviction of psychic mediums that they are able, under certain conditions, to act as a channel for information from sources other than their normal selves." Wouter J. Hanegraaff, *New Age Religion and Western Culture* (Brill, 1996), 23. See Suzanne Riordan, "Channeling: A New Revelation?," in *Perspectives on the New Age*, ed. James R. Lewis and J. Gordon Melton (State University of New York Press, 1992); Michael F. Brown, *The Channeling Zone: American Spirituality in an Anxious Age* (Harvard University Press, 1997).

12. Kent, "The Magical Music of Iasos," 18.

13. Advertisement, *Yoga Journal*, January 1978, 57.

14. Steven Halpern, interview by author, April 26, 2024. See also Underwood, *World Music and Inner Transformation*, H-13.

15. Laraaji, interview by author, May 8, 2024.

16. Robert Venosa interview, in *True Visions*, ed. Massimiliano Geraci and Federica Timeto (Betty Books, 2006), 105.

17. Steve Roach, interview by author, May 14, 2024.

18. Stephanie Davis, "Kat Epple," *Florida Weekly: Fort Myers Edition*, September 18, 2019, https://fortmyers.floridaweekly.com/articles/kat-epple/.

19. Kat Epple, interview by author, July 17, 2024.

20. Epple, interview.

21. Epple, interview.

22. Underwood, *World Music and Inner Transformation*, D-13–14. Peter Davison traveled to Bali in 1979 to study Gamelan music and while there had a number of experiences with psilocybin mushrooms. "I found this palm tree, and we made really good friends," he recalled. "That was a really good day," he said. "What I try to capture in my music is moments like that." Peter Davison, interview by author, July 25, 2024.

23. George Deuter, interview by author, April 25, 2024.

24. Peter Michael Hamel, *Through Music to the Self: How to Appreciate and Experience Anew* (Element Books, 1978), 3. Steve McLinn, who released New Age cassettes under the name Ojas, stated that "LSD and the other psychoactive chemicals really opened me up, but I had no explanations for these experiences." He turned to practices like yoga and meditation to continue those experiences. Underwood, *World Music and Inner Transformation*, O-4. Iasos provides another example; he tried drugs in the late 1960s but found that they did more harm than good. In 1968, he began to practice transcendental meditation, which had more long-term and sustainable results. "People Playing Music (KPFA)," Iasos.com, accessed, July 12, 2024, https://iasos.com/media/mp3/PeoplePlayingMusic(KPFA)InterviewsIasos-1975.mp3. The flutist Paul Horn began his study of transcendental meditation in the 1960s before celebrities like the Beatles and Donovan made it chic. The "essence of meditation" and the essence of New Age music is the same, he wrote: "Meditation is what serious New Age music is all about." Paul Horn with Lee Underwood, *Inside Paul Horn* (HarperCollins, 1990), 85.

25. Hanegraaff asserts that "one of the most characteristic elements of the counterculture was the widespread use of psychedelic drugs." Wouter Hanegraaff, *New Age Religion and Western Culture: Esotericism in the Mirror of Western Thought* (State University of New York Press, 1998), 11. One indication that the psychedelic experience was a major pathway to visionary experience can be found in the fact that the designation "psychedelic art" is sometimes synonymous with visionary art. In 1968, Robert Masters and Jean Houston wrote that "the psychedelic artist is an artist whose work has been significantly influenced by psychedelic experience and who acknowledges the impact of the experience on his work" and defined psychedelic art as "works of art attempting in some sense to communicate psychedelic experience, or to induce psychedelic experience, or at least to alter consciousness so as to approximate aspects of the

chemically induced state." Robert E. L. Masters and Jean Houston, *Psychedelic Art* (Balance House, 1968), 17–18.

26. James Kent writes that "the one artistic medium which can be expressed immediately in psychedelic intoxication without disrupting the quality of the shamanic experience is music," which is "the traditional method for binding psychedelic memory into physical space. The act of singing, drumming, or dancing also drives feedback and amplifies the energy of the psychedelic experience, thus making music the primary medium of psychedelic information compression and transmission." Music, he writes is "a cross-cultural technology for real-time encoding and transmission of nonlinear psychedelic information." James L. Kent, *Psychedelic Information Theory: Shamanism in the Age of Reason* (PIT Press, 2010), 127–28. On "occulture" and psychedelics, see Christopher Partridge, *The Re-enchantment of the West*, vol. 2 (Continuum, 2005), 97–98, 127–28.

27. Such an experience could, as Aldous Huxley wrote, be treated as a fleeting novelty rather than something deeply significant and life-changing. Aldous Huxley, "Visionary Experience," in *The Highest State of Consciousness*, ed. John White (Anchor Books, 1972), 56–57. Carl Jung wrote that the value of having a visionary experience depended on the attitude that the recipient took toward it: "When a primordial idea presents itself in visionary terms, the task of the individual is to translate the spontaneous and symbolic picture or dramatic sequence into an individual statement." Andrew Samuels, Bani Shorter, and Fred Plaut, *A Critical Dictionary of Jungian Analysis* (Routledge, 1986), 159.

28. On the "sacralization of popular music," made explicit by New Age musicians like Steve Roach and Steve Hillage, see Partridge, *The Re-enchantment of the West*, vol. 1, 147, 153. On the New Age movement as "a significant spiritual subculture," see James R. Lewis, introduction to *The Encyclopedic Sourcebook of New Age Religions*, ed. James R. Lewis (Prometheus Books, 2004), 13. Also see David J. Hess, *Science in the New Age* (University of Wisconsin Press, 1993), 3, 174.

29. "Soul Space Interviews Iasos," www.youtube.com/watch?v=dPhhztN6Bow, Accessed, July 12, 2024.

30. Steve Roach, interview by author, August 27, 2024. Iasos made a similar comparison between music and painting: if a painter can create a work alone, why do they need someone else to paint the clouds, the trees, and the landscape? "Soul Space Interviews Iasos," www.youtube.com/watch?v=dPhhztN6Bow, accessed, July 12, 2024. "Red Bull Music Academy Fireside Chat with Iasos," https://iasos.com/media/mp3/RedBullMusicAcademyRadio-FiresideChatWithIasos-Sept2014.mp3, accessed, July 12, 2024.

31. Steve Roach, interview by author, May 14, 2024. Deuter is another New Age pioneer who realized early in his career that studio recording "doesn't work for me. I cannot make music that way," he said (Deuter, interview). See also Underwood, *World Music and Inner Transformation*, D-8.

32. Andreas Kitzmann and Einar Engstrom, introduction to *Modular Synthesis: Patching Machines and People*, ed. Ezra J. Teboul, Andreas Kitzmann, and Einar Engstrom (Routledge, 2024), 1.

33. Suzanne Ciani worked with Buchla starting in the late 1960s and later used modular synths to create her successful New Age albums of the 1980s.

34. Stan Levine, "A Sample of Serge Tcherepnin," *Synapse* 1, no. 4 (November–December 1976): 5.

35. "Nobody could afford a Moog system at that time, or a Buchla really," Braheny Fortune said. Braheny Fortune, interview by author, August 27, 2024.

36. Braheny Fortune, interview.

37. TONTO is an acronym for "The Original New Timbral Orchestra," and Cecil and his partner, Bob Margouleff, released an album called *Zero Time* (1971) under the name "Tonto's Expanding Head Band." Tracks from *Zero Time* were played on the seminal New Age radio show *Music from the Hearts of Space*, and it stands as a precursor to the New Age genre. The TONTO synthesizer can be seen as a prop in Brian DePalma's film *Phantom of the Paradise* (1974). Stevie Wonder heard *Zero Time* and subsequently hired Cecil and Margouleff to produce his classic albums of the early 1970s. Malcolm Cecil was thus an A-list producer and proto-New Age synth artist when Kevin Braheny Fortune began working with him in the mid-1970s. "Being with Malcolm was like getting kicked upstairs," Braheny Fortune remembered.

38. Suzanne Ciana, interview by author, August 13, 2024.

39. Epple, interview.

40. New Age composer Joanna Brouk discovered analog synths at Mills College in the early 1970s and shifted her focus from sound poetry to recording. In a 1980 interview, Brouk recalled that the first day she worked with the synthesizer, she jumped back in astonishment. "This can make the sounds I hear," she said, "without having to study. I can just make sounds. . . . It's really wonderful." KPFA, June 24, 1980, Redcrystal.org, https://redcrystal.org/2020/08/20/joanna-brouk/.

41. See David Jay Brown and Rebecca Ann Hill, *Women of Visionary Art* (Park Street Press, 2018).

42. Epple, interview.

43. Trevor Pinch and Frank Trocco, *Analog Days: The Invention and Impact of the Moog Synthesizer* (Harvard University Press, 2002), 45.

44. Rich Gold, with Darrel Johansen and Marina LaPalma, *An Introduction to the Serge Modular Music System*, https://communiteq-eu5.nbg1.your-objectstorage.com/uploads/db8181/original/3X/1/5/154e8c42d2a37e291596ffacb8595d68b6e45c2e.pdf, 83.

45. Martin Russ, *Sound Synthesis and Sampling*, 3rd ed. (Focal Press, 1996), 106–7.

46. Musicologist Jonathan De Souza echoes the sentiments of my interviewees when he writes that modular synths not only enabled musicians to produce novel sounds but also established new conceptual models for what creating music could be. Jonathan De Souza, "Modular Synthesizers as Conceptual Models," in *Modular Synthesis: Patching Machines and People*, ed. Ezra J. Teboul, Andreas Kitzmann, and Einar Engstrom (Routledge, 2024), 82–83. See also Alexander Rehding on the monochord: Alexander Rehding, "Instruments of Music Theory," *MTO: A Journal of the Society for Music Theory* 22, no. 4 (December 2016): 6–7.

47. Halpern, interview. He was inspired by playing a gig with Herbie Hancock in San Francisco: "Herbie is warming up and plays a glissando that sounded just like what I heard in the woods in meditation, and I look around and I walk right up and say, 'What is that?' He said, 'That's a Fender Rhodes, the electric piano Miles (Davis) made me play.' I go, 'Oh, man! I gotta get one of those!'" Halpern had heard Herbie Hancock playing the Rhodes on Miles Davis's album *Miles in the Sky* (1968). He saved his money and, in late 1970, could afford both a Fender Rhodes and a station wagon to transport it.

48. "Athol Cassidy Interviews Iasos," Iasos.com, accessed, July 12, 2024, https://iasos.com/media/mp3/AtholCassidy-interviews-Iasos-8-13-2020.mp3.

49. The numerology related to the instrument is also significant to Laraaji: 36 is composed of the digits 3 and 6; 3 plus 6 is 9, which is the "number of the complete universe," When he's playing the autoharp, therefore, he feels that he is "using the language of the complete universe." Laraaji, interview.

50. Epple, interview.

51. Carlos R. Nakai, interview by author, August 5, 2025.

52. Nakai, interview.

53. Anna Turner and Stephen Hill, *Music from the Hearts of Space: Guide to Cosmic, Transcendent and Innerspace Music* (Music from the Hearts of Space, 1981), 2.

54. For Paul Heelas, this means that "New Agers can 'draw' on traditions whilst bypassing their explicit authoritative doctrines, dogmas and moral codes." Paul Heelas, *The New Age Movement: Religion, Culture, and Society in the Age of Postmodernity* (Blackwell, 1996), 27–28. Colin Campbell makes

a similar point about the mysticism of the cultic milieu: "The religious ideal is a state of unity with the divine," he writes, and since there is felt to be "an underlying unity of all consciousness and life," the result is that all spiritual paths "can lead to the same all-encompassing truth." Colin Campbell, "The Cult, the Cultic Milieu and Secularization," in *The Cultic Milieu: Oppositional Subcultures in an Age of Globalization*, ed. Jeffrey Kaplan and Helene Loow (Altamira Press, 2002), 16. On perennialism in transpersonal psychology, see Jorge N. Ferrer, *Revisioning Transpersonal Theory: A Participatory Vision of Human Spirituality* (State University of New York Press, 2002).

55. On the "affirmative" form of orientalism in the tradition of Western occultism, see Christopher Partridge, "The Occult and Orientalism," in *The Occult World*, ed. Christopher Partridge (Routledge, 2015), 622.

56. Turner and Hill, *Music from the Hearts of Space*, 25. Iasos made similar comments in a 1979 documentary, "Inter-Dimensional Music thru Iasos," dir. Clark Higgins, 1979, https://vimeo.com/41939043, July 15, 2024. Similarly, synth pioneer Isao Tomita stated, "I believe [electronic music] is as natural as other sounds. As you know, electricity is an energy which flows quite naturally, just like wind blows in the air and water runs in the stream. These phenomena are natural, and so is electricity. So an art which uses electricity is as natural as other kinds of music." From an interview in *Synapse*, November–December 1977, cited in Underwood, *World Music and Inner Transformation*, 26–27. Iasos gave talks entitled "High Tech Audio for Ancient Temple Music." "Bliss Interview with Iasos," Iasos.com, https://iasos.com/articles/bliss_interview/.

57. Peter Michael Hamel, *Through Music to the Self* (Element Books, 1978), 127.

58. Hamel, *Through Music to the Self*, 129.

59. Hamel, *Through Music to the Self*, 141.

60. Hamel, *Through Music to the Self*, 142–43. Hamel defined minimalism as "the repetition of short motifs which alter almost imperceptibly and are varied only minimally."

61. Kent, *Psychedelic Information Theory*, 45.

62. Kent, *Psychedelic Information Theory*, 78.

63. One way to understand the minimalism/disco/New Age relationship is through the categories of highbrow, lowbrow, and middlebrow. If minimalism and disco ended up occupying, respectively, highbrow and lowbrow cultural positions, New Age music occupied the middlebrow. As the middlebrow has tended to be scorned by critics, it is not surprising that New Age applications of minimalist techniques have been slow to be appreciated. On minimalism's influence, see Robert Fink, *Repeating Ourselves: American Minimal Music as*

Cultural Practice (University of California Press, 2005); Kerry O'Brien and William Robin, *On Minimalism: Documenting a Musical Movement* (University of California Press, 2023), 3–5.

64. Turner and Hill, *Music from the Hearts of Space*, xi. One musicologist described this tendency in New Age music as representing a "new tonality": "This music is very tonal and very consonant. In fact, it goes to the extremes in these two parameters, the composers feeling that their music should sooth the listener and produce positive, healthful effects on the human body by reducing tensions, lowering blood pressure and tension, and engendering relaxation. Obviously, this is a very radical approach to music compared to what composers have been doing in the past 25 or more years." Robert C. Ehle, "New Age Music," *American Music Teacher* 32, no. 6 (June–July 1983): 36–37. A writer for the *San Francisco Chronicle* described space music as being "based in harmony, sounds are harmonic with one another to give a sense of completion and completeness." John Sunier, "Space Music Offers Excitement and Relaxation," *San Francisco Chronicle*, October 10, 1982, 11.

65. Academic training of this kind is notable in the context of visionary art, which has tended to be placed in the same category as outsider art, with an assumption that the artist has a lack of training or formal education. Erik Davis argues that visionary art broadens the notion of outsider art since many visionary artists are, in fact, well-trained and "self-consciously locate their work within a lineage of inspired image-makers that stretches back through generations of Surrealist dreamscapes, mystic abstractionists, and medieval iconography." Erik Davis, "Visionary Art: The Vanguard of Tradition," in *True Visions*, ed. Massimiliano Geraci and Federica Timeto (Betty Books, 2006), 5–6. W. J. T. Mitchell notes the limitations of the outsider artist designation for William Blake. "To qualify as an outsider artist," Mitchell writes, "one should be either untrained or mentally ill, preferably both." Blake, Mitchell notes, is "arguably the first and most famous outsider artist in the Western canon," but he does not fit the model, since he was "far from untrained," apprenticing as a journeyman engraver, making his living in that trade, and studying for a time at the Royal Academy. W. J. T. Mitchell, "Inside Out: Reflections on Outsider Art," *Brooklyn (NY) Rail*, July–August 2018, https://brooklynrail.org/2018/07/criticspage/Inside-Out-Reflections-on-Outsider-Art.

66. Davison, interview.

67. Davison, interview.

68. Noah Johnson, "A Mind-Bending Journey with the Mystic Master of New Age Music," *GQ*, June 6, 2023. "Avant-garde music, it sounds kind of ugly. . . . There's very little color. It's just kind of all brown. I just had it with writing

atonal, arrhythmic music that nobody wants to hear. . . . One of the reasons I stopped doing the new music," he said, is that it's "music that people don't want to hear." Peter Davison, interview by author, July 19, 2024.

69. Davison, July 19, 2024, interview.

70. Davison, July 19, 2024, interview.

71. Underwood, *World Music and Inner Transformation*, DR-8.

72. A similar aesthetic can be heard on Laraaji's *Unicorns in Paradise* (1981).

73. Susan Jacobs, "Stephen Halpern: Exploring the Farthest Reaches of Sound," *Yoga Journal*, November-December 1984, 38–39.

74. Steven Halpern with Louis Savary, *Sound Health: The Music and Sounds That Make Us Whole* (Harper & Row, 1985), 143.

75. Halpern and Savary, *Sound Health*, 144.

76. See also Iasos on New Age music's break with musical conventions: Iasos, "What Is New Age Music?," Iasos.com, https://iasos.com/articles/new-age-music/.

77. For one example of prog-esque "swords and sorcery" themes, see Emerald Web's first album, *Dragon Wings and Wizard Tales* (1979). On prog rock and spirituality, see Partridge, *The Re-enchantment of the West*, vol. 1.

78. Edward Macan, *Rocking the Classics: English Progressive Rock and the Counterculture* (Oxford University Press, 1997). Also see Kevin Holm-Hudson, introduction to *Progressive Rock Reconsidered*, ed. Kevin Holm-Hudson (Routledge, 2002).

79. "Soul Space Interviews Iasos," YouTube video, https://www.youtube.com/watch?v=dPhhztN6Bow, accessed July 12, 2024.

80. Steven Halpern, "Notes on New Age Music," in *The New Age Music Guide*, ed. Patti Jean Birosik (Collier Books, 1989), xix. The musicologist Peter Doyle describes an "ancient nexus" between reverberant spaces and the sacred or magical, as exemplified in "the sacred grottoes and caves of preurban societies, and later by the acoustic properties present in temples, shrines, mausoleums." Peter Doyle, *Echo and Reverb* (Wesleyan University Press, 2005), 42.

81. Kevin Braheny Fortune, interview by author, August 27, 2024.

82. Eckart Rahn, interview by author, November 28, 2024.

83. James Newton, interview by author, January 9, 2025.

84. Newton, interview. In an email to the author on April 26, 2025, Hill remembered that

> you had to walk more than half a mile uphill over a narrow, bumpy path to get to the actual canyon. We had 300 pounds of the latest digital recording equipment and cables—too much to carry in and out three times. The solution was to rent a stainless steel location sound cart in Los Angeles. It weighed over a hundred

pounds, but it had big wheels and could handle the path with all our equipment tied onto it. . . . Once we had the mechanics down, the actual recording was relatively easy, although we had to wait until midnight for the traffic on the road to subside to the point we could get takes with just flute and crickets (Stephen Hill, email to author, April 26, 2025).

85. Newton recalled praying with the monks in the church before he recorded, and feeling like "the Holy Spirit was leading me and guiding me" on the sessions. Both his Celestial Harmonies albums are saturated with natural reverberation and spiritual references like the title of the final track on *In Venice*, "Of the Most High." Tracks from Newton and Horn's albums are among those collection on the label's CD *The Sound Inside: Music and Architecture* (1998).

86. Nakai, interview.

87. "Iasos—Tips for Aspiring Musicians," Vimeo, accessed July 12, 2024, https://vimeo.com/69443467; "Athol Cassidy Interviews Iasos," Iasos.com, accessed July 12, 2024, https://iasos.com/media/mp3/AtholCassidy-interviews-Iasos-8-13-2020.mp3,.

88. My theorization of New Age musical temporality is based on the work of musician Randall McClellan, about whom there will be more in chapter 2. You can hear his lecture on music, "Music as a Healing Force Lecture," on *The Healing Music of Rana—Vol. IV* (1981).

89. On visionary art and transpersonal time, see Erik Davis, "Visionary Art: The Vanguard of Tradition," in *True Visions*, 6–7. Mitchell describes "uncertainty" about William Blake's "proper historical location": "If Blake did not quite fit in his own time, it is largely because he located himself and his work outside of or across time altogether, in an atemporal region he called 'Eternity.'" W. J. T. Mitchell, "Blake Now and Then," in *William Blake and the Age of Aquarius*, ed. Stephen F. Eisenman (Princeton University Press, 2017), 200.

90. The New Age musical pioneer Wilburn Burchette put non-ordinary temporal experience at the center of his work. "I considered music to be an art form of time, through time, and in time. I assumed that everything was time . . . the breakthrough to Higher Reality is outside of time. When you break through time, that is revelation, that is breaking through to the Godhead." Douglas Mcgowan, liner notes to *I Am the Center* CD (Light In the Attic Records, 2013). See also Brad Steiger, "Music and the Occult," *Woodland Daily Democrat*, December 9, 1971, 7.

91. McClellan, "Music as a Healing Force."

92. Braheny Fortune, interview. Michael Stearns talked about using sequencers to create a kind of sonic tapestry, with the goal being that "you

give up your sense of ego, and surrender to the tapestry of all of these threads going through." The music then creates a context for being in a different state of awareness: "The possibility that is presented in this music is to lose your sense of self within it." Michael Stearns, interview by author, April 9, 2024. Halpern writes that "New Age music is not based on pulse. . . . This shift has created an extraordinary sense of timelessness for listeners, who no longer have the same perceptual and contextual cues to help them to anticipate the next beat. No longer are music or musicians slaves of 'the time machine.'" Halpern, "Notes on New Age Music," xviii.

93. Alex Grey interview, in *True Visions*, ed. Massimiliano Geraci and Federica Timeto (Betty Books, 2006), 33. On psychedelics and "all-in-one-ist" experiences, see Partridge, *The Re-enchantment of the West*, vol. 2, 127.

94. According to Kent, one of the most commonly reported visual effects of psychedelics is grid-like geometric patterns. Kent, *Psychedelic Information Theory*, 81–82. "The hallucinogenic perception of a complex embedded symbolic grid or kinetic fractal superstructure is unique to the psychedelic experience," he writes, and "may be the visual essence of what makes an experience authentically psychedelic," 87–88. We might also compare the tape delay effects of minimalists like Terry Riley to the time effects and visual echoes of psychedelic experience; see Kent, *Psychedelic Information Theory*, 75–76, 101.

95. McClellan, "Music as a Healing Force."

96. Walter Hopps, introduction to *Visions* (Pomegranate Publications, 1977), xiii.

CHAPTER 2: HOLISTIC SOUNDS

1. Douglas Mcgowan, "New Age Music," in *The Acid Archives*, ed. Patrick Lundborg (Lysergia, 2010), 382.

2. John Sippel, "Distributor Nurtures New Vistas," *Billboard*, June 9, 1984, 6; Eckart Rahn, interview by author, November 28, 2024.

3. Wouter J. Hanegraaff, *New Age Religion and Western Culture: Esotericism in the Mirror of Secular Thought* (Brill, 1996), 119–20. Alternative healing, Hanegraaff writes, involves healing the whole person by giving "attention to the interaction between physical, emotional, mental and spiritual aspects of the patient's experience, as well as to social factors and the influence of the wider environment" (43). Religious studies scholar J. Gordon Melton writes that "holistic" is a ubiquitous term in New Age discourse and refers to a view of the universe as a complex set of systems that are "intricately connected and

interdependent, with each part reflective of the whole"; J. Gordon Melton, *New Age Encyclopedia* (Gale Research, 1990), xx. Olav Hammer, "Contradictions of the New Age," in *The Encyclopedic Sourcebook of New Age Religions*, ed. James R. Lewis (Prometheus Books, 2004), 412–13. The transpersonal psychologist Stanislav Grof defined "holotropic" states of consciousness as those that are "moving in the direction of wholeness." "In our everyday state of consciousness, we are fragmented and identify with only a small fraction of who we really are," Grof writes. Holotropic states allowed people to transcend those narrow boundaries and reclaim their full identity. New Age musicians explored such holotropic states and communicated them to listeners eager to unify and integrate their fractured lives. See Stanislav Grof, *The Cosmic Game:: Explorations of the Frontiers of Human Consciousness* (State University of New York Press, 1998), 4–5; Stanislav Grof, "Brief History of Transpersonal Psychology," *International Journal of Transpersonal Studies* 27, no. 1 (2008): 48.

4. James A. Beckford, "Holistic Imagery and Ethics in New Religious and Healing Movements," *Social Compass* 31, no. 2–3 (1984): 261.

5. Patti Jean Birosik, *The New Age Music Guide* (Collier Books, 1989), ix. For musician Suzanne Doucet, New Age music caught on because it provided "an ideal accompaniment for meditation, yoga, physical workouts, and therapy." Suzanne Doucet, "Commentary: Success Has Diluted New Age Music," *Billboard* 100, no. 25 (June 18, 1988): 9.

6. Kirpal Singh, *Naam or Word* (Sant Bani Ashram, 1978), 20, 29–30. New age musician Constance Demby studied Surat Shabd Yoga and wrote that vibration is "the fundamental creative force": "Every leaf, atom, particle, planet, galaxy, every cell in our body is humming its own tune." https://web.archive.org/web/20050309062929fw_/http://www.constancedemby.com/healing_f.html, accessed July 14, 2024.

7. Victor Szabo, *Turn On, Tune In, Drift Off: Ambient Music's Psychedelic Past* (Oxford University Press, 2023), 144.

8. Paul Horn with Lee Underwood, *Inside Paul Horn: The Spiritual Odyssey of a Universal Traveler* (HarperCollins, 1990), 265.

9. McClellan describes the human body as a series of "interlocking and interdependent vibrational systems," a "virtual symphony" of "biological, mental and emotional rhythms" that seek "the state of perfect balance and equilibrium." Randall McClellan, *The Healing Forces of Music* (Element Books, 1991), 38.

10. McClellan, *The Healing Forces of Music*, 38. "There is no split between spirit and matter for both are vibration," he explains, adding that emotions are frequency vibrations that affect the organs, and thoughts are electromagnetic waveforms.

11. Peggy Taylor, "Relaxation Tapes: A Conscious Consumer's Guide," *New Age Journal* 7, no. 6 (January 1982): 60.

12. Peggy Taylor, "Aural Samadhi," *New Age Journal* 7, no. 10 (May 1982), 60–61, 63.

13. In one of the first discussions of New Age music in the industry trade journal *Billboard*, we read that an underground music from Northern California had first gotten exposure through "specialty bookstores, health food retailers and extensive mail order business." Jack McDonough, "Music for a 'New Age' Surfacing in California," *Billboard* 95, no. 3 (January 22, 1983): 63. Suzanne Doucet, "Commentary: Success Has Diluted New Age Music," *Billboard* 100, no. 25 (June 18, 1988): 9.

14. Connie Zweig, "Bodhi Tree Bookstore: Timeless Retreat," *Los Angeles Times*, February 14, 1987, D3. See also John Dart, "Bookstore Offers a Way Station for Minds," *Los Angeles Times*, May 9, 1981, A30.

15. Shirley MacLaine, *Out on a Limb* (Bantam, 1983), 46. The Bodhi Tree was one of several listings in a 1977 guide to "occult" bookstores in Los Angeles, along with Aleph Books in Glendale, where New Age cassettes shared space with candles, incense, Tarot decks, and crystal balls. The Bodhi Tree can be seen in Shirley MacLaine's New Age biopic *Out on a Limb*. Leight Charlton, "The Occult Cult," *Los Angeles Times*, January 4, 1977, I10.

16. Georgia Kelly, interview by author, February 21, 2025. See Underwood, GK-10–12.

17. Georgia Kelly, interview by author, August 8, 2024. Kevin Braheny Fortune, interview by author, August 27, 2024.

18. Peter Davison, interview with author, July 25, 2024.

19. Davison, interview. On Horn's album *Inside the Great Pyramid* (1976) and his research into pyramid power, see Horn and Underwood, *Inside Paul Horn*, 198.

20. Davison, interview.

21. Davison, interview.

22. Ethan Edgecombe, interview by author, June 21, 2025.

23. Edgecombe, interview, June 21, 2025. His father worked as a farmer during the winters and went to Mackinac Island in Michigan to work in the summers where he operated a bike chair company at the Grand Hotel. Ethan remembers getting on the Greyhound Bus in Fort Lauderdale and driving through the South, "which was challenging at those times." Ethan Edgecombe, interview by author, July 12, 2025.

24. Edgecombe, interview, June 21, 2025.

25. Edgecombe, interview, July 12, 2025.

26. Edgecombe, interview, June 21, 2025.

27. Edgecombe, interview, June 21, 2025.

28. He found himself drawn to what was then known as "international" music at record stores and head shops, records of Japanese shakuhachi flute, for example, and releases by the Nonesuch and Lyrichord labels (Edgecombe, interview, June 21, 2025). "I was hungry for a new way of life, a new way of thinking and being," he said (Edgecombe, interview, July 12, 2025).

29. The Bay Area "was the place" for this music he recalled. "The musicians were there . . . and *Hearts of Space* was there." He also remembered that German musicians would regularly come through town on their way to visit the Rajneesh/Osho community in Oregon. "All these folks came to the States to be close to their teacher, and they would always come through the Bay Area," he said. "Many of them crashed at our house." Edgecombe, interview, June 21, 2025.

30. Edgecombe, interview, June 21, 2025. Edgecombe would reply to classified ads in the *New Age Journal*, where musicians had ads for their cassettes, buy one, and respond to see if they were interested in working with him to distribute their music. "That's how I met Laraaji. That's how I met Ramananda [Ed Christmas]."

31. Edgecombe, interview, June 21, 2025.

32. Edgecombe, interview, June 21, 2025.

33. The New Age musician William Aura had a similar trajectory, working for Eden Foods in Michigan before becoming part of the New Age scene. William Aura, interview by author, July 1, 2025. In a variation on this theme, R. Carlos Nakai sold his first cassettes at "Indian trading posts" around the Navajo Hopi Indian Reservation in Arizona. R. Carlos Nakai, interview by author, August 5, 2025.

34. Kat Epple, interview by author, November 18, 2024.

35. Chris Morris, "New Outlet Caters Solely to New Age Aficionados," *Billboard* 99, no. 6 (February 7, 1987): 39.

36. Steven Halpern with Lous Savary, *Sound Health: The Music and Sounds That Make Us Whole* (Harper & Row, 1985), 140. Haplern and Savary write: "if it is true that you are what you eat, it may just as accurately be said that you are what you listen to" (viii).

37. Anna Turner and Stephen Hill, *Music from the Hearts of Space: Guide to Cosmic, Transcendent and Innerspace Music* (Music from the Hearts of Space, 1981), xii. In the same guide, *Hearts of Space* cohost Stephen Hill refers to music that serves as "a form of spatial food for our finer being bodies." Turner and Hill, *Music from the Hearts of Space*, xv. They are likely drawing here from an essay written by New Age musician Jordan De La Sierra, found in a booklet to

his album *Gymnosphere* (1978). In the essay, titled "The Sound of Our Life," De La Sierra writes, "Sound is a form of food, a food for our finer being bodies; a food served in many varieties with many possible powers." See Discogs, www.discogs.com/release/553161-Jordan-De-La-Sierra-Gymnosphere-Song-Of-The-Rose.

38. As with health food, radio provided a metaphor for describing the vibrational ontology of sound. Kirpal Singh, whose Surat Shabd Yoga we encountered above, wrote that "our human body is a receiving set for catching the Sound Current and like a radio, has to be adjusted properly to bring it in tune with the ethereal waves." Singh, *Naam or Word*, 155. Iasos also used a radio metaphor: "Sound can be used as a channel-tuner for your consciousness. . . . Rather than the dial of your consciousness being 'stuck' most of the time on only one station—this physical dimension, you can exercise your ability to access different realms. . . . You can use sound as a 'wave guide' to harmonically align with the higher octaves of your own being—your Higher Self." Iasos, "Music as Light Waves," Iasos.com, https://iasos.com/articles/index.html#Music_as_Light_Waves.

39. Douglas Mcgowan, "A New Age for New Age?," interview on *Arkivet Podcast*, April 9, 2017.

40. Lee Underwood, *World Music and Inner Transformation* (unpublished manuscript, 1984), h/t 17. See also Ann Turner and Stephen Hill, "Brahms Does the Dishes," in *Spacemusic: Music by Mail 1984 from Heart of Space* (San Francisco, 1984), 45.

41. The flutist Larkin, whom we will meet in chapter 4, recalled first hearing his music played on *Music from the Hearts of Space*. "I was in Santa Cruz, in the Santa Cruz Mountains. . . . You can look from Santa Cruz all the way back and see San Francisco. I was in my Volkswagen van, listening to the show, and I heard him put on [my album] and, the metamorphosis that took place in me, looking back and then seeing the music being transmitted into the cosmos, was amazing." Larkin Stentz, interview by author, February 17, 2025.

42. "New Age Radio: Syndicated Shows Blaze Cosmic Trail to Format of the Future," *Billboard* 98, no. 43 (October 25, 1986): N8. Interviews with New Age musicians could be heard on William Noffke's Bay area radio shows *The Meeting of the Ways* (1972–74) and *New Dimensions* (1975–79). Tom Lopez's New Age radio serials produced by the media commune ZBS featured the music of New Age composer Tim Clark. See my essay "Travels with Jack: ZBS's Post-Network Radio Adventure," *Resonance* 1, no. 1 (2020).

43. Ethan Edgecombe of Fortuna Records told *Billboard* that in addition to promotion in New Age magazines and at New Age fairs, he relied on *Music*

from the Hearts of Space to promote his cassette releases. See John Sippel, "Distributor Nurtures New Vistas," *Billboard*, June 9, 1984, 6.

44. Goldman writes, "With this word, *intent*, we are really talking about the consciousness of the sound being created. This encompasses the overall state of the person making the sound and involves the physical, mental, emotional, and spiritual aspects of that person." *Healing Sounds: The Power of Harmonics* (Healing Arts Press, 1992), 18. See also Dane Rudhyar: "Will and Sound are vehicles for concretizing or exteriorizing needs, emotions, ideas, and subjective states of being or consciousness in general. Will and Sound are carrier-waves, bringing what is potential into a condition of actualization and effectual manifestation." *The Magic of Tone and the Art of Music* (Shambhala, 1982), 10. Iasos stated that an artist's intent rides on a sound wave "just as one water wave can ride on top of another, larger wave." Iasos, "Music as Light Waves," Iasos.com, https://iasos.com/articles/index.html#Music_as_Light_Waves.

45. Underwood, *World Music and Inner Transformation*, ph-9. Suzanne Doucet stated that there is "a certain state of consciousness that people have who do this music" and that state is "transferred through the music." "Visionary art is bringing a higher consciousness into the art, and transmitting that through the art," she said. Suzanne Doucet, interview by author, April 18, 2024. For Constance Demby, "The listener can only go as high, as deep and as wide as the composer went when receiving and composing the music." Web Archive, accessed July 14, 2024, https://web.archive.org/web/20050309062929fw_/http://www.constancedemby.com/healing_f.html. Steve McLinn, who recorded under that name Ojas, said that "the higher and more integrated my consciousness is, the higher and more integrated the music will be." Underwood, *World Music and Inner Transformation*, o-10.

46. Horn and Underwood, *Inside Paul Horn*, 198.

47. Susan Jacobs, "Stephen Halpern: Exploring the Farthest Reaches of Sound," *Yoga Journal*, November–December 1984, 40.

48. Summer gives the example of Beethoven rewriting a symphony fifty times. Rather than existing in a detached state of higher consciousness, Beethoven was primarily occupied with solving technical problems in the score.

49. Lisa Summer, *Music: The New Age Elixir* (Prometheus Books, 1996), 53.

50. The Sufi musician and philosopher Hazrat Inayat Khan, whose mystical writings on music were an influence on the visionary school, wrote that instrumental music "depends upon the evolution of man who expresses with the tips of his fingers upon the instrument his grade of evolution; in other words, his souls speaks through the instrument." Hazrat Inayat Khan, *The Mysticism of Sound and Music: The Sufi Teaching of Hazrat Inayat Khan* (Shambhala, 2022), 198.

51. In the words of Erik Davis, this approach to visionary art deepens the sense of the artist "as a mediator, and the artwork as a transmission rather than an object." Erik Davis, "Visionary Art: The Vanguard of Tradition," in *True Visions*, ed. Massimiliano Geraci and Federica Timeto (Betty Books, 2006), 8.

52. Chris Morris, "New Outlet Caters Solely to New Age Aficionados," *Billboard* 99, no. 6 (February 7, 1987): 39. Michael Stearns stated that New Age musicians "do not strive to become the object or the focal point for the audience's energy. Instead, we strive to create a context, in which each member of the audience can take responsibility for his or her own energy." "The music is not the artwork. The *artist* is the artwork. The music is just a metaphor for the growth and development of the artist, and for the depth of participation going on within that artist." Underwood, *World Music and Inner Transformation*, s-7–8, s16–17.

53. Helfried C. Zrzavy, "Issues of Incoherence and Cohesion in New Age Music," *Journal of Popular Culture* 24, no. 2 (Fall 1990): 41–46.

54. Paul Heelas, *The New Age Movement: Religion Culture, and Society in the Age of Postmodernity* (Blackwell, 1996), 83.

55. Malcolm Hamilton, "An Analysis of the Festival for Mind-Body-Spirit, London," in *Beyond New Age*, ed. Steven Sucliffe and Marion Bowman (Edinburgh University Press, 2000), 188–89. See also Christopher Partridge, *The Re-enchantment of the West*, vol. 1 (Continuum, 2004), 65–66. Partridge also discusses music festival culture (156–66).

56. "60 Noted Authorities to Speak at Pasadena Convention Center," *San Marino Tribune*, January 18, 1979, 12.

57. William McKibben, "The Whole Life," *The New Yorker*, December 5, 1982, 40–41.

58. Michael Stearns, interview by author, April 9, 2024.

59. Kelly, interview, August 8, 2024.

60. Edgecombe, interview, June 21, 2025.

61. Colin Campbell, "The Cult, the Cultic Milieu and Secularization," in *The Cultic Milieu: Oppositional Subcultures in an Age of Globalization*, ed. Jeffrey Kaplan and Helene Loow (Altamira Press, 2002), 14.

62. Campbell, "The Cult," 23. Hanegraaf writes that the New Age movement was "a manifestation of popular culture criticism . . . a reaction to the ideas and values which are perceived as having dominated western culture during the last two thousand years." Hanegraaff, *New Age Religion and Western Culture*, 302.

63. Bob Larson, *Straight Answers on the New Age* (Thomas Nelson, 1989), 176. Larson also writes that New Age composers "believe they can vibrate the

body's psychic energy centers to awaken and transform the spiritual awareness of the human spirit. They also hope to alter the listener's consciousness to induce a state of 'globalistic realization.' All these goals are contrary to Holy Scripture" (177). On subcultures and moral panic, see Sarah Thornton, *Club Cultures, Music Media and Subculture Capital* (Wesleyan University Press, 1996), 136–37.

64. Frank King, "New Age Music: Does It Soothe the Soul or Summon Satan?," *Calgary Herald*, February 16, 1991, 94.

65. In his analysis of the Festival for Mind-Body-Spirit, Malcolm Hamilton argues that the event provided a "plausibility structure" for the New Age subculture. "In gathering together such a large number of like-minded people," Hamilton writes, the festival "creates a strong sense of the force and significance of this alternative world view." Malcolm Hamilton, "An Analysis of the Festival for Mind-Body-Spirit, London," in *Beyond New Age*, ed. Steven Sutcliffe and Marion Bowman (Edinburgh University Press, 2000), 194.

66. New Age music can also be compared with Jamaican dub music of the 1970s, which had a marked spiritual valence, a studio-centric composition process, and the producer as the primary author. On dub and spirituality, see Christopher Partridge, *The Re-enchantment of the West*, vol. 1, 175–77. Thanks to an anonymous reader for bringing this to my attention.

67. "Steve Hill from Music from the Hearts of Space Interviews Iasos," Iasos .com, accessed July 12, 2024, https://iasos.com/media/mp3/HeartsOfSpace -Interview9-20-79.mp3.

68. New Age spirituality, Heelas writes, is a "highly optimistic, celebratory, utopian and spiritual form of humanism." Heelas, *The New Age Movement*, 28. See also Robert C. Ehle, "New Age Music," *American Music Teacher* 32, no. 6 (June–July 1983): 36–37. Turner and Hill, *Music from the Hearts of Space*, xi.

69. Patti Jean Birosik, *The New Age Music Guide* (Collier Books, 1989), xi, ix. The music critic Lee Underwood wrote in 1982 that New Age music appeals to positive emotions like "love, creativity, spiritual serenity and world brotherhood." By contrast, mass audiences "revel in the music of aggression, rebellion, heartache, sexual desire and Bacchanalian frenzy." Lee Underwood, "Mellowing Out with New Age Music," *Los Angeles Times*, July 11, 1982, M89.

70. "Soul Space Interviews Iasos," https://www.youtube.com/watch?v=dPhhztN6Bow, accessed July 12, 2024. See also "Jane Heaven, KPFA Radio, interviews Iasos," Iasos.com, accessed July 12, 2024, https://iasos.com/media /mp3/JaneHeaven-interviews-Iasos-KPFA-7-15-2012-.mp3.

71. Distortion from "Soul Space Interviews Iasos," https://www.youtube .com/watch?v=dPhhztN6Bow, accessed July 12, 2024. Clapping from

"Inkarose Interviews Iasos," https://www.youtube.com/watch?v=oPSn2_bMSeU, accessed July 12, 2024.

72. Kat Epple of Emerald Web talked about the need to make "angry music" as well as peaceful or uplifting music. Kat Epple, interview by author, August 15, 2024. See also Alex Grey interview, in *True Visions*, ed. Massimiliano Geraci and Federica Timeto (Betty Books, 2006), 34.

73. More can be said about the relationship between surrealism and visionary art. In their book on *Psychedelic Art*, Masters and Houston write that psychedelic art "proclaims the long overdue news that Freud, in the sense of most present use of his ideas, is dead!" Psychedelic artists, they continue "are concerned with depth probes of the psyche" but unlike surrealism, "psychedelic art makes a basic tenet of spiritual harmony with the universe. Psychedelic art is not antagonistic to the religious art of the past and does not find its affinities with daemonic and heretical art as such. It is more mature than surrealism in declining to equate the beautiful with the bizarre. It has no fascination with madness or the hallucinations of madness. It seeks out the images and other phenomena to be found in the depths of the normal but expanded mind." Robert E. L. Masters and Jean Houston, *Psychedelic Art* (Balance House, 1968), 96–97. Canonical visionary painters like Ernst Fuchs and Robert Venosa studied with Salvador Dali, and the curator Walter Hopps lists surrealism as precursor to the California visionary school of artists. Walter Hopps, introduction to *Visions* (Pomegranate, 1977), xiii. In the introduction to a collection of Gilbert Williams's works, Peny North writes that what distinguishes visionary art from surrealism is that, to count as visionary art, not only must a work "include at least two distinctly unique paradigms of reality represented naturalistically" but it must express a positive and uplifting message, with "spiritual content" that points to "the highest ideals of humankind." Peny North, "Illuminations," in *Illuminations: The Visionary Art of Gilbert Williams* (Visionary, 1986), 1–2. To take the example of Gilbert Williams's *The Healing Temple*, we see an almost photorealistic naturalistic depiction of a waterfall and cloudy night sky, paired with the "disparate reality" of a luminous temple. These realities collide not to create a shocking surrealist nightmare, but a soothing invocation of healing and transcendence.

74. The physicist David Bohm, an influence on New Age thinking, points out that the word "health" comes from the Anglo-Saxon "hale," which means "whole." "To be healthy is to be whole," Bohm writes. Bohm also notes that "holy" is based on the same root as "whole," and this entire network of meaning indicates that people have always sensed that "wholeness or integrity is an

absolute necessity to make life worth living." David Bohm, *Wholeness and Implicate Order* (Routledge, 1980), 3–4.

75. Sarah M. Pike, *New Age and Neopagan Religions in America* (Columbia University Press, 2004), 23.

76. Iasos, "Music as Light Waves," https://iasos.com/articles/index.html#Music_as_Light_Waves; Constance Demby, "The Healing Power of Sound," webpage, 1999–2000, Web Archive, accessed July 14, 2024, https://web.archive.org/web/20050309062929fw_/http://www.constancedemby.com/healing_f.html.

77. Note that *The BodyMind Energizer* grounds its claims in references to scientific research. Nomeika explains that the healing concepts presented on the cassette are "taken from quantum physics. Many scientists that have written about these concepts have won Nobel prizes for their work. If you do not believe them, who will you believe? This is a New Age, our understanding of life is different now. Our understanding is that all is one, that there is intelligence within the cells, the particles, the subatomic matter of the universe." On the New Age movement's high regard for modern science, see Hanegraaff, *New Age Religion and Western Culture*, 62.

78. See Mitch Horowitz, *One Simple Idea: How the Lessons of Positive Thinking Can Change Your Life* (Skyhorse, 2016). Horowitz writes that "in many ways, New Age spirituality is an update of New Thought" (259).

79. Barbara Ehrenreich, *Bright-Sided: How Positive Thinking Is Undermining America* (Picador, 2009), 4–5.

80. Iasos asserts that sound can heal through the "physical resonance" of vibrating air, which synchronizes the systems of the body. Iasos, "Music as Light Waves," Iasos.com, https://iasos.com/articles/index.html#Music_as_Light_Waves. McClellan writes that "atoms, molecules, cells, organs . . . are in a state of continuous vibration. The wave forms resulting from vibration are neither random nor chaotic but produce patterns of complex unity. . . . Disease is the result of a change in the fundamental frequency of vibration." McClellan, *The Healing Forces of Music*, 52–53.

81. "Through the principle of resonance, sound can be used to change disharmonious frequencies of the body back to their normal, healthy vibrations." Goldman, *Healing Sounds*, 13–14.

82. For Iasos, Jenny's "ground-breaking work, shows how sound and vibrations can create order and symmetry out of randomness and chaos." Manuel Montes, "Iasos: Interview to a Theoretician/Practitioner of the New Age," Amazings.com, www.amazings.com/articles/article0014.html. For other

references to cymatics, see Don Campbell, *The Mozart Effect: Tapping the Power of Music to Heal the Body, Strengthen the Mind, and Unlock the Creative Spirit* (Harper, 2001), 34; Khan, *The Mysticism of Sound and Music*, 91–92; Summer, *Music*, 187.

83. The introduction to the book is framed in terms of holism. We read that cymatics "seeks to understand people as unified energy fields . . . as wholes." "Our physical body, emotions, and thought processes are like cymatic forms which are organized by underlying vibrational fields, the densest (the physical), being animated by the subtler vibrations (emotions and thoughts)." John Beaulieu, "A Commentary on Cymatics," in *Cymatics: A Study of Wave Phenomena and Vibration*, ed. Hans Jenny (MACROmedia, 2001), 12, 17.

84. "Cymatics Full Documentary (Part 2 of 4). The Healing Nature of Sound," https://www.youtube.com/watch?v=57JpuMnWS1I&list=PLQ45lh-DF4Ajz_wRDqkMkoLRrEHIo4aBt&index=2.

85. "We're interested in holistic medicine, and the patient is an individual not a case," Manners says. Cymatics "seeks to understand people as unified energy fields . . . as wholes."

86. See, for example, Wikipedia, "Vibroacoustic Therapy," last updated November 2, 2025, 16:49 (UTC), https://en.wikipedia.org/wiki/Vibroacoustic_therapy. Ken Jenkins recalled that Anna Turner of *Music from the Hearts of Space* was involved with a company that manufactured sound healing beds.

87. McKibben, "The Whole Life," 40–41. Potentials Unlimited cassettes were advertised in *New Age Journal*; see *New Age Journal* 4, no. 2 (July 1978): 65.

88. The presence of subliminal messages in the media had been a topic of popular anxiety and speculation since the publication of Vance Packard's *The Hidden Persuaders* (1957). Discussion of subliminal advertising resurfaced in the 1970s, with writers such as Wilson Bryan Key claiming that advertising images were full of hidden messages. Audio producers have explored the potential of transmitting "subaudible" messages to help listeners lose weight or quit smoking. See my essay "Turn Me On, Dead Media: A Backwards Look at the Re-enchantment of an Old Medium," *Television and New Media* 12, no. 6 (November 2011): 531–51.

89. See *New Age Journal* 6, no. 13 (July 1981): 5.

90. Steven Halpern, interview by author, April 26, 2024.

91. Halpern, interview.

92. On the Human Potential movement and its relationship to the New Age movement, see Hanegraaff, *New Age Religion and Western Culture*, 48. On Esalen and the Human Potential movement, see Marilyn Ferguson, *The*

Aquarian Conspiracy (Penguin, 1980), 134–35. At Esalen, Kelly got to know the jazz musician Charles Lloyd, and they worked together on the album *Big Sur Tapestry* (1979). Kelly, interview, August 8, 2024.

93. Georgia Kelly, interviews by author, August 8, 2024, and February 21, 2025.

94. Rick Ingrasci, "Healing Tapes by Emmett E. Miller, M.D.," *New Age Journal* 6, no. 6 (December 1980): 57. See also Peggy Taylor, "The Power of Positive Listening," *New Age Journal* 7, no. 9 (April 1982): 80–81; and Peggy Taylor, "Portable Pep Talks," *New Age Journal* 7, no. 11 (June 1982): 78.

95. "Music itself does not do the healing," Kelly said, but it slows down bodily processes in a manner similar to meditation. "The music gives you an environment and a mood which facilitates relaxation and tranquility, enabling you to free yourself from the attachment to pain." In this context, she concluded, the term "therapeutic" is more appropriate than the term "healing." Underwood, *World Music and Inner Transformation*, gk-6–7. See also Margaret Draper, "Georgia Kelly: Temple Musician," *New Age Journal* 7, no. 2 (September 1981): 21. Compare Kelly's comments with Hanegraaff's discussion of the difference between curing disease and healing illness. Hanegraaff, *New Age Religion and Western Culture*, 42–43.

96. Kelly, interview, August 8, 2024. Underwood, *World Music and Inner Transformation*, gk-5–6.

97. Pamela Bloom, "Soul Music," *New Age Journal*, March/April 1987, 59–60.

98. Jon Kabot-Zinn, *The World of Relaxation: A Guided Mindfulness Meditation Practice for in the Hospital and/or at Home* (BetterListen, 2013).

99. Kabot-Zinn, *The World of Relaxation*.

100. Steve McLinn/Ojas created *Trance Tape* (1982) for a psychologist who needed stress-reduction music for his patients and *Rebirth* (1982) as a relaxing aid to childbirth. See Underwood, *World Music and Inner Transformation*, o-2.

101. Ferguson, *The Aquarian Conspiracy*, 2. Partridge writes that a key theme of New Age spirituality is that "the self is divine or that the self can, by some means or other, become divine." Partridge, *The Re-enchantment of the West*, vol. 1, 32.

102. Grof, "Brief History of Transpersonal Psychology," 49.

103. Grof, "Brief History of Transpersonal Psychology," 49. John C. Lilly compared an LSD session to "a 'pupation' period. The caterpillar forms the cocoon and then proceeds to total reorganization as a pupa. Only after a period of apparent disorganization and reformation can the butterfly form. . . . The

LSD session itself is the pupation, the period of organized disorganization, in which things are moving around with a fluidity and a plasticity that one normally does not experience." John C. Lilly, *The Centre of the Cyclone: An Autobiography of Inner Space* (Paladin, 1972), 28–29.

104. Gregory Bateson and Mary Catherine Bateson, *Angels Fear: Towards an Epistemology of the Sacred* (Hampton, 2005), 52.

105. Nina Sun Eidsheim, *Sensing Sound: Singing and Listening as Vibrational Practice (Sign, Storage, Transmission)* (Duke University Press, 2015), 3, 9, 167. See music theorist Brian Kane's thought-provoking critique of the vibrational ontology and an "ontological turn" in sound studies that sets itself against the linguistic emphasis in the humanities. Brian Kane, "Sound Studies Without Auditory Culture: A Critique of the Ontological Turn," *Sound Studies* 1, no. 1 (2015): 3, 7.

106. I refer here to Jonathan Sterne's notion of audile technique. See Jonathan Sterne, *The Audible Past: Cultural Origins of Sound Reproduction* (Duke University Press, 2003).

107. Bateson and Bateson, *Angels Fear*, 208.

108. Bateson and Bateson, *Angels Fear*, 52.

109. Bateson and Bateson, *Angels Fear*, 51.

110. That Bateson had conflicted feelings about the New Age movement is clear from an essay that explores the possibility of being "neither Supernatural nor Mechanical." Bateson and Bateson, *Angels Fear*, 50.

111. Bateson and Bateson, *Angels Fear*, 51–42.

112. Bateson and Bateson, *Angels Fear*, 64.

CHAPTER 3: LUMINOUS SOUNDS

1. Aldous Huxley, "Visionary Experience," in *The Highest State of Consciousness*, ed. John White (Anchor Books, 1972), 50–51.

2. Huxley, Huxley, "Visionary Experience," 36.

3. Huxley, "Visionary Experience," 56–57.

4. See Patrick Feaster and Jacob Smith, "Reconfiguring the History of Early Cinema Through the Phonograph," *Film History* 21, no. 4 (2009): 311–25, at 312. See also "Phonograph Toys and Early Sound Cartoons: Towards a History of Visualized Phonography," *Animation* 7, no. 2 (July 2012).

5. Gene Youngblood, *Expanded Cinema* (Fordham University Press, 1970), 45, 54.

6. Kirpal Singh, *Naam or Word* (Sant Bani Ashram, 1978), 155.

7. Lee Underwood, *World Music and Inner Transformation* (unpublished manuscript, 1984), Dem-12–13. Demby wrote that "Sound and Light are the building blocks of the universe, the very framework upon which all of creation is hung." Constance Demby, "The Healing Power of Sound," Web Archive, https://web.archive.org/web/20050309062929fw_/http://www.constancedemby.com/healing_f.html, accessed July 14, 2024.

8. Gaston Bachelard, *Earth and Reveries of Will: An Essay on the Imagination of the Matter* (Dallas Institute Publications, 2002), 246.

9. Ken Jenkins, interview by author, July 24, 2024.

10. John L. Rennick, "Homemade Color Organ," *Popular Science*, April 1936, 52.

11. Don Lancaster, "Psychedelia 1," *Popular Electronics*, September 1969, 27. In another article published that year, *Popular Science* announced that psychedelic light shows were "making the scene" and provided instructions for a build-it-yourself color organ. "Even if you are over 30, these gadgets popular with the kids are worth looking at with tolerance," the article explained, since they both enhanced music and served as lessons about color, light, and optics. W. Stevenson Bacon and Sam Shatavsky, "Tune-in with Psychedelic Light-Show System You Can Build," *Popular Science*, May 1969, 158–59. The video synthesizer pioneer Stephen Beck also created a color organ as a child, hooking up the lights on a Christmas tree to blink in time with Christmas music playing on the family stereo. Stephen Beck, interview by author, July 8, 2025.

12. On the history of luminescence in art, see E. Newton Harvey, *A History of Luminescence* (American Philosophical Society, 1957), 18. Articles from the 1930s and '40s with titles like "Homemade Ultra-Violet Produces Magic Black Light" suggested domestic uses for blacklights, such as producing stage effects for puppet theatres. See Douglas Leechman, "Homemade Ultra-Violet Produces Magic Black Light," *Popular Science*, December 1932, 75; Walter E. Burton, "Mystifying Black Light Experimentism," *Popular Science*, March 1934, 52; Judith Richardson, "Color Magic with Black Light," *Popular Mechanics*, June 1945, 106–7; Judith Richardson, "Black Light Reveals Secrets and Mystifies," *Popular Mechanics*, September 1935, 450–51.

13. Wesley S. Griswold, "His Magic Makes the World Glow," *Popular Science*, May 1953, 156, 238.

14. Griswold, "His Magic Makes the World Glow," 238.

15. James L. Kent, *Psychedelic Information Theory: Shamanism in the Age of Reason* (PIT Press, 2010), 38. See also Stanislav Grof, "Brief History of Transpersonal Psychology," *International Journal of Transpersonal Studies* 27, no. 1 (2008): 49.

16. Albert Hofmann, *LSD: My Problem Child* (McGraw-Hill, 1980).

17. John C. Lilly, *The Centre of the Cyclone: An Autobiography of Inner Space* (Paladin, 1972), 24.

18. Cei Richardson, "Enter the Supercolors," *Sun*, April 26, 1970, SM23.

19. Houston Blacklight made a number of popular poster designs, and several depict the Houston music scene. J D Emmanuel, interview by author, July 26, 2024. See Sara Gredler, "Love Street Light Circus Feel Good Machine," Texas State Historical Association (TSHA), www.tshaonline.org/handbook/entries/love-street-light-circus-feel-good-machine.

20. Emmanuel, interview.

21. Walter Hopps, introduction to in *Visions* (Pomegranate Publications, 1977), vii. See also Thomas Albright, "Visuals," *Rolling Stone*, September 2, 1971, 50.

22. Dan Donahue, *Ultraviolet: 69 Blacklight Posters from the Aquarian Age and Beyond* (Abrams, 2009), 2–3.

23. Jenkins, interview, July 24, 2024.

24. Jenkins, interview, July 24, 2024.

25. "Soundless Symphonies from Keys of 'Organ' Projected on Screen," *Popular Mechanics*, April 1924, 515. See Andrew R. Johnston, *Pulses of Abstraction: Episodes from a History of Animation* (University of Minnesota Press, 2020), 64, 72–73.

26. Keely Orgeman, "A Radiant Manifestation in Space: Wilfred, Lumia, and Light," in *Lumia: Thomas Wilfred and the Art of Light* (Yale University Press, 2017), 21. See also William Moritz, "Abstract Film and Color Music," in *The Spiritual in Art: Abstract Painting 1890–1985*, ed. Maurice Tuchman (Abbeville Press, 1986); Kerry Brougher, Jeremy Strick, Ari Wiseman, and Judith Zilczer, eds., *Visual Music: Synesthesia in Art and Music Since 1900* (Los Angeles Museum of Contemporary Art, 2005). One writer described Wilfred's lumia as jewels "poured out of invisible cornucopias." Kenneth Peacock, "Instruments to Perform Color-Music: Two Centuries of Technological Experimentation," *Leonardo* 21, no. 4 (1988): 397–406, at 405.

27. Peacock, "Instruments to Perform Color-Music," 405.

28. Donna M. Stein, *Thomas Wilfred: Lumia* (Corcoran Gallery of Art, 1971), 61. Andrew Robert Johnston, "The Color of Prometheus: Thomas Wilfred's Lumia and the Projection of Transcendence," in *Color and the Moving Image: History, Theory, Aesthetics, Archive*, ed. Simon Brown, Sarah Street, and Liz Watkins (Routledge, 2013), 69.

29. Thomas Wilfred, "Composing in the Art of Lumia," *Journal of Aesthetics and Art Criticism* 7, no. 2 (December 1948): 79–80. On the use of the "dream

ship" metaphor, see Keely Orgeman, "A Radiant Manifestation in Space: Wilfred, Lumia, and Light," in *Lumia: Thomas Wilfred and the Art of Light* (Yale University Press, 2017), 26; Wilfred, "Composing in the Art of Lumia," 79–80.

30. Gregory Zinman, "Thomas Wilfred's Aesthetic Legacy," in *Lumia: Thomas Wilfred and the Art of Light*, by Keely Orgeman (Yale University Press, 2017).

31. Jenkins, interview, July 24, 2024.

32. Ad, *Radio-Electronics Magazine* 41, no. 4 (April 1970): 99.

33. Jenkins, interview, July 24, 2024.

34. Jenkins, interview, July 24, 2024.

35. Dorothy Fadiman, interview by author, March 6, 2025.

36. Jenkins, interview, July 24, 2024

37. Hill recalled that he had started working on the film as an audio engineer, but as it evolved, he became more of a music director. "Because of doing the radio program, I was aware of a lot of early American and European New Age and electronic music that would work with the film and give it a contemporary sound," he said. Stephen Hill, email to author, April 26, 2025.

38. Script available at Concentric Media (website), www.concentric.org/films/radiance.html.

39. "The message that we are all radiant beings reaches more than the intellect—it rushes directly to the heart," the reviewer stated. Bud Brainard, "Radiance: The Experience of Light," *New Age Journal* 4, no. 5 (October 1978): 20.

40. Gene Youngblood, *Expanded Cinema* (Fordham University Press, 1970): 158–59.

41. Youngblood, *Expanded Cinema*, 388–90. William Moritz, "Jordan Belson Last of the Great Masters," in *Animation: Critical and Primary Sources*, vol. 4, *Key Individuals*, ed. Chris Pallant (Bloomsbury Academic, 2021), 25, 28. See also K. C. Yu, K. D. Williams, Gaston L. Neafus, and G. Downing, "Gaia Journeys: A Museum-Based Immersive Performance Exploration of the Earth," *International Journal of Digital Earth* 2, no. 1 (2009): 44–58. John Hare, "(In-House) Laser Shows: A Long Term Proposition," *Planetarian* 13, no. 1 (March 1984): 8.

42. Dennis W. Sunal and Cynthia Szymanski Sunal, "The Planetarium in the American School Experience," *School Science and Mathematics* 77, no. 3 (1977): 203–13, at 207.

43. Sunal and Sunal, "The Planetarium in the American School Experience," 203, 209. Film scholar Alison Griffiths notes that planetarium shows had always been "heavily intertextual multimedia performances." Alison Griffiths, "A Moving Picture of the Heavens: The Planetarium Space Show as Useful

Cinema," in *Useful Cinema*, ed. Charles R. Acland and Haidee Wasson (Duke University Press, 2011), 231.

44. Interview with Larry Sturhahn, *Filmmaker's Newsletter*, May 1975, www.jordanbelson.info/copy-2-of-texts.

45. Scott MacDonald, *A Critical Cinema: Interviews with Independent Filmmakers*, vol. 3 (University of California Press, 1988), 73. Alfred Frankenstein, "Vortex: The Music of the Hemispheres," *High Fidelity* 9, no. 5 (May 1959): 46.

46. Cindy Keefer, "Cosmic Cinema and the Vortex Concerts," in *Cosmos: En Busca de los Origenes* (TEA Tenerife Espacio de las Artes, 2009), 472.

47. Frankenstein, "Vortex," 46.

48. Jordan Belson, transcript of tape, 1959, CineFiles, University of California Berkeley Art Museum and Pacific Film Archive, www.jordanbelson.info/copy-2-of-texts.

49. MacDonald, *A Critical Cinema*, 73–74.

50. Doug McKechnie, interview by author, August 7, 2025.

51. In one review, San Francisco music critic Ralph J. Gleason's comments recall Thomas Wilfred's spacecraft metaphor for lumia art. He writes that a "swirling mass of light particles flows away from a central point, giving one the illusion of being in the observation bubble of a jet fighter or a rocket." Ralph J. Gleason, "Vortex Music Goes Round and Round," *San Francisco Chronicle*, January 14, 1958, 19. See also Junius Adams, liner notes to *Highlights of Vortex* (Folkways Records, 1959).

52. Frankenstein, "Vortex IV Sounds Better Than Ever," *San Francisco Chronicle*, May 19, 1958, 39. Paine Knickerbocker, "Vortex Film Producer Discusses His New Art," *San Francisco Chronicle*, December 15, 1958, 43. Keefer, "Cosmic Cinema and the Vortex Concerts," 475.

53. In 1976, the journal *Planetarian* provided a list of "planetarium hits" that included Beethoven's Piano Sonata No. 14 in C-sharp Minor ("Moonlight"), Vivaldi's *The Four Seasons*, Gustav Holst's *The Planets*, Debussy's *Clair De Lune*, and Richard Strauss's *Also Sprach Zarathustra*. Jack Dunn, "Add Some Music to Your Day (Night)," *Planetarian* 5, no. 1 (Spring 1976): 19–25, at 20.

54. Tim Clark, interview by author, June 4, 2024.

55. Clark, interview.

56. Tim Clark, "Some Thought on Planetarium Show Music," *Planetarian* 3, nos. 1 & 2 (Spring/Summer 1974): 51.

57. "They Dreamed of Staying Up," *Rochester Democrat and Chronicle*, February 27, 1972, 7B. Jack Garner, "Mixed Media Show Is a Giant Sleep-In,"

article in Strasenburgh Planetarium scrapbook. "Cine Dreams" is a precursor to New Age musician Robert Rich's "sleep concerts" of the 1980s, which similarly used music as a tool to explore states of consciousness that exist between wakefulness and sleep. More on Rich in chapter 6.

58. *Science Center News*, November 1973. That same year, the electronic music pioneer Morton Subotnick brought an experimental "four-dimensional concrete poem" called "Game for Two Players" to the planetarium, which involved a process related to the kind of biofeedback devices on display at the Kohoutek Celebration. "Planetarium Show Is a 'Game for Two Players,'" scrapbook. Mark Starr, "New Game Two People Play," article in Strasenburgh Planetarium scrapbook. See also Visual Studies Workshop (website), www.vsw.org/collections/watch-portable-channel-videos/summer-fun/.

59. Hardham studied film and experimental video at San Francisco State College, where he was influenced by experimental filmmakers like Jordan Belson and John Whitney. In the mid-1960s, Hardham had become excited about the poster art connected to the rock scene in San Francisco, and when he saw what was happening with light shows at concerts, he thought, "Wow, I really want to do that." In 1972 he teamed up with Joan Chase and Mary Ann Meyer to form Heavy Water. In San Francisco, Hardham did shows with the San Francisco Tape Music Center, Don Buchla, and early synth pioneer Doug McKechnie. John Hardham, interview by author, September 26, 2024.

60. Hardham, interview.

61. Hardham, interview.

62. A Strasenburgh newsletter describes the event: "Imagine two Moog Synthesizers being played simultaneously by the planetarium's music director, Tim Clark. Imagine that Tim and the synthesizers are on the Zeiss projector elevator, rising up into the center of the Star Theater. Surrounding them is a cascade of light, projected on the dome by the Heavy Water Lightshow of San Francisco." Clark's score contains "original jazz and rock oriented pieces composed on the Moog synthesizer" and he accompanied himself with prerecorded tracks. See "Moog Light," *Science Center News*, May 1975. Heavy Water returned to the Strasenburgh in 1978 with a show called "Astral Perceptions," which utilized kaleidoscopic lenses, prisms, and mylar reflectors. The audience also got a free pair of 3-D glasses with their ticket, which was said to heighten the sensation of flying or the ability to reach out and touch the images that accompanied a musical score by Clark. See *Science Center News*, April 1978.

63. Underwood, *World Music and Inner Transformation*, Dem-12–13.

64. Anna Van Der Heide, "Central Maine Musicians Play 'Not Music' Music," *Central Maine Morning Sentinel*, 1974; Ad, *Boston Globe*, April 17,

1975, A13. "From the Vaults: Constance Demby born 9 May 1939," May 9, 2023, https://fromthevaults-boppinbob.blogspot.com/2023/05/constance-demby-born-9-may-1939.html; Ray Murphy, "Maine Power Co. an Electrifying Experience," *Boston Globe*, September 11, 1975, 31. The group appeared at the Boston Hayden Planetarium in 1975, presenting a "sound and light program" titled *Cosmic Resonances*. A review of the show stated, "The concerts are intended as space trips, both inner and outer space, or spaced-out trips, seeking to find a moment outside of time where there exists a perfect suspension of soul and mind, and where the spiritual values come all together into a perfect union." "Multi-media Orchestra to Perform," *Mass Media in Boston*, April 8, 1975, 18.

65. Laddy Kite, "Electronic Ceremonies in Rochester," *Afterimage* 2, no. 4 (October 1974): 2–3. See Randy Cohen, "Synthesized Video," *Synapse* 2, no. 2 (July–August 1977): 14–15; Murphy, "Maine Power Co.," 31.

66. Kite, "Electronic Ceremonies in Rochester," 2–3. A Rochester-based nonprofit video documentary operation filmed the event, allowing us to see how video images of faces and hands strumming instruments were distorted using the video synthesizer and merged with planetarium slides of clouds and outer space. See https://vimeo.com/showcase/7677439?video=367351648.

67. Clark, interview.

68. Iasos took part in a revival of the Vortex concerts in 1974. That revival also featured electronic musician Doug McKechnie and Maggi Payne. John L. Wasserman, "Light plus Sound Equals a Hit," *San Francisco Chronicle*, November 13, 1974, 57.

69. Other New Age planetarium collaborations include Kevin Braheny Fortune's album *Galaxies* (1988), created for the Hanson Planetarium in Salt Lake City, which was a project connected to Timothy Ferris's coffee table book *Galaxies* (1982) and Steve Roach's performances at the Seattle Pacific Science Center and the Ruben H. Fleet Space Theatre in San Diego. Kevin Braheny Fortune, interview by author, August 27, 2024; Steve Roach, interview by author, August 27, 2024. Kat Epple recalled that like the Central Maine show at the Strasenbrugh, they would plan a whole show that would start with the depiction of sunset and the appearance of the stars. Kat Epple, interview by author, August 15, 2024.

70. Jonn Serrie, interview by author, October 3, 2024.

71. Serrie, interview.

72. Serrie, interview.

73. Dennis Mammana, "Music from the Hearts of Space," *Planetarian* 13, no. 1 (March 1984): 30. See also John Sunier, "Space Music Offers Excitement and Relaxation," *San Francisco Chronicle*, October 10, 1982, 11.

74. Jenkins, interview, July 24, 2024.
75. Jenkins, interview, July 24, 2024.
76. Jenkins, interview, July 24, 2024.
77. Jenkins, interview, July 24, 2024.
78. Jenkins, interview, July 24, 2024.
79. Jenkins thought of color as a way to match the temporality of music. "Music is constantly changing," he said, "even in the slow, ambient world there's change going on constantly." The color palette of his visual music is also changing constantly (Jenkins, interview, October 4, 2024).
80. Jenkins, interview, July 24, 2024.
81. See MacDonald, *A Critical Cinema*, 76–77.
82. Belson also made films titled *Seapeace* (1980), which likely uses music from Georgia Kelly's album *Seapeace*; *Pisces/Blues* (1980), which likely uses tracks from Steven Halpern's album *Zodiac Suite*; and *Eleusis/Crotona* (1980), which likely uses tracks from Halpern and Kelly's *Ancient Echoes*.
83. Manuel Montes, "Iasos: Interview to a Theoretician/Practitioner of the New Age," Amazings (website), www.amazings.com/articles/article0014.html. "Bliss Interview with Iasos," https://iasos.com/articles/bliss_interview/. In one interview, Iasos said that in his vision of the future, records would be made obsolete by video technology, and he foresaw a future in which "in the safety and sacredness" of a person's own living room, one could have "a very profoundly moving spiritual experience." Interview with Will Noffke, Noffke archive.
84. The use of fabric to create visual accompaniment for New Age music can also be seen in Lynn Augstein's collaborations with Steve Roach. See https://www.youtube.com/cobaltsunvideo.
85. Roach also made *Kairos* (2006), a collaboration with visual artists Lynn Augstein, Steven Rooke, and John Vega.
86. MacLaine and the producers had originally wanted each mandala to remain in the chakra's assigned color, but Jenkins convinced them to only begin and end with the primary color and in between to move through his usual prismatic patterns to avoid color fatigue. Ken Jenkins, interview by author, August 10, 2024. A precursor to MacLaine's *Inner Workout* can be seen in the 1983 VHS tape *YogaMoves with Alan Finger*, which features video effects by Ron Hays. See https://www.youtube.com/watch?v=HAFq_Nd003s.
87. "Shirley MacLaine's TV Special Is, as Usual, Not Your Ordinary Fare," *Sun*, March 8, 1977, B4.
88. Angela Schill, "Laserium Two," *Synapse* 1, no. 6 (March–April 1977): 33. A review noted that Tim Clark's music was "made up of the combined timbres

of a synthesizer and tuned water glasses" and "was very complimentary with the textures in the darkness above us."

89. Kim Blair, "Laser Box Puts Music in Color on Beam," *Los Angeles Times*, March 21, 1971, D5. Patricia Daukantas, "A Short History of Laser Light Shows," *OPN Optics & Photonics News*, May 2010, 45–46. See also the chapter on Garmire in Colin Williamson, *Drawn to Nature: American Animation in the Age of Science* (University of Minnesota Press, 2025).

90. Daukantas, "A Short History of Laser Light Shows," 45–46. Not everyone was happy about the success of planetarium laser shows. Planetarium execs were concerned about rowdy and stoned youth audiences, and old school visual artists, like Doug McKechnie, who worked on the revival of the Vortex Concerts in 1974, remembered feeling disgusted that more elaborate and complicated visual performances were dropped in favor of Laserium, which he characterized as "one little box with a green squiggly line." Doug McKechnie, interview by author, August 7, 2025.

91. John Leonard, "Starring a Concentration of Light," *New York Times*, June 25, 1976, 52. Dan Sullivan, "Beaming In on a Laser Light Show," *Los Angeles Times*, September 25, 1974, G13.

92. Sullivan, "Beaming In on a Laser Light Show," 3. The *San Francisco Chronicle* described "delicate skeins of color that rippled like waves through foggy nimbuses propelled across the dome by softly blowing breezes." Thomas Albright, "A Lightweight Light Show," *San Francisco Chronicle*, November 26, 1974, 41. "The experience is dreamlike and defies verbalization. The joy lies in the personal sensation of abstract visual stimulation with colors as pure and rich as a rainbow." Charles Edison Jr., "Astral Fireworks in Laserium II," *Los Angeles Times*, November 5, 1976, E23. Newspaper ads proclaim, "Laserium is the closest thing to tripping out in inner space." "Display Ad," *Los Angeles Times*, Jan 9, 1977, R44.

93. Duncan Fallowell, "Laser Light Shows," *The Spectator*, July 2, 1977, 24. "Had it not been for psychedelic experience in my Timothy Leary days I could well have been taken aback." Abstraction was felt to be part of Laserium's appeal. "This generation has heard too many words," one journalist wrote. "It wants to turn off the subtitles and go with the images." Sullivan, "Beaming In on a Laser Light Show."

94. Glenn Edward Thomas, *The Laserium Laserist: The Greatest Job on Earth* (International Laser Display Association, 2023), 33, hwww.ilda.com/thomas.htm.

95. Thomas, *The Laserium Laserist*, 37.

96. Ken Jenkins, email to author, October 14, 2024.

97. In press accounts and Laserium promotional materials, the laser light show was described as a new art form. The national sales manager for Laserium told a reporter that laser shows were "a new entertainment medium for the coming century," and that he envisioned a cohort of "master laserists emerging from the 20th Century consciousness as Leonardo and Raphael did in their age of graphic arts." Calvin Ahlgren, "Laserium Concert Began on a Simulated Universe Stardrop," *San Francisco Chronicle*, December 1, 1974, 15. "This is an instrument which hasn't yet found its Beethoven," wrote journalist Dan Sullivan. "Beaming In on a Laser Light Show," *Los Angeles Times*, September 25, 1974, G13.

98. Interview in *Laserium: The Gods of Light* (2022). See also Charles Solomon, "Laser Artistry: Right on Beam," *Los Angeles Times*, November 24, 1983, H2.

99. Roach observed that laserists carried themselves very much like musicians. "They took on the kind of swagger of a musician," he recalled, which had something to do with the fact that they entertained large crowds of people with sounds and images in darkened theaters, much like popular musicians. Roach recalled that his colleagues at Laserium had an ARP 2600 synth, but they were using it to create visuals that they could colorize and control (Roach, interview).

100. The Who, Wings, ELO, and Led Zeppelin were early adopters of lasers in the domain of arena rock.

101. Mary Ann Meyer, "Concert Reviews: Tangerine Dream," *Variety* 286, no. 10 (April 13, 1977): 62. The synth magazine *Synapse* published a review of Laserium in 1977 in which we read that "lasers and synthesizers both have an enticing beauty and a technical flawlessness that when experienced together, the final sum product is enhanced several hundred times. . . . The dynamic duo will certainly advance by great leaps toward a more perfect fusion of this type of expression." Angela Schill, "Laserium Two," *Synapse* 1, no. 6 (March–April 1977): 33.

102. Epple remembers getting busted at one show by the Bureau of Radiological Health, who asked to see their license for operating a laser. They didn't have one and were let go with a warning. They soon got their BRH official laser operator license (Epple, interview).

103. Richard Horn, "The Lighter Side of Laser," *New York Times*, September 30, 1979, SM224. At least one person—Hugh Hefner—installed a home laser projection system in his bedroom in the Playboy mansion. Ed Auswachs, interview by author, August 1, 2025.

104. David Moore, "Laser Images and Blood-Red Heart Throbs," *San Francisco Chronicle*, August 19, 1979, 36. The success of Laserium was a mixed

blessing for light shows like Heavy Water, as it came to dominate audiovisual entertainment at planetariums. The Strasenburgh Planetarium launched its own in-house laser show in 1982. Furthermore, the Laserium business model moved away from New Age and classical toward current Top 40 hits, heavy metal, and classic rock during the 1980s.

105. Another point of intersection between Jackson and the visionary school can be found in visionary artist Gilbert Williams's artwork for the album *Triumph* (1980), by the Jacksons.

106. Kirpal Singh, *Naam or Word* (Sant Bani Ashram, 1978), 155.

CHAPTER 4: COSMIC SOUNDS

1. The Cosmic Beam, also known as the Blaster Beam, was originally designed by John Lazelle, who had been inspired by American composer and instrument builder Harry Partch.

2. Positive Media Paul, "Francisco Lupica Interview," https://web.archive.org/web/20051219055003/http://www.virtualvenice.info/music/francisint.htm. In an article on Lupica from 1973, he is described performing dressed entirely in white and playing with "religious simplicity." His music, we read, "deals directly with the elements and their spiritual qualities." Len Lyons, "Cosmic Beam Experience Isn't Meant for the Concert Stage," *San Francisco Examiner*, December 9, 1973, 16.

3. Pat Hartman, "Francisco and His Cosmic Beam," https://web.archive.org/web/20051219044216/http://www.virtualvenice.info/music/francisco.htm. John Lilly, famous for his research into dolphin intelligence, LSD, and isolation tanks, is quoted on the back of the album: "If you are one of the people who establishes far out states of being and domains of consciousness through listening to music, then Francisco's music is the best prescription I know." Web Archive, https://web.archive.org/web/20050405085408/http://www.virtualvenice.info.

4. Lupica also established a relationship with the director Terrence Malick in the 1970s that led to the Beam being used in *The Thin Red Line* (1998) and *The Tree of Life* (2011). See https://www.youtube.com/watch?v=tvFDqZHbSMM; and Web Archive, https://web.archive.org/web/20161025002541/http://francescocosmicbeamexperience.com/the-journey-of-the-consmic-beam-exprience/.

5. See Julie Hubbert, *Celluloid Symphonies* (University of California Press, 2011).

6. Kathryn Kalinak, *Film Music: A Very Short Introduction* (Oxford University Press, 2023), 75. See Jeff Smith, *The Sounds of Commerce* (Columbia University Press, 1998). On Williams's Romantic style, see Emilio Audissino, *The Film Music of John Williams* (University of Wisconsin Press, 2021), 37–54.

7. Mervyn Cooke, *A History of Film Music* (Cambridge University Press, 2008), 478.

8. Cooke, *A History of Film Music*, 469–70.

9. Kalinak, *Film Music*, 77–78. See also Terry Atkinson, "Scoring with Synthesizers," *American Film* 7, no. 10 (September 1982): 67–17.

10. Kat Epple, interview by author, November 18, 2024. In a 1980 interview, Bob Stohl of Emerald Web was asked how to define their music. He replied, "It's not progressive rock. It's like . . . progressive imagery music. It's hard to give it a name. Acoustic electronic music? Cosmic music?" David Lieber, "Flying Towards Fame on the Wings of Music," *News-Press* (Fort Myers, Florida), May 16, 1980, 49. In an article in *New Age Journal* from 1982, the music is referred to as "New Age music, innerspace music, cosmic music, environmental music, meditation music, etc." Peggy Taylor and Rick Ingrasci, "The Cosmic Connection," *New Age Journal* 7, no. 8 (March 1982): 82.

11. On the characteristic of universal correspondences in Western Esotericism, see Antoine Faivre, *Western Esotericism: A Concise History* (State University of New York Press, 2010), 11–12. Joscelyn Godwin, *The Greater & Lesser Worlds of Robert Fludd* (Inner Traditions, 2018), 30. On the ecological dimension to the term "cosmos," see Laura Dassow Walls, "Cosmos," in *Keywords for Environmental Studies*, ed. Joni Adamson, William A. Gleason, and David N. Pellow (New York University Press, 2016), 48.

12. The front cover of the Kohoutek Celebration program states that the coming of the comet "reminds us of our essential connection with the cosmos." Kohoutek Celebration of Consciousness program, annotated, Paul Mariah Papers, Yale University Library, GEN MSS 2096, box 7, folder 134.

13. One of the models for *Koyaanisqatsi* was Hilary Harris's short film *Organism* (1975), which is even more sympatico with Continuum, in its intercutting between time-lapse city scenes and the flow of blood cells.

14. Kalinak, *Film Music*, 75. Mervyn Cooke agrees, writing that "the mechanical nature" of Glass's repetition "could readily foster emotional neutrality and distanciation." Cooke, *A History of Film Music*, 478.

15. Scott MacDonald, "Celebration and Warning," in *The Qatsi Trilogy* DVD booklet (Criterion Collection, 2012), 10.

16. Later, *Koyaanisqatsi* was seen as a precursor to New Age video. See, for example, "VH-1's 'New Visions' Helps Expand Horizons," *Billboard* 98,

no. 43 (October 25, 1986): N8; Chris McGowan, "Instrumental Inroads: Outburst of Quiet Fusion Signals That New Age Has Arrived," *Billboard* 98, no. 43 (October 25, 1986): N3; Linda Kohanov, "The Sight of Music," *New Age Journal*, January/February 1990, 91–92.

17. Scott MacDonald, *The Sublimity of Document: Cinema as Diorama* (Oxford University Press, 2019), 27–28.

18. Michael Stearns, interview by author, April 9, 2024.

19. Susan Harper, interview by author, January 7, 2025. Stearns, interview, April 9, 2024; Michael Stearns, interview by author, March 4, 2025.

20. See Emilie Conrad, *Life on Land: The Story of Continuum* (North Atlantic Books, 2007). See also the audio documentary produced by Gary David, "The Movement of Movements," Continuum Movement Arts (website), www.continuummovementarts.org/portfolio-item/movement-of-movement/. See also Lee Underwood, *World Music and Inner Transformation* (unpublished manuscript, 1984), s-3–4.

21. At one point, he was working with Robert Moog to create a custom-designed twenty-two-tone synthesizer. Gary David, interview by author, January 28, 2025. In the 1960s, David worked as a professional musician, singing and playing piano with a trio in a San Francisco club, and later made several albums with an experimental group called The Sound of Feeling.

22. David, interview. The first Continuum class David attended had music by Don Preston, the keyboard player with Frank Zappa's Mothers of Invention. Preston was playing a Buchla synthesizer, and David recalled that "it was raining sound, it was just beautiful."

23. During the workshop, Stearns recognized that David had created a tape piece that featured excerpts from Ken Nordine's spoken word album *Word Jazz* (1957) played backward and at half speed. After the session, Stearns approached David and asked, "How did you think to take that cut from that record, turn it into a loop, and then play it backwards at half speed?" David looked at him in amazement, and said, "You're the only person in the world who would have known that!" Stearns, interview, April 9, 2024.

24. Harper, interview.

25. Harper, interview.

26. Georgianne Cowan, who was a student and then a teacher at Continuum, remembered that Conrad was "a very powerful presence" and had a "shamanic energy," with jet black hair and piercing eyes. "She was powerful, sharp as an eagle, and very influential. She really commanded attention." Georgianne Cowan, interview by author, May 30, 2025. One student remembered an hour-long Continuum session dedicated to laying on the floor and turning

the body over while "being aware of every single part that's engaged in turning, and where you're blocked, where you can't turn, where you need to push a little." Jeanette Stobie, interview by author, May 25, 2025.

27. Conrad, *Life on Land*, 6–7, 96–97. Conrad had been influenced by Theodor Schwenk's book *Sensitive Chaos: The Creation of Flowing Forms in Water and Air* (1962), which connected the "cosmic qualities and movements of water" with a host of other phenomena, such as the movements of air, the formation of biological structures, and the flow of thought. Theodor Schwenk, *Sensitive Chaos: The Creation of Flowing Forms in Water and Air* (Sophia Books, 1962), 95–96.

28. Susan Harper, interviews by author, February 13, 2025, and January 7, 2025.

29. Georgianne Cowan, email to author, May 29, 2025.

30. David, interview.

31. "We would work the sound into a fluid wave" (David, interview).

32. Harper, interview, January 7, 2025.

33. For Georgianne Cowan, the music at Continuum "did not impose itself." Rather, it was "the scaffolding for the raw expression of the dancer. Because it did not dictate, there was permission to let emerge whatever energies needed to be exorcized or expressed. . . . It was healing at its core. . . . It held you safely in its arms." Georgianne Cowan, email to author, May 29, 2025.

34. Larkin Stentz, interview by author, February 17, 2025.

35. Stentz, interview.

36. Kevin Braheny Fortune, interview by author, August 27, 2024.

37. Hill met Michael Stearns around 1977, a time when he was experiencing distress from overwork. Stearns saw Hill's poor condition and suggested that he meet with Emilie Conrad at Continuum. Hill found Conrad to be one of the most impressive people he'd ever encountered and dropped everything to take classes with her for a month. "In addition to her unique movement practice, she talked about practical and philosophical principles for living," he said. "I loved it." Stephen Hill, email to author, April 26, 2025. Hill was a fan of Larkin as well and has a blurb on his album: "Larkin's pure, clear music will make you aware of the pace of your life and provide you with the space to return to the natural rhythms of the cosmos."

38. Anna Turner and Stephen Hill, *Music from the Hearts of Space: Guide to Cosmic, Transcendent and Innerspace Music* (Music from the Hearts of Space, 1981), 76, 20.

39. Underwood, *World Music and Inner Transformation*, s-26–27. Harper recalls that Conrad had spoken about the notion of a planetary unfolding,

which referred to the idea that "the planet wasn't done, the cosmos wasn't done, and that we were part of a creative unfolding." These ideas inspired the music on Stearns's album. Harper, interview, January 7, 2025.

40. After gaining an awareness of the resonance of the cosmos as a whole, David's dream ends with him waking up to the small, "moist breath" of the Earth. Stearns told an interviewer that "we are part of a much larger whole and a much larger system," and that in *Planetary Unfolding*, he "wanted the music to take it from the planet Earth, out into a much larger system, and then bring it back." Underwood, *World Music and Inner Transformation*, s-26–27. Liner notes on the cassette state that the music "transports us to the far reaches of deep space. Gently we return with new ears to our unfolding planet Earth alive, in an ever-changing universe."

41. Braheny Fortune, interview.

42. Wouter J. Hanegraaff, *New Age Religion and Western Culture* (Brill, 1996), 119–20. The drone/sequencer technique of cellular wave music is the sonic equivalent to visual techniques of the visionary artist Alex Grey. Grey depicts translucent bodies whose realistic anatomy coexists with "the glowing subtle energies visible to clairvoyants," a manifestation of his belief that "the human anatomy is a microcosm of the many systems and levels of order in nature." Grey hoped that this double description would inspire viewers to broaden their sense of self beyond the physical body to allow an "influx of healing energies from a more perfect spiritual template." Grey's images, like Continuum's cellular wave music, are a variation on the alchemical depiction of the human body as a system of nested cosmic circles. Alex Grey interview, in *True Visions*, ed. Massimiliano Geraci and Federica Timeto (Betty Books, 2006), 34.

43. Harper, interview, January 7, 2025. The label was originally named Continuum Tape Montage, because they were only making cassettes. Braheny Fortune tried his hand at self-releasing cassettes but admitted that he was "terrible at business and self-promotion." Stephen Hill from "Music from the Hearts of Space" was a big fan, and played his music on the air, especially a track titled "Perelandra." Hill eventually released it on his Hearts of Space record label. Braheny Fortune interview. Another of his early tracks, "Lullaby for the Hearts of Space," was recorded at a fundraiser for Hill and Turner's KPFA show.

44. Stearns, interview, March 4, 2025. Stearns was working at this time with Craig Huxley, who had been a child actor on television shows like *Bewitched*, *Gunsmoke*, and *Star Trek*. Huxley was also an accomplished jazz pianist and studied musical harmony with Gary David. Through David, he became part of the Continuum musical scene. Huxley and Stearns saw Francesco Lupica

performing with his Cosmic Beam and decided to build a more portable version of the instrument using lightweight aluminum. Stearns used one of those Beams on *Planetary Unfolding.* When Huxley left Continuum, he opened his own studio and began working on scoring music for films.

45. Edward Guthman, "'Chronos': A Visual Symphony of the World," *San Francisco Chronicle*, June 29, 1986, 24.

46. Steve Winn, "Passing Time in a Big Way," *San Francisco Chronicle*, July 3, 1986, 68.

47. MacDonald, *The Sublimity of Document*, 24. MacDonald notes that Fricke's titles reflect his spiritual interests: "In Buddhism samsara is the repetitive cycle of birth and death that characterizes earthly life; in Islam baraka is the divine force that flows through people and things attuned to God."

48. MacDonald, *The Sublimity of Document*, 43.

49. MacDonald, *The Sublimity of Document*, 38.

50. MacDonald, *The Sublimity of Document*, 32.

51. Lee Underwood, "Mood Elevator Music," *LA Weekly*, September 5, 1985, 49. In the same interview, Stearns stated that "throughout *Chronos*, we see and hear and feel the vast slow time of nature, the gradual acceleration of time during the evolution of Western man, and the highspeed technological time we live in today. Historical, psychological and spiritual time all exist together, simultaneously, in this present moment. I tried to permeate the music with that feeling."

52. MacDonald, *The Sublimity of Document*, 37. Fricke stated that "if there's one person who understands what I'm doing, it's Michael [Stearns]; we're very much on the same wavelength, blending images and music together with the same outcome in mind."

53. On IMAX, see Charles R. Acland, "IMAX Technology and the Tourist Gaze," *Cultural Studies* 12, no. 3 (1998): 431. The first IMAX theater was opened in Toronto in 1971, and in 1994, "museum sites accounted for 59 per cent of all IMAX theatres," and "documentary and educational films predominate the IMAX film library" (432–33). See also Alison Griffiths, "Time Traveling IMAX Style," in *Virtual Voyages: Cinema and Travel*, ed. Jeffrey Ruoff (Duke University Press, 2006), 240–41.

54. Stephen Hunter, "'Chronos': Visual Poem on an Imax Screen," *Baltimore Sun*, November 3, 1989, F13. Fricke stated that Jeffery Kirsch, the director of the Reuben H. Fleet Theater, "saw the potential in making an innovative, large-format film for a very small budget. . . . The OmniMax theater at the museum could easily recoup the Hall of Science's investment by playing the film as long as they wanted." MacDonald, *The Sublimity of Document*, 32.

55. Stearns did considerable work at planetariums. See, for example, his album *Music for the Dome* (2016).

56. Jody Jacobs, "KCET Plans Stellar Fund-Raiser," *Los Angeles Times*, June 29, 1980, H4.

57. "That was a big step, because a lot of people had such a prejudice against synthesizers . . . when *Cosmos* came out, that had an influence on people saying, 'Well, maybe it's not so bad'" (Epple, interview). "In fact, there were a couple of times when we would bring synthesizers on stage and people would come up and pretend like they were going to kick the stand over, because this is the reviled synthesizer they'd heard about."

58. Keay Davidson, *Carl Sagan: A Life* (John Wiley & Sons, 1999), 264.

59. The center of Sagan's research was the search for extraterrestrial life, but he was an ardent UFO skeptic, frequently debunking claims made during the peak years of UFO sightings. Sagan was drawn to television in part because he hoped it would lure the public away from pseudoscience.

60. Jon Lomberg, interview by author, February 7, 2025.

61. Lester Grinspoon, ed., *Marihuana Reconsidered* (1971), essay by "Mr. X."

62. Davidson, *Carl Sagan*, 236.

63. John Lomberg, "Cosmos: A Personal Voyage by John Lomberg, *Ciencia, y el "Cosmos" del Signo XXI* (blog), accessed November 28, 2024, https://cienciayelcosmosdelsigloxxi.blogspot.com/2020/01/cosmos-personal-voyage-by-jon-lomberg.html.

64. The Seth MacFarlane Collection of the Carl Sagan and Ann Druyan Archive, Library of Congress, box 17.

65. Lomberg was inspired in part by a concept album made by members of the San Francisco psychedelic band Jefferson Airplane, *Blows Against the Empire* (1970).

66. The Seth MacFarlane Collection of the Carl Sagan and Ann Druyan Archive, Library of Congress, box 17.

67. Lomberg, interview.

68. Lomberg, interview.

69. His early influences as an artist were psychedelic poster art, comic book art, album covers, Salvador Dali, M. C. Escher, and the California Visionary Art School. Lomberg, interview.

70. Lomberg, interview. The International Association of Astronomical Artists (IAAA) defines space art as "a genre of modern artistic expression emerging from knowledge and ideas associated with outer space, both as a source of inspiration and as a means for visualizing and promoting space travel." IAAA.org, https://iaaa.org/page-18089. See also Donald Davis, "Space

Art," Donald Davis.com, www.donaldedavis.com/PARTS/SPACEART.html. See also the website of the International Association of Astronomical Artists, https://iaaa.org.

71. "I see the universe very much as one thing," he said. "There's not the biological universe and then somewhere out there, the astronomical universe." Lomberg was interested in finding visual patterns that connected these realms. Lomberg, interview.

72. Lomberg, interview; Jon Lomberg, email to author, February 9, 2025. "The microcosm and the macrocosm are not separated," Lomberg said. "They're part of a continuum" (Lomberg, interview).

73. Lomberg, interview.

74. Lomberg, "Cosmos: A Personal Voyage." The project began to take shape when Adrian Malone was hired as executive producer. Malone had worked on a show that was a model for the Sagan project, the BBC documentary *The Ascent of Man* (1973).

75. Lomberg, interview.

76. Thomas Wilfred, "Composing in the Art of Lumia," *Journal of Aesthetics and Art Criticism* 7, no. 2 (December 1948): 79–80. See also Donna M. Stein, *Thomas Wilfred: Lumia* (Corcoran Gallery of Art, 1971), 63; Thomas Wilfred, "Light and the Artist," *Journal of Aesthetics and Art Criticism* 5, no. 4 (June 1947): 247–55, at 247.

77. "Caltech enabled us to work with one of their electron microscope scientists in taking electron micrographs of what dandelion fluff really looks like and using that . . . as a model for the little animation that we did of the ship wafting through the universe. . . . Carl was not a big fan of *Star Wars* and was not a big fan of manned space flight. Anything that smacked of astronauts and spacesuits and the look of spaceships that *Star Wars* and *Star Trek* had put into people's minds, he wanted to be as far away from that as possible. That's why the dandelion worked." Lomberg, interview.

78. Carl Sagan, *The Dragons of Eden* (Random House, 1977), 13–17.

79. Lomberg, interview.

80. Don Davis, interview by author, October 30, 2024.

81. Davis, interview.

82. Lomberg, interview; Davis, interview.

83. Susan Brown from the *Cosmos* team was a big fan of the progressive rock band Yes, whose members had worked with Vangelis, and who had an ongoing artistic collaboration with the artist Roger Dean. Dean's sci-fi landscapes were "very simpatico to us," Lomberg said. The *Cosmos* artists went to a Yes concert in Long Beach during the production (Lomberg, interview).

84. Davis said that the painting, titled *Initiation*, was "imagining human civilization uniting and functioning as a worldwide entity in harmony with the ecosystem making contact with interstellar civilizations and joining them." It was one of the first works Davis showed to Carl Sagan when they met. Sagan thought the work was "too traditionally religious." Davis said that Olaf Stapeldon's science fiction classic *Star Maker* was an inspiration. Don Davis, email to author, March 2, 2025.

85. Chandler grew up near Palo Alto, close to Ken Jenkins, and the two knew each other growing up. He got a BFA from Oakland's California College of Arts and Crafts. Chandler told an interviewer that he began painting scenes of outer space because he was fascinated by the beauty of the universe. "I see the universe on a different level, unlike scientists who view it as evidence and information," he said. Chandler had a show of his work at the Oakland Museum in 1977–78 titled *The Universe: Celestial Paintings*. Martha McGuire, "Darth, Are You There?," *Oakland Museum Magazine*, 1977, 6–7.

86. Chandler also created the cover image for Constance Demby's album *Novus Magnificat* (1986). Aeoliah is another New Age musician who is also an airbrush artist.

87. Lomberg, "Cosmos: A Personal Voyage."

88. The Seth MacFarlane Collection of the Carl Sagan and Ann Druyan Archive, Library of Congress, box 17.

89. "Computer graphics at that point existed only in a few laboratories around the world," Lomberg said. "They were not commercial. They were a research project of computer scientists." The JPL was one of the centers of that work and Kohlhase's day job was to be the design director for the Voyager Mission. "He plotted the trajectory of Voyager," Lomberg said. "That was his main job, but he was helping invent computer graphics on the side" (Lomberg, interview).

90. Lomberg went to the evolutionary biologist Stephen Jay Gould for a sequence of organisms, and then the *Cosmos* research staff found illustrations or photographs of each organism. Then one of the artists on the team, Susan Brown, made drawings of them. Lomberg, "Cosmos: A Personal Voyage."

91. Lomberg, "Cosmos: A Personal Voyage"; Lomberg, interview.

92. Lomberg, interview.

93. The Seth MacFarlane Collection of the Carl Sagan and Ann Druyan Archive, Library of Congress, box 569.

94. "Cosmos Track on RCA," *Variety* 302, no. 8 (March 25, 1981): 153. The liner notes to the *Cosmos* LP begin with a letter from a truck driver, one of the viewers who had written to PBS about the show's music. "The musical content of *Cosmos* seemed to create a message of its own," the viewer wrote, "almost as

though it were the collective intelligence of the universe pleasantly calling our attention to the lessons at hand."

95. Cary Darling, "RCA Aiming 'Cosmos' LP at Wide Market," *Billboard* 93, no. 16 (Apr 25, 1981): 17.

96. Stephen Hill wrote that *Cosmos* introduced the "much older Public Television audience to the genre" and "kick-started or upgraded the careers of a number of the featured artists, especially Vangelis. And it was a major fund-raising hit for PBS stations. It was one of those rare instances where everyone involved won." Hill, email to author.

97. Edgecombe recalled that though artists like Vangelis and Jean Michel Jarre were more popular and "mainstream-y," than his usual artists, metaphysical bookstores still wanted them. Ethan Edgecombe, interview by author, June 21, 2025.

98. Epple, interview. Jonn Serrie agreed and said that "it was a really good time for the audience to get a glimpse of what this electronic music was all about. . . . It wasn't just the beeps and the boops or funny sounds used in a soundtrack. . . . It really had character." Jonn Serrie, interview by author, June 13, 2025.

99. Epple, interview.

100. On music in *Cosmos*, see the Seth MacFarlane Collection of the Carl Sagan and Ann Druyan Archive, Library of Congress, boxes 510, 569, 622, 1254.

101. Epple, interview.

102. "We were his go-to production team for music" (Kat Epple, interview by author, November 18, 2024). "The fact that we were able to record, compose, and produce music that could find a place on TV and movies was unheard of before that time. . . . Before that, somebody with a four-track that records in their home would not be really considered for a film. You had to be one of the sanctioned film composers" (Epple, interview).

103. Peter Davison, interview by author, August 6, 2024.

104. "Television Reviews: Cosmos," *Variety* 300, no. 9 (Oct 1, 1980): 78. William Poundstone, *Carl Sagan* (Henry Holt, 1999), 261. Don Davis recalled that the show was sometimes referred to as "Cost-most" because it was "the most expensive PBS show ever made up to that time" (Davis, interview).

105. In Don Davis's words, the show was "a warning to the world to always treasure and safeguard knowledge and make it a continuing priority" (Davis, interview).

106. Lomberg, interview. *Cosmos* was hailed as the most widely viewed public television series in history during the 1980s, but it was eclipsed by Ken Burns's *The Civil War* (1990). William Dicke, "Carl Sagan, an Astronomer

Who Excelled at Popularizing Science, Is Dead at 82," *New York Times*, December 21, 1996, 1. There is something telling in that movement, on either side of the Reagan '80s, from *Cosmos* to *The Civil War*. It shows a narrowing in scope and ambition, both in terms of content and style, from the cosmic to the historical and national and from extreme long shots of faraway galaxies to extreme close-ups of archival photographs.

107. The show links micro- and macrocosmic scales in a manner similar to New Age philosophies but maintains Sagan's critical edge, as in sequences that debunk theories about UFOs and astrology. Sagan does not simply discount deviant or borderline science but uses it to capture the imagination and start the discussion. For example, *Cosmos* has an entire episode dedicated to Johannes Kepler, an astronomer who practiced astrology. "By including Kepler," writes Sagan biographer Keay Davidson, Sagan "showed that scientific ideas occasionally emerge from a pseudoscientific context." Davidson, *Carl Sagan*, 335.

CHAPTER 5: ENVIRONMENTAL SOUNDS

1. Kohoutek Celebration of Consciousness Program, annotated, in Paul Mariah Papers, Yale University Library, GEN MSS 2096, box 7, folder 134.

2. Benjamin Kline, *First Along the River: A Brief History of the U.S. Environmental Movement* (Rowman & Littlefield, 2022), 227. On *Bambi*, see David Whitley, *The Idea of Nature in Disney Animation* (Routledge, 2008).

3. On ecocinema, see Stephen Rust et al., eds., *Ecocinema Theory and Practice* (Routledge, 2012); Robin L. Murray and Joseph K. Heumann, *Ecology and Popular Film: Cinema on the Edge* (State University of New York Press, 2009). There was also an ecological sensibility to the happenings, psychedelic multimedia events, and "environments" in art galleries taking place at the time. See James Nisbet, *Ecologies, Environments, and Energy Systems in Art of the 1960s and 1970s* (MIT Press, 2014).

4. On punk and the natural world, see David Ingram, *The Jukebox in the Garden: Ecocriticism and American Popular Music Since 1960* (Editions Rodopi, 2010), 169; John Parham, "A Concrete Sense of Place: Alienation and the City in British Punk and New Wave, 1977–1980," *Green Letters* 15, no. 1 (2012): 76.

5. Underwood played lead guitar with singer-songwriter Tim Buckley during the late 1960s and early '70s and released his own New Age album, *California Sigh* (1988).

6. Greg Garrard, *Ecocriticism* (Routledge, 2012), 199. On Gaia, see Fritjof Capra and Pier Luigi Luisi, *The Systems View of Life: A Unifying Vision*

(Cambridge University Press, 2014), 163–64. Ernest Callenbach, *Ecology: A Pocket Guide* (University of California Press, 2008), 67. See also Kline, *First Along the River*, 98. On Gaia theory and "occulture," see Christopher Partridge, *The Re-enchantment of the West*, vol. 2 (Continuum, 2005), 61–63.

7. Lee Underwood, *World Music and Inner Transformation* (unpublished manuscript, 1984), 13.

8. These attributes combined and interacted, as when a cosmic perspective supported an environmental one. "Just as our cells, tissues, organs, toes and fingers are interconnecting parts of ourselves," Underwood wrote, "so we and all beings, land, waters, and air are interconnecting parts of the living planetary organism. The planet is not a lifeless thing to be plundered and exploited. It is our larger body." Underwood, *World Music and Inner Transformation*, 13.

9. On the systems view and the New Age movement, see Wouter Hanegraaff, *New Age Religion and Western Culture* (State University of New York Press, 1998), 107–8, 133, 137.

10. Bruce Clarke, "Neocybernetics," in *More Posthuman Glossary*, ed. Rosi Braidotti et al. (Bloomsbury, 2022), 281–82.

11. The systems view could be applied to all scales of reality allowing, for example, cities to be compared to living systems, as in Hilary Harris's short film *Organism* (1975), which intercuts between time-lapse city scenes and the flow of blood cells, and predates better-known sequences in *Koyaanisqatsi*.

12. Peter Harries–Jones, "'From Anthropology to Epistemology': Extensions to an Autobiography of Gregory Bateson," in *Encyclopédie internationale des histoires de l'anthropologie* (Bérose, 2021), 4.

13. Daniel Belgrad, *The Culture of Feedback: Ecological Thinking in '70s America* (University of Chicago Press, 2019), 311.

14. Underwood, *World Music and Inner Transformation*, O-6.

15. Steve Roach, interview by author, August 27, 2024. Mead talked about varieties of ecological thinking in comparison to tending an aquarium; see Irving Morrissett and Karen B. Wiley, eds., *The Environmental Problem: Selections from Hearings on the Environmental Education Act of 1970* (Social Science Education Consortium, 1971), 79. On systems theory and the dichotomy of human and nonhuman, see Cary Wolfe, "In Search of Posthumanist Theory: The Second-Order Cybernetics of Maturana and Varela," in *Observing Complexity: Systems Theory and Postmodernity*, ed. William Rasch and Cary Wolfe (University of Minnesota Press, 2000), 175. See also Bruce Clarke, *Neocybernetics and Narrative* (University of Minnesota Press, 2014), xi.

16. Bateson was an early researcher on whale and dolphin communication. Belgrad, *The Culture of Feedback*, 1.

17. Lawrence Buell, *The Environmental Imagination: Thoreau, Nature Writing, and the Formation of American Culture* (Harvard University Press, 1995), 220–21.

18. In my interviews, Don Slepian, Kevin Braheny Fortune, and Robert Rich all mentioned *Sonic Seasonings*. See also Ric Levine, "Wendy Carlos: Planting New Seeds . . . Again," *Cymbiosis* 1, no. 4 (1987).

19. Suzanne Doucet, interview by author, April 9, 2025.

20. Suzanne Doucet, interview by author, April 18, 2024. If Doucet had continued this approach to working with field recordings, she might have developed something akin to Irv Teibel's *Environments* albums (1969–79): albums that feature recordings of seashores, birds, thunderstorms, wind, and rain, and that have become canonical in histories of ambient music. On Irv Teibel, see Mack Hagood, *Hush: Media and Sonic Self-Control* (Duke University Press, 2019); and Victor Szabo, *Turn On, Tune In, Drift Off: Ambient Music's Psychedelic Past* (Oxford University Press, 2023).

21. Doucet, interview, April 18, 2024.

22. Doucet, interview, April 9, 2025.

23. Some of the spiritual writers that influenced the visionary school supported such a numinous approach to listening to the natural world as a kind of music. The Sufi mystic Hazrat Inayat Khan wrote that "nature's music is more perfect than that of art. It gives us a sense of exaltation to be moving about in the woods, to be looking at the green, to be standing near the running water that has its rhythm, its tone, and its harmony. The swinging of the branches in the forest, the rising and falling of the waves—all has its music. Once we contemplate and become one with nature, our hearts open to its music." Hazrat Inayat Khan, *The Mysticism of Sound and Music* (Shambhala, 2022), 15.

24. George Deuter, interview by author, April 25, 2024.

25. Eckart Rahn, interview by author, November 28, 2024.

26. On the track "Oh, How Deeply Do I Love You?" (1979), Iasos added his angelic synth environments to a recording of a bird singing outside his window. He released the unadorned bird recording on a cassette titled *Paradise Bird of Endless Melodies* (1980). Iasos talked about his process of creating "paradise music" by concentrating on photographs of natural spaces that "struck a chord with [his] soul." "Christopher Toussant Interviews Iasos," accessed, July 12, 2024, https://vimeo.com/38694958,. The first side of Michael Stearns's album *Morning Jewel* (1980) combines modular synthesizer with field recordings of dawn in the desert outside Tucson and in Puerto Vallarta, Mexico. Tracks on Steve Roach's classic albums *Structures from Silence* and *Quiet Music* feature field recordings. Natural sounds were central to the aesthetic of the Japanese

New Age star Kitaro. "The trees, the woods, the grass, the air, the winds—everything is living in God," he told an interviewer. Don Heckman, "Mixing Blunt Words with New Age Serenity," *Los Angeles Times*, April 1, 1990, F68. Kitaro's home studio in the 1970s and '80s was near Mount Fuji in Japan, and he explained how he would open the windows when he recorded to let in the sounds of birds and rustling leaves: "Nature informs the music," he said, "and the music travels outdoors to inform nature." Lynn Van Matre, "Kitaro Builds New Bridge from Japan," *Chicago Tribune*, November 18, 1986, D3. Kitaro's early albums often contain field recordings; *Astral Trip* (1978) begins with waves crashing on the beach and ends with gusting winds, *Full Moon Story* (1979) begins with tranquil flowing water and the call of a cuckoo, and on *Oasis* (1979), ocean waves introduce the track "Aqua." Alice Damon's *Windsong* (1981) features natural sounds on the track "Waterfall Winds" and on the twenty-five minute closing track "Path to the Cave of the Bear." Other New Age artists who use field recordings in a similar manner include Joanna Brouk, William Aura, and David Naegele.

27. Stanislav Grof, "Brief History of Transpersonal Psychology," *International Journal of Transpersonal Studies* 27, no. 1 (2008): 46–54, at 49.

28. Thomas Albright, "Visuals," *Rolling Stone*, September 2, 1971, 48–49.

29. See Leo Marx, *The Machine in the Garden: Technology and the Pastoral Idea in America* (Oxford University Press, 1964). David Ingram uses this kind of intellectual framework to make the case for Wendy Carlos's *Sonic Seasonings*, which for him employs a "slippage between electronically synthesized sounds and real sounds" that avoids the "prettiness and securities" of simple pastoral. "This is ambient music that is complex and tonally unsettling," he writes. Ingram, *The Jukebox in the Garden*, 209.

30. Peter Davison, interview by author, April 29, 2025. Emerald Web took a similar approach on their album *Nocturne* (1983). Kat Epple said that on that album, they created the sounds of birds and crickets with synthesizers. Kat Epple, interview by author, June 5, 2025. James Newton and Peter Michael Hamel also mentioned the influence of Olivier Messiaen in my interviews.

31. Bernie Kraus, *The Great Animal Orchestra: Finding the Origins of Music in the World's Wild Places* (Profile Books, 2012), 39, 68.

32. Kraus, *The Great Animal Orchestra*, 27, 33–34. See Bryan C. Pijanowski et al., "Soundscape Ecology: The Science of Sound in the Landscape," *BioScience* 61, no. 3 (March 2011): 203–16; Jérôme Sueur and Almo Farina, "Ecoacoustics: The Ecological Investigation and Interpretation of Environmental Sound," *Biosemiotics* 8 (2015): 493–502; Almo Farina, *Soundscape Ecology: Principles, Patterns, Methods, and Applications* (Springer, 2014); Almo Farina

and Stuart H. Gage, eds., *Ecoacoustics: The Ecological Role of Sounds* (Wiley and Sons, 2017).

33. Jon Carroll, "Songs of the Humpbacked Whale," *Rolling Stone*, August 6, 1970, 34.

34. See Alaina Claire Fledman, "Minor Listening, Major Influence," *e-flux Journal* 118 (May 2021): 1.

35. Roger Payne, *Among Whales* (Scribner, 1995), 20–21.

36. Payne, *Among Whales*, 144–45. Cited in David Rothenberg, *Whale Music: Thousand Mile Songs in a Sea of Sound* (Terra Nova Press, 2023), 11.

37. Gary David, "Music of the Humpback Whale," *Los Angeles Free Press*, September 4, 1970, 59.

38. David, "Music of the Humpback Whale," 59.

39. In fact, this article helped bring David together with Emilie Conrad. When they met in 1973, "she told me that it was the article that caught her attention beyond our prior cursory meeting. . . . It was love at first read." Gary David, email to author, April 7, 2025.

40. Carl Sagan was also on the "whale trip." Sagan consulted with Payne, included humpback songs on the Voyager Golden Disc and dedicated a good portion of one episode of *Cosmos* (1980) to whale vocalization. See Carl Sagan, *Cosmos* (Random House, 1980), 270–73; also see Carl Sagan, *The Cosmic Connection* (New Dell, 1973).

41. Rex Weyler, *Song of the Whale* (Anchor Press/Doubleday, 1986), 6. Jason M. Colby, *Orca: How We Came to Know and Love the Ocean's Greatest Predator* (Oxford University Press, 2018), 121, 126.

42. Ron Percical, "Friend Wants Skana Freed," *Vancouver (BC) Sun*, June 4, 1969, 4.

43. Tom Ardies, "Skinny Dipping Spong Skirmishes for Skana," *Vancouver (BC) Sun*, June 16, 1969, 7. Spong was quoted as saying: "I wanted to swim in the nude with Skana. I wanted to play electronic music to her. I wanted the whole bloody city to know she loves electronic music" (Colby, *Orca*, 127).

44. "Heaviest Act in Town," *Times Colonist* (Victoria, British Columbia), June 11, 1971, 13.

45. Weyler, *Song of the Whale*, 101. Tom Shandel, dir., *We Call Them Killers*, www.nfb.ca/film/we-call-them-killers/.

46. Underwood, *World Music and Inner Transformation*, ph-9.

47. Spong wrote of his experience being "deconditioned" to fear orcas by his interactions with the orca Skana. Paul Spong, "The Whale Show," in *Mind in the Waters*, ed. Joan McIntyre (Charles Scribner's Sons, 1974), 173–74.

48. Weyler, *Song of the Whale*, 127.

49. Pat Dufour, "Giant Eggnog Down the Hatch," *Times Colonist* (Victoria, British Columbia), November 14, 1972, 19.

50. Paul Horn with Lee Underwood, *Inside Paul Horn* (HarperCollins, 1990), 180.

51. Erich Hoyt, *Orca: The Whale Called Killer*, 5th ed. (Firefly Books, 2019), 145.

52. Horn expresses a Sagan-esque connection between extraterrestrials and whales: "At a time when man is penetrating ever deeper into outer space, he may well find one of his greatest discoveries right here in the depths of our oceans, as he explores the consciousness of these gentle giants."

53. See also Horn and Underwood, *Inside Paul Horn*, 183–84.

54. Jesper Hoffmeyer, *Biosemiotics* (University of Scranton Press, 2008), 4. Also see Timo Maran, "Biosemiotics," in *Keywords for Environmental Studies*, ed. Joni Adamson et al. (New York University Press, 2016), 29.

55. Thomas A. Sebeok, *Signs: An Introduction to Semiotics*, 2nd ed. (University of Toronto Press, 2001), 3.

56. Thomas Sebeok, *I Think I Am a Verb* (Plenum Press, 1986), 82.

57. Sebeok, *I Think I Am a Verb*, 92–93.

58. Bateson, *Steps to an Ecology of Mind* (University of Chicago Press, 2000) 141, 177-81.

59. Spong, "The Whale Show," 176.

60. Spong, "The Whale Show," 175.

61. Weyler, *Song of the Whale*, 239. Also see the work of Jim Nollman. His album *Playing Music with Animals* (Folkways, 1982), was reviewed by Stephen Davis in "Jamming with the Animals," *New Age Journal* 8, no. 5 (December 1982): 72.

62. Relationship was also Gregory Bateson's guiding interest in cetacean communication. "Lecture by Gregory Bateson part 2 1975," from "Orders of Change, Naropa," https://archive.org/details/Lecture_by_Gregory_Bateson_part_2_1975_75R004. See also D. Graham Burnett, "A Mind in the Water," *Orion* magazine, https://orionmagazine.org/article/a-mind-in-the-water/. Also see Gregory Bateson, "Observations of a Cetacean Community," in *Mind in the Waters*, ed. Joan McIntyre (Charles Scribner's Sons, 1974), 159, 163.

63. Colby, *Orca*, 231. On Hunter's conversion experience putting his head in the mouth of the orca Skana, see William E. Jackson, *Once upon a Greenpeace* (Infinity, 2010), 24–26.

64. Jackson wrote that "the strategy was to lead the whales away from slaughter" by playing synth sounds underwater that mimicked whale vocalization, which might attract the animals away from the whalers. Will Jackson,

"Synthesizers on the Eco-Front," *Synapse* 1, no. 6 (March–April 1977): 16–17. Also see Jackson's memoir, *Once upon a Greenpeace*, for a sense of how whales at that time could be considered as psychic, telepathic, spiritual teachers.

65. Erich Hoyt, interview by author, April 8, 2025.

66. On Project Apex, see McIntyre, *Mind in the Waters*, 184.

67. Hoyt, interview.

68. Hoyt, interview.

69. "False intimacy" is a reference to Derek Bouse's work on wildlife documentaries. See Derek Bouse, "False Intimacy: Close-Ups and Viewer Involvement in Wildlife Films," *Visual Studies* 18, no. 2 (2003).

70. Hoyt, interview.

71. McIntyre, *Mind in the Waters*, 184.

72. Erich Hoyt, email to author, April 23, 2025. Scott Macrae, "Had Whale of a Time, Hope Whales Will, Too," *Vancouver (BC) Sun*, December 29, 1973, 35.

73. Another track on Paul Horn's *Inside II* is "Centaur," which is Horn's score for a film of the same title on human-horse interactions produced by The National Film Board of Canada.

74. Erich Hoyt went on to dedicate his life to studying, writing about, and protecting orcas, most recently as a research fellow with the UK nonprofit organization Whale and Dolphin Conservation. His early experiments with orca mimicry dovetailed with emerging discoveries about the specific dialects of orca pods and the ways in which they learned their dialects. Hoyt composed the score for the low-budget horror film *The Keeper* (1976), starring Christopher Lee, which features simulated orca sounds created with his ARP synth.

75. Paul Winter, interview by author, March 30, 2025.

76. Paul Winter, interview by author, February 5, 2025.

77. Winter, interview, February 5, 2025.

78. Underwood, *World Music and Inner Transformation*, PW-5.

79. Peter Barry Chowka, "The Healing Power of Music," *New Age Journal* 4, no. 6 (November 1978): xx.

80. Underwood, *World Music and Inner Transformation*, PW-7–8.

81. Chowka, "The Healing Power of Music"

82. Winter, interview, March 30, 2025.

83. Chowka, "The Healing Power of Music," xx.

84. Winter, interview, February 5, 2025.

85. Winter, interview, February 5, 2025.

86. Winter, interview, February 5, 2025.

87. Winter, "A Tribute to David Darling," Paul Winter.com, January 2021, https://paulwinter.com/wp-content/uploads/2021/02/Remembering-David-Story.pdf.

88. Winter, interview, February 5, 2025.

89. Winter, interview, February 5, 2025.

90. See, for example, Colby, *Orca* 240; and William E. Jackson, *Once upon a Greenpeace* (Infinity, 2010).

91. Winter, interview, February 5, 2025.

92. Adi Gevins and Sam Silver, "Breaking the Species Barrier," *Berkeley Barb*, November 25–December 2, 1976, 3.

93. Monica Bay, "A Whale of a Benefit Concert," *Rolling Stone*, December 30, 1976, 16. Winter, February 5, 2025.

94. Winter, interview, February 5, 2025. See David Rothenberg, *Whale Music: Thousand Mile Songs in a Sea of Sound* (Terra Nova, 2023), 49–50. Underwood, *World Music and Inner Transformation*, PW-8–9.

95. Winter, interview, February 5, 2025.

96. Winter, "A Tribute to David Darling." Winter, interview, February 5, 2025. Chowka, "The Healing Power of Music," xx. Underwood, *World Music and Inner Transformation*, PW-2–3.

97. On different kinds of animal charisma, see Jamie Lorimer, *Wildlife in the Anthropocene: Conservation After Nature* (University of Minnesota Press, 2015), 40–41, 49.

98. Winter, interview, March 30, 2025.

99. Chowka, "The Healing Power of Music," xx.

100. Winter, interview, March 30, 2025.

101. Winter, interview, March 30, 2025.

102. Winter had worked with Columbia Records and Epic Records for the Consort releases of the late 1960s. About *Common Ground*, he said, "I produced that on my own, and then we placed it with A&M. That was the last time I did anything with a major label." Winter interview, March 30, 2025.

103. Winter, interview, March 30, 2025.

104. Winter, interview, March 30, 2025.

105. Winter, interview, March 30, 2025.

106. Winter, interview, March 30, 2025.

107. "I would do . . . workshops. Some of those places would have a little store, and they'd have a few albums." Winter, interview, March 30, 2025.

108. Stephen Davis, "Paul Winter and Friends," *New Age Journal* 6, no. 9 (March 1981): 71.

109. The booklet begins with a map that depicts the journey taken by a seal named Silkie around North America. Silkie's journey serves as an organizing structure for the album. Silkie was inspired by an encounter with a sea lion pup in Baja, California, which motivated Winter to study seals, North American ecosystems, and British folklore about seal-human "silkies." Silkie is "a messenger between the ocean world and the land," we read in the booklet, "calling us back to a world we once shared, luring us into our own inner oceans." "I thought of her as a link between us and our more distant cousins of the sea—just as the wolf is, for me, our closest link with the wild animals of the land."

110. McIntyre, *Mind in the Waters*. Underwood, *World Music and Inner Transformation*, PW-10.

111. Payne, *Among Whales*, 145.

112. Underwood, *World Music and Inner Transformation*, PW-10.

113. Rex Weyler, "Paul Winter's Earth Mass," *New Age Journal* 8, no. 1 (August 1982): 28.

114. Sarah M. Pike, *New Age and Neopagan Religions in America* (Columbia University Press, 2004), 74. Also see Paul Heelas, *The New Age Movement* (Blackwell, 1996), 22.

115. Underwood, *World Music and Inner Transformation*, PW-28.

116. Underwood, *World Music and Inner Transformation*, PW-11–12. David Darling, the cellist in the Winter Consort, had a brother-in-law who was a scientist and astronaut who worked on the Apollo 15 mission in 1971, which undertook the fourth moon landing. Because of that connection, a cassette of the Winter Consort's album *Road* (1970) was taken on the mission, and by some accounts, the cassette was left on the surface of the moon. Paul Winter, interview by author, February 5, 2025. See also Winter, "A Tribute to David Darling."

117. Winter, interview, March 30, 2025.

118. Captain Kirk (William Shatner) recites lines from D. H. Lawrence that begin *Mind in the Waters*.

119. Winter, interview, March 30, 2025. See also Geoff Mayfield, "Video Retailing: 'Star Trek' Inspires Drive," *Billboard* 99, no. 44 (October 31, 1987): 48.

120. Winter, interview, March 30, 2025.

CHAPTER 6: NOW AGE

1. Chris Morris, "New Outlet Caters Solely to New Age Aficionados," *Billboard* 99, no. 6 (February 7, 1987): 39.

2. Morris, "New Outlet Caters Solely to New Age Aficionados," 39.

3. Suzanne Doucet, interview by author, April 18, 2024.

4. Morris, "New Outlet Caters Solely to New Age Aficionados," 39.

5. Jennifer C. Lena, *Banding Together* (Princeton University Press, 2012), 6.

6. Lena, *Banding Together*, 23.

7. Lena, *Banding Together*, 41.

8. Aeoliah and Laraaji both used the phrase "now age" in my interviews. See also Victor Szabo, *Turn On, Tune In, Drift Off: Ambient Music's Psychedelic Past* (Oxford University Press, 2023), 241.

9. Lena, *Banding Together*, 46–47.

10. José Argüelles, *The Mayan Factor: Path Beyond Technology* (Bear, 1987), 212.

11. Dick Roraback. "Resonating with Jose Arguelles, a New Age Scholar," *Los Angeles Times*, August 12, 1987, OCD1. Philip J. Hilts and Mary Battiata, "Planets Won't Attend Astronomical Celebration," *Washington Post*, August 16, 1987, A1. Jonathan Weisman, "New Age Believers Greet a New Day," *Los Angeles Times*, August 17, 1987, F.

12. Argüelles stated that 144,000 rainbow humans were needed to create the signal. José Argüelles, "Open Letter to 144,000 Rainbow Humans," in *The Encyclopedic Sourcebook of New Age Religions*, ed. James R. Leis (Prometheus Books, 2004), 588–89. Also see Eric Zorn, "Hold On! Age of Aquarius Soon at Hand," *Chicago Tribune*, August 9, 1987, A1.

13. Bob Sipchen and Jonathan Weisman, "Harmonic Convergence: A Braver New World?," *Los Angeles Times*, August 12, 1987, F1. Also see James Barron, "Dancing at Dawn in Rite of Cosmic Harmony: Harmony Is Sought All Over," *New York Times*, August 17, 1987, A1.

14. Eric Zorn, "Hold On! Age of Aquarius Soon at Hand," *Chicago Tribune*, August 9, 1987, A1; Paul Weingarten, "World Peace Is OK, but Fun Begins When UFOs Get Here," *Chicago Tribune*, March 20, 1990, D1. Ben Fong-Torres, "Why the Stars in Hollywood Turn to the Stars in the Cosmos," *San Francisco Chronicle*, April 28, 1988, B3.

15. Jonathan Weisman, "New Age Believers Greet a New Day," *Los Angeles Times*, August 17, 1987, F. Michael Collins, "Ohio's Serpent Mound Attracts 3,000," *Sentinel Tribune* (Bowling Green, Ohio), August 17, 1987, 4.

16. Ben Fong-Torres, "Journey into the New Age," *San Francisco Chronicle*, April 28, 1988, B3; Meg Sullivan, "New Age Will Dawn in August, Seers Say," *Wall Street Journal*, June 23, 1987, 1.

17. Michael Walsh, "Music: New Age Comes of Age," *Time*, September 1, 1986, xx; Chris McGowan, "Instrumental Inroads: Outburst of Quiet

Fusion Signals That New Age Has Arrived," *Billboard* 98, no. 43 (October 25, 1986): N3.

18. Rick Ingrasci, "The View from Windham Hill," *New Age Journal*, May/June 1988, 74.

19. Ethan Edgecombe's Fortuna was distributing Windham Hill records for a period before the breakout success of Winston's albums. Ethan Edgecombe, interview by author, June 21, 2025.

20. Ingrasci, "The View from Windham Hill," 74. "Windham Hill: A Business with Heart and Style," *New Age Journal* 8, no. 12 (July 1983): 34.

21. Ingrasci, "The View from Windham Hill," 74. See also "Windham Hill: A Business with Heart and Style."

22. The article makes a comparison between Windham Hill and the German label ECM. Stephen Davis, "California Strummin'," *New Age Journal* 7, no. 11 (June 1982): 72–73.

23. Rex Weyler, "George Winston's Pure Piano," *New Age Journal* 8, no. 12 (July 1983): 60–61.

24. Weyler, "George Winston's Pure Piano," 60.

25. "Windham Hill: A Business with Heart and Style," 34.

26. In her guide to New Age music, P. J. Birosik includes Windham Hill in the subcategory of New Age folk. Patti Jean Birosik, *The New Age Music Guide* (Collier Books, 1989), 36.

27. Ingrasci, "The View from Windham Hill," 74.

28. Zan Stewart, "New Age Music Money Machine," *Los Angeles Times*, January 31, 1988, M22; Ingrasci, "The View from Windham Hill," 74.

29. Zan Stewart, "Spotlight: New Age Music," *Billboard* 99, no. 44 (October 31, 1987): N1, N10; Sam Sutherland, "Geffen Maps Massive Push for Kitaro," *Billboard* 97, no. 33 (August 17, 1985): 6.

30. David L. Morton, *Sound Recording: The Life Story of a Technology* (Johns Hopkins University Press, 2004), 172–73. Andre Millard, *America on Record: A History of Recorded Sound*, 2nd ed. (Cambridge University Press, 2005), 353–55.

31. In a *Wall Street Journal* article from 1987, we read that "many New Age fans first heard the music at stereo stores, which used the high-quality pressings to show off high-end equipment. Audiophiles love effects like those on the Living Music label, which records in such places as the Grand Canyon and inside a reverberant stone cathedral." Meg Cox, "New Age Music Wins Wider Following as Many People Grow Too Old for Rock," *Wall Street Journal*, April 1, 1987, 1. Ackerman boasted that Windham Hill was "right on the cutting edge. We made some of the very first digital recordings. . . . We made

the first domestically manufactured Compact Disc, beating out Warner Brothers for that." Lee Underwood, *World Music and Inner Transformation* (unpublished manuscript, 1984), Ack-16b. See also Ken Terry, "Major Labels Joining New Age Parade," *Variety* 324, no. 4 (August 20, 1986): 77; Stewart, "Spotlight," N1, N10.

32. Eckart Rahn, interview by author, November 28, 2024. Ethan Edgecombe had discovered Kitaro's import albums and told Eckart Rahn about them (Edgecombe, interview).

33. Rick Ingrasci, "A Little Light Music," *New Age Journal*, November/December 1987, 71. A documentary about Kitaro's 1987 tour is available on YouTube, https://www.youtube.com/watch?v=RQLJ46qbDjU.

34. "Billboard Introduces New Age Albums Chart," *Billboard* 100, no. 44 (October 29, 1988): 4.

35. Bill Holdship and Adam White, "A New Age Primer," *Radio and Records* no. 739 (May 27, 1988): 3. Before joining KMET, Cody developed the *Jazz Show with David Sanborn* for NBC Radio. Kim Freeman, "KMET Gives Up on Rock; New Age/Jazz Format Seen," *Billboard* 99, no. 8 (February 21, 1987): 1.

36. "New Respect for New Age," *Broadcasting* 114, no. 12 (March 21, 1988): 55; Cox, "New Age Music Wins Wider Following," 1. Bill Holland, "'Wave' Takes TAB by Storm," *Billboard* 99, no. 39 (September 26, 1987): 1.

37. Suzanne Ciani, interview by author, August 13, 2024.

38. Ciani, interview.

39. I'm basing my characterization of conventional music video style on the work of Carol Vernallis. See Carol Vernallis, *Experiencing Music Video: Aesthetics and Cultural Context* (Columbia University Press, 2004).

40. Jim McCullaugh, "New Age Video," *Billboard* 99, no. 44 (October 31, 1987): N6. "VH-1's 'New Visions' Helps Expand Horizons," *Billboard* 98, no. 43 (October 25, 1986): N8.

41. Peter Davison, interview by author, August 6, 2024. The period 1986–87 was a monumental time for Davison, who in addition to starting his work with Living Arts sold the rights to his first independently released albums to the company Higher Octave. Peter Davison, interview by author, April 29, 2025. On Living Arts and Steven Adams, see "Serenity for Sale," *Forbes*, April 19, 1999, www.forbes.com; Catherine Cella, "Home Video: Business Is Soaring for New Age Dealers," *Billboard* 101, no. 35 (September 2, 1989): 45.

42. On New Age music and home video, see Rick Ingrasci, "Video Meditation," *New Age Journal*, March/April 1988, 63–64; Linda Kohanov, "The Sight of Music," *New Age Journal*, January/February 1990, 91–92.

43. Miramar's videos were sold in catalogs for outdoor gear and in national park gift shops. New Age music videos like these were also sold in Suzanne Doucet's Only New Age record store, metaphysical bookstores, national park gift shops, electronics catalogs, chains like Tower Records, and got airplay on VH1 and a satellite network for hospital patients. Ingrasci, "Video Meditation," 63–64. Steven Dupler, "VH-1 Prepares to Enter 'New Age,'" *Billboard* 97, no. 50 (December 14, 1985): 29. By 1990, big chains like Tower Records were carrying New Age videos. Linda Kohanov, "The Sight of Music," *New Age Journal*, January/February 1990, 91–92.

44. Kat Epple, interview by author, June 5, 2025.

45. Lena, *Banding Together*, 23.

46. Lena, *Banding Together*, 15.

47. Bill Holdship and Adam White, "A New Age Primer," *Radio and Records* no. 739 (May 27, 1988): 3; Ken Terry, "Major Labels Joining New Age Parade," *Variety* 324, no. 4 (August 20, 1986): 77.

48. Steve Morse, "New Age Music Finds Market as Mellow Alternative to Punk Rock," *Chicago Tribune*, June 9, 1985, L14. See also Freeman, "KMET Gives Up on Rock," 1.

49. Jon Pareles, "New Age Music Booms, Softly," *New York Times*, November 29, 1987, H1.

50. Cox, "New Age Music Wins Wider Following," 31; Lee Underwood, "Mellowing Out with New Age Music," *Los Angeles Times*, July 11, 1982, M89. Terry Wood, "New Age Has Affected Baby Boomers," *Billboard* 101, no. 43 (October 28, 1989): 11.

51. Walsh, "Music," xx.

52. Mark Prendergast, *The Ambient Century: From Mahler to Moby—The Evolution of Sound in the Electronic Age* (Bloomsbury, 2000), 144. Also see Ryan Hibbett, "The New Age Taboo," *Journal of Popular Music Studies* 22, no. 3 (2010): 296; Szabo, *Turn On, Tune In, Drift Off*, 30. Pendergast's "hot tub" put-down is typical of critical suspicion of New Age music's holistic and functional aesthetic. As I mentioned in chapter 2, one of the dangers of promoting your music as a blend of art and science, medicine and entertainment, is that such an approach risks being condemned as too functional to be art and too entertaining to be science.

53. As Szabo writes, "Critics' reduction of New Age media to their commodification—and accordingly, to their complicity in the rise of neoliberalism—ultimately deflates and flattens what was originally a transpersonal and humanistic world-building affair. Participants in the New Age movement assiduously built alternative media networks and markets not just to

promote individual healing, but also to populate a universally transformative planetary environment." Szabo, *Turn On, Tune In, Drift Off*, 31.

54. Suzanne Doucet, "Commentary: Success Has Diluted New Age Music," *Billboard* 100, no. 25 (June 18, 1988): 9.

55. Doucet, "Commentary," 9.

56. Terry Wood, "New Meet for New Age," *Billboard* 101, no. 9 (March 4, 1989): 6. At the second conference in 1990, Doucet still seemed optimistic about bringing together traditional music-industry people with people who had been "working for fifteen years making music in their garages, building their own instruments." The Crystal Awards that year went to both business-people (distributor Michael Anderson of Pyramid Distributors; broadcaster Stephen Hill) and creatives (Iasos for music; Ken Jenkins for video). Don Heckman, "Opposites Attract at International New Age Conference," *Los Angeles Times*, February 12, 1990, xx.

57. John Diliberto, "I Am Not a New-Age Artist," *Pulse*, July 1991, 87. Diliberto quipped that "it's the only conference where instead of being awaken by loud TVs or parties, you are roused by chanting from the next hotel room" (86). Will Ackerman of Windham Hill was not a fan of the "New Age" label. "I think of monotonal, soporific music. I almost bleed when I hear the term," he said; Stewart, "New Age Music Money Machine," M22. Ackerman told an interviewer in 1988 that he "insists on a distinction between New Age and the music produced by Windham Hill Records. . . . I'm just not in the business of selling philosophies." Rena Fruchter, "Shhh! Don't Call His Music 'New Age,'" *New York Times*, September 11, 1988, 19.

58. Diliberto, "I Am Not a New-Age Artist," 87.

59. Don Slepian, interview by author, April 19, 2024.

60. Slepian, interview, April 23, 2025.

61. Slepian, interview, April 23, 2025.

62. Slepian, interview, April 23, 2025.

63. Slepian, interview, April 23, 2025.

64. Music writer Liz Pelly argues that functional music for wellness and productivity is part of "late 2010s wellness culture, like CBD sodas and skincare routines. . . . It spoke to a generation that was anxious and overworked, engaged in cycles of trying to focus hard and chill hard." Liz Pelly, *Mood Machine: The Rise of Spotify and the Costs of the Perfect Playlist* (Atria, 2025), 44. On Spotify and mood music, see Maria Eriksson et al., *Spotify Teardown: Inside the Black Box of Streaming Music* (MIT Press, 2019), 115. According to program director Frank Cody, KTWV/the Wave refined the concept of "radio as a mood service." In that regard, KTWV can be seen as a precursor to Spotify.

65. Marc Masters, *High Bias: The Distorted History of the Cassette Tape* (University of North Carolina Press, 2023), 153–58.

66. "Sounds of Dawn," https://www.youtube.com/@soundsofthedawn.

67. Steve Roach emphasized the significance of the "Eurorack explosion," which he recalled happening in the early 2000s. Steve Roach, interview by author, May 20, 2025.

68. US Department of Health and Human Services, National Center for Complimentary and Integrative Health, "Meditation and Mindfulness: Effectiveness and Safety," www.nccih.nih.gov/health/meditation-and-mindfulness-effectiveness-and-safety.

69. Hilary Potkewitz, "Headspace vs. Calm: The Meditation Battle That's Anything but Zen," *Wall Street Journal*, December 15, 2018. See also Liz Hartman, "Calm Is Sleeping Its Way to Success," *Publishers Weekly*, August 19, 2019, 10–11.

70. Christine Lagorio-Chafkin, "Michael Acton Smith," *Inc.*, Winter 2023/2024, 77.

71. Aeoliah, interview by author, April 25, 2024.

72. Amanda Petrusich, "The Transcendence of Laraaji," *The New Yorker*, February 27, 2023; Gunseli Yalcinkaya, "A Conversation with Laraaji About Laughter, Music and Wellbeing," *Crack*, November 5, 2017, https://crackmagazine.net/article/long-reads/conversation-laraaji-laughter-music-wellbeing/; also, Ben Beaumont-Thomas, "Laraaji: The Brian Eno of Laughter," *The Guardian*, July 8, 2014; Mary Cleary, "A Guide to Laughter Meditation with Laraaji," *Wallpaper*, October 8, 2022, www.wallpaper.com/beauty-grooming/laraaji-teaches-laughter-meditation.

73. Simon Kauffman, "Studies Show Most Americans Are Sleep Deprived," *Scripps News*, February 20, 2023, www.scrippsnews.com/science-and-tech/studies-show-most-americans-are-sleep-deprived.

74. Recall the Cine Dreams event at the Strasenburgh Planetarium in 1972, described in chapter 3, when the experimental filmmaker Stan VanDerBeek held an all-night, multi-media event in which planetarium visitors were encouraged to sleep. On hypnagogic and hypnopompic states, see Stanley Krippner, "Altered States of Consciousness," in *The Highest State of Consciousness*, ed. John White (Anchor Books, 1972), 2.

75. Robert Rich, interview by author, September 23, 2024.

76. Rich, interview.

77. Interview with Robert Rich by Thierry Moreau for the French magazine *Dreaming* in 1992.

78. Rich, interview.

79. Steven Halpern, interview by author, April 26, 2024.

80. Halpern, interview.

81. James Fadiman and Jordan Gruber, *Microdosing for Health, Healing, and Enhanced Performance* (St. Martin's, 2025), 8.

82. Fadiman and Gruber, *Microdosing*, xvii–xviii.

83. Andrew Leonard, "LSD Microdosing," *Rolling Stone* no. 1249 (December 3, 2015): 51; Steven Halpern, email to author, May 1, 2025.

84. Szabo, *Turn On, Tune In, Drift Off*, 30.

85. Berna Rauch, "Surviving a Cosmic Convention," *San Francisco Examiner*, May 19, 1974, 21–30.

86. See, for example, Christina Welch. "Appropriating the Didjeridu and the Sweat Lodge: New Age Baddies and Indigenous Victims?," *Journal of Contemporary Religion* 17, no. 1 (2002): 21–38; Christopher Partridge, "The Occult and Orientalism," in *The Occult World*, ed. Christopher Partridge (Routledge, 2015); Rachel Fell McDermott, "New Age Hinduism, New Age Orientalism, and the Second-Generation South Asian," *Journal of the American Academy of Religion* 68, no. 4 (December 2000): 721–31.

87. Otto Friedrich, "New Age Harmonies," *Time*, December 7, 1987.

88. Colin Campbell, "The Cult, the Cultic Milieu and Secularization," in *The Cultic Milieu: Oppositional Subcultures in an Age of Globalization*, ed. Jeffrey Kaplan and Helene Loow (Altamira Press, 2002), 16. On New Age tolerance, also see Michael Hill, "The New Age: A Sociological Assessment," in *The Encyclopedic Sourcebook of New Age Religions*, ed. James R. Lewis (Prometheus Books, 2004), 386–87. On New Age individualism, eclecticism, and "supermarket spirituality," see Christopher Partridge, *The Re-enchantment of the West*, vol. 1 (Continuum, 2004), 32.

89. "Taraka Larson Interviews Iasos," Iasos.com, accessed May 15, 2025, https://iasos.com/media/mp3/Taraka-interviews-Iasos-4-26-12.mp3; "Inkarose Interviews Iasos," accessed July 12, 2024, https://www.youtube.com/watch?v=oPSn2_bMSeU.

90. On conspirituality, see Charlotte Ward and David Voas, "The Emergence of Conspirituality," *Journal of Contemporary Religion* 26, no. 1 (2011): 108; Egil Asprem and Asbjørn Dyrendal, "Conspirituality Reconsidered: How Surprising and How New Is the Confluence of Spirituality and Conspiracy Theory?," *Journal of Contemporary Religion* 30, no. 3 (2015): 367–82; Derek Beres, Matthew Remski, and Julian Walker, *Conspirituality* (PublicAffairs, 2023).

91. Ken Jenkins, interview by author, April 17, 2025.

92. Jenkins, interview.

93. Jenkins, interview.

94. Jenkins, interview.

95. Jenkins, interview.

96. Don Davis, "Challenger and the End of the Dream," January 2011, Don Davis website, accessed November 2024, www.donaldedavis.com/STS025/ENDOFDREAM.html.

97. Georgia Kelly, interview by author, February 21, 2025.

98. Kelly, interview. On Praxis Peace Institute, see https://praxispeace.org.

99. Kelly, interview.

100. Kelly, interview.

101. Paul Roquet, *Ambient Media: Japanese Atmospheres of Self* (University of Minnesota Press, 2016), 171–72.

102. Peter Davison, interview by author, July 19, 2024.

103. Davison, interview, April 29, 2025.

104. I'm adapting Victor Szabo's statement that ambient artists should address the "catastrophic conditions" of the twenty-first century, "not just through the quiet creation of interiorized trips, but also through loudly engaging with the spread, out there, of a new ecological sympathy." Szabo, *Turn On, Tune In, Drift Off*, 51.

105. Pelly, *Mood Machine*, 44, 40. Eriksson et al., *Spotify Teardown*, 124. On functional music, see also Mack Hagood, *Hush: Media and Sonic Self-Control* (Duke University Press, 2019).

106. Iasos, "Music as Light Waves," https://iasos.com/articles/index.html#Music_as_Light_Waves.

107. Don Slepian, interview by author, April 23, 2025.

108. Doucet, interview.

109. C. G. Jung, *Modern Man in Search of a Soul* (Mariner Books, 1933), 155–56, 158.

110. Ernst Fuchs interview in *True Visions*, ed. Massimiliano and Federica Timeto (Betty Books, 2006), 16.

111. See Lauren Jackson, "Americans Haven't Found a Satisfying Alternative to Religion," *New York Times*, April 18, 2025. See also Ruth Graham, "Orthodox Church Pews Are Overflowing with Converts," *New York Times*, November 19, 2025. On declining traditional religions and New Age spirituality, see Partridge, *The Re-enchantment of the West*, 1:37.

112. Kevin Lozano, "Where Weird Music Meets Mindfulness: At Church, Apparently," *Pitchfork*, June 21, 2017. Craig Hubert, "Electronic Music Finds Spiritual Home in Brooklyn's Churches," *Brownstoner*, October 18, 2017;

August Brown, "At Ambient Church, a Sacred Setting for Radically Meditative Music," *Los Angeles Times*, August 1, 2018.

113. Roach, interview, May 20, 2025.

114. Churches were important venues for New Age musicians in the 1970s and '80s as well. Kat Epple remembered that Emerald Web would frequently play at "New Age churches" like Unity, Church of Religious Science, and other spiritual centers. "There were so many New Age churches," she recalled. "They were such an amazing resource for a musician who was maybe traveling. . . . You could play a Sunday morning service, sell cassettes, and make enough gas money to get to your next concert" (Epple, interview).

115. Roach, interview, May 14, 2024. More on Eric Epstein here can be found at Najork.net, https://najork.net/index.html. In a 2023 documentary, Roach talked about composing the piece with the rhythms of the breath in mind: "If you're going to sit at an instrument that's made of metal and plastic and a bunch of components . . . I realized that there has to be a deeper connection, and there has to be an interface that comes from your physicality. . . . That's when the whole feeling of breath and playing and breathing while playing, and then having that model guide as you're playing, and then having that sigh where you pause, and you have that space between the notes and the chords. Then it returns." Kurt Lancaster, dir., *Steve Roach: Life in the Soundcurrent* (2023).

116. Roach's first release was called *Now*. He said, "I have about five albums with 'Now' in the title. . . . When I play live, I'm really in the front side of now. . . . It's like the feeling of life in your consciousness blooming, fractalizing forward." Steve Roach, interview by author, May 20, 2025.

117. Kevin Braheny Fortune, "Music Channeling," accessed August 2, 2025, https://kevinbrahenyfortune.com/music-channeling-1.

118. C. G. Jung, foreword to *The I Ching*, trans. Richard Wilhelm (Princeton University Press, 1950), xxiv. For more on Jung and the *I Ching*, see Roderick Main, "Magic and Science in the Modern Western Tradition of the *I Ching*," *Journal of Contemporary Religion* 14, no. 2 (1999): 263–75. The *I Ching* was an important tool in the avant-garde musical scene of the postwar years due to John Cage's use of it in composition. See Marc G. Jensen, "John Cage, Chance Operations, and the Chaos Game: Cage and the I Ching," *Musical Times* 150, no. 1907 (Summer 2009): 97–102; Peter Jaeger, *John Cage and Buddhist Ecopoetics* (Bloomsbury, 2013).

119. On channeling, see Suzanne Riordan, "Channeling: A New Revelation?," in *Perspectives on the New Age*, ed. James R. Lewis and J. Gordon Melton (State University of New York Press, 1992), 105–6. Also see Michael F. Brown,

The Channeling Zone: American Spirituality in an Anxious Age (Harvard University Press, 1997); Wouter J. Hanegraaff, *New Age Religion and Western Culture* (Brill, 1996), 23.

120. Kevin Braheny Fortune, interview by author, January 31, 2025.

121. Braheny Fortune, interview.

122. Braheny Fortune, "Music Channeling."

123. Kevin Braheny Fortune, "The Bridge," https://kevinbrahenyfortune.bandcamp.com/album/the-bridge.

124. Braheny Fortune, interview.

125. Braheny Fortune, interview.

126. C. G. Jung, foreword to *The I Ching*, xxxix.

SELECTED BIBLIOGRAPHY

The information in this book is drawn from interviews, articles, and archival materials. Full citations for all primary sources appear in the notes. In this bibliography, I list the key secondary sources that shaped the book's arguments.

Bateson, Gregory, and Mary Catherine Bateson. *Angels Fear: Towards an Epistemology of the Sacred*. Hampton Press, 2005.

Belgrad, Daniel. *The Culture of Feedback: Ecological Thinking in '70s America*. University of Chicago Press, 2019.

Birosik, Patti Jean. *The New Age Music Guide*. Collier, 1989.

Brown, David Jay, and Rebecca Ann Hill. *Women of Visionary Art*. Park Street, 2018.

Campbell, Colin. "The Cult, the Cultic Milieu and Secularization." In *The Cultic Milieu: Oppositional Subcultures in an Age of Globalization*, edited by Jeffrey Kaplan and Helene Loow. Altamira, 2002.

Caruana, L. *The First Manifesto of Visionary Art*. Recluse, 2001.

Davis, Erik. "Visionary Art: The Vanguard of Tradition." In *True Visions*, edited by Massimiliano Geraci and Federica Timeto. Betty Books, 2006.

DeConnick, April D. *The Gnostic New Age: How a Countercultural Spirituality Revolutionized Religion from Antiquity to Today*. Columbia University Press, 2016.

Faivre, Antoine. *Western Esotericism: A Concise History*. State University of New York Press, 2010.

Ferguson, Marilyn. *The Aquarian Conspiracy: Personal and Social Transformation in Our Time*. Penguin, 1987.

Ferrer, Jorge N. *Revisioning Transpersonal Theory: A Participatory Vision of Human Spirituality*. State University of New York Press, 2002.

Goldman, Jonathan. *Healing Sounds: The Power of Harmonics*. Healing Arts, 1992.

Grey, Alex. *The Mission of Art*. Shambala, 1998.

Grof, Stanislav. *The Cosmic Game: Explorations of the Frontiers of Human Consciousness*. State University of New York Press, 1998.

Halpern, Steven, with Louis Savary. *Sound Health: The Music and Sounds That Make Us Whole*. Harper & Row, 1985.

Hamel, Peter Michael. *Through Music to the Self*. Element Books, 1978.

Hanegraaff, Wouter. *New Age Religion and Western Culture: Esotericism in the Mirror of Secular Thought*. State University of New York Press, 1997.

Heelas, Paul. *The New Age Movement: Religion Culture, and Society in the Age of Postmodernity*. Blackwell, 1996.

Hess, David J. *Science in the New Age: The Paranormal, Its Defenders and Debunkers, and American Culture*. University of Wisconsin Press, 1993.

Hibbett, Ryan. "The New Age Taboo." *Journal of Popular Music Studies* 22, no. 3 (2010): 283–308.

Holm-Hudson, Kevin, ed. *Progressive Rock Reconsidered*. Routledge, 2002.

Horn, Paul, with Lee Underwood. *Inside Paul Horn: The Spiritual Odyssey of a Universal Traveler*. HarperCollins, 1990.

Huxley, Aldous. "Visionary Experience." In *The Highest State of Consciousness*, edited by John White. Anchor Books, 1972.

Jung, C. G. *Modern Man in Search of a Soul*. Mariner Books, 1933.

Jung, C. G. *The Spirit in Man, Art, and Literature*. Princeton University Press, 1966.

Kent, James L. *Psychedelic Information Theory: Shamanism in the Age of Reason*. PIT Press, 2010.

Lewis, James R., and J. Gordon Melton, eds. *Perspectives on the New Age*. State University of New York Press, 1992.

Macan, Edward. *Rocking the Classics: English Progressive Rock and the Counterculture*. Oxford University Press, 1997.

Masters, Robert E. L., and Jean Houston. *Psychedelic Art*. Balance House, 1968.

McClellan, Randall. *The Healing Forces of Music: History, Theory, and Practice*. Element Books, 1991.

Mcgowan, Douglas. "New Age Music." In *The Acid Archives*, edited by Patrick Lundborg. Lysergia, 2010.

McIntyre, Joan. *Mind in the Waters: A Book to Celebrate the Consciousness of Whales and Dolphins*. Scribner's Sons, 1974.

Melton, J. Gordon. *New Age Encyclopedia*. Gale Research, 1990.

Partridge, Christopher. *The Re-enchantment of the West: Alternative Spiritualities, Sacralization, Popular Culture, and Occulture.* 2 vols. Continuum, 2004, 2005.
Pike, Sarah M. *New Age and Neopagan Religions in America.* Columbia University Press, 2004.
Pinch, Trevor, and Frank Trocco. *Analog Days: The Invention and Impact of the Moog Synthesizer.* Harvard University Press, 2002.
Roszak, Theodore. *Unfinished Animal: The Aquarian Frontier and the Evolution of Consciousness.* Harper & Row, 1974.
Rudhyar, Dane. *The Magic of Tone and the Art of Music.* Shambhala, 1982.
Russ, Martin. *Sound Synthesis and Sampling.* 3rd ed. Routledge, 2008.
Summer, Lisa. *Music: The New Age Elixir.* Prometheus Books, 1996.
Sutcliffe, Steven, and Marion Bowman, eds. *Beyond New Age: Exploring Alternative Spirituality.* Edinburgh University Press, 2000.
Szabo, Victor. *Turn On, Tune In, Drift Off: Ambient Music's Psychedelic Past.* Oxford University Press, 2022.
Teboul, Ezra J., Andreas Kitzmann, and Einar Engström, eds. *Modular Synthesis: Patching Machines and People.* Focal Press, 2024.
Turner, Anna, and Stephen Hill. *Music from the Hearts of Space: Guide to Cosmic, Transcendent and Innerspace Music.* Music From the Hearts of Space, 1981.
Youngblood, Gene. *Expanded Cinema.* Fordham University Press, 1970.

INDEX

Founded in 1893,
UNIVERSITY OF CALIFORNIA PRESS
publishes bold, progressive books and journals on topics in the arts, humanities, social sciences, and natural sciences—with a focus on social justice issues—that inspire thought and action among readers worldwide.

The UC PRESS FOUNDATION
raises funds to uphold the press's vital role as an independent, nonprofit publisher, and receives philanthropic support from a wide range of individuals and institutions—and from committed readers like you. To learn more, visit ucpress.edu/supportus.

www.ingramcontent.com/pod-product-compliance
Lightning Source LLC
LaVergne TN
LVHW090749030926
847095LV00029B/300